The Policing of Families

THE POLICING
OF FAMILIES

Jacques Donzelot

With a Foreword by Gilles Deleuze

Translated from the French by Robert Hurley

Hutchinson of London

Hutchinson & Co.(Publishers) Ltd
3 Fitzroy Square, London W1P 6JD

London   Melbourne   Sydney   Auckland   Johannesburg   and   agencies
throughout the world

La Police des Familles first published by Les Éditions de Minuit 1977
© Les Éditions de Minuit 1977
This translation first published in Great Britain as *The Policing of Families* 1980

Translation © Random House, Inc. 1979
Preface © Jacques Donzelot 1979

Set in Times Roman

Printed in the United States of America and bound by Wm Brendon & Sons Ltd, Tiptree,
Essex

BRITISH LIBRARY CATALOGUING IN PUBLICATION DATA
Donzelot, Jacques
    The policing of families.
    1. Family — France — History
    I. Title
    301.42′1′0944   HQ623   79-1888

ISBN 0 09 140950 0 cased
     0 09 140951 9 paper

for Alice

Contents

Foreword

The Rise of the Social

Clearly it is not a question of the adjective that qualifies the set of phenomena which sociology deals with: *the* social refers to a *particular sector* in which quite diverse problems and special cases can be grouped together, a sector comprising specific institutions and an entire body of qualified personnel ("social" assistants, "social" workers). We speak of social scourges, from alcoholism to drugs; of social programs, from repopulation to birth control; of social maladjustments or adjustments, from predelinquency, character disorders, or the problems of the handicapped to the various types of social advancement. Jacques Donzelot's book is a forceful one, because it proposes a genesis of this strange sector, of recent formation and growing importance, *the* social: a new landscape has risen up around us. As the contours of this domain are nebulous, one has to recognize it first by the way it took form, beginning in the late eighteenth and early nineteenth centuries, by the way it sketches out its own originality in relation to older sectors, so that it is able to react on them and effect a new distribution of their functions. Among Donzelot's most remarkable pages are those wherein he describes the workings of the "juvenile court," an agency that exemplifies *the* social *par excellence*. At first glance, it might be taken for nothing more than a miniaturized jurisdiction; but, as sometimes happens when one studies an engraving through a magnifying glass, Donzelot discovers a different organization of space, other ends, other personages, even though the last are disguised or assimilated into the juridical apparatus: notables as assessors, educators as witnesses, a whole circle of tutors and technicians who press closely in upon the shattered or "liberalized" family.

The social sector does not merge with the judicial sector, even if it does extend the field of judicial action. And Donzelot shows that the social does not merge with the economic sector either, since in point of fact it invents an entire social economy and lays new foundations for marking the distinction between the rich and the poor. Nor does it merge with the public sector or the private sector, since on the contrary it leads to a new hybrid form of the public and the private, and itself produces a repartition, a novel interlacing of interventions and withdrawals of the state, of its charges and discharges. The question is not at all whether there is a mystification of the social, nor what ideology it expresses. Donzelot asks how the social takes form, reacting on other sectors, inducing new relationships between the public and the private; the judicial, the administrative, and the customary; wealth and poverty; the city and the country; medicine, the school, and the family; and so on. We are shown how it cuts across and reshapes previously existing or independent divisions, providing a new field for the forces already present. Donzelot is then perfectly justified in leaving the reader to draw his or her own conclusions as to the pitfalls and machinations of the social.

As the social is a hybrid domain, particularly in regard to relations between the public and the private spheres, Donzelot's method consists in isolating *pure little lines of mutation* which, acting successively or simultaneously, go to form a contour or surface, a characteristic feature of the new domain. The social is located at the intersection of all these little lines. But the milieu on which these lines act, investing and transforming it, still needs to be defined. This milieu is the family—not that the family is itself incapable of being a motive force of evolution, but when this is the case, of necessity it is by virtue of a coupling with other vectors, just as the other vectors enter into relations of coupling or intersection in

order to act on the family. So Donzelot has *not* written another book on the crisis of the family: the crisis is simply the
negative effect of the emergence of these little lines; or rather,
*the rise of the social and the crisis of the family are the twofold
political effect of these same elementary causes.* Whence the
title, *The Policing of Families,* which expresses above all this
whole correlation, escaping the double danger of a sociological analysis that is too global and a moral analysis that is too
summary.

Next it was necessary to show how, at each intersection of
these causes, mechanisms are assembled to function in such
and such a manner, slipping into the interstices of bigger or
older apparatuses, which then undergo a mutation as a result.
It is here that Donzelot's method is akin to that of engraving,
for he delineates a new scene set within a given frame (for
example, the scene of the juvenile court within the judicial
framework; or the "philanthropic visit"—and these pages are
also among Donzelot's finest—which has slipped into the
framework of the "charitable" institutions). Finally, it was
necessary to determine the consequences these lines of mutation and new interworkings were to have on the field of
forces, the alliances, the hostilities, the resistances, and above
all the collective processes [*les devenirs collectifs]* that change
the value of a term or the meaning of a statement. In sum,
Donzelot's method is genealogical, functional, and strategic,
which bespeaks his considerable debt to Michel Foucault and
also to Robert Castel. But the way Donzelot establishes his
lines, the way he sets them working in a scene or a portrait,
drafting an entire strategical map of the social, gives his book
a profound originality.

Donzelot shows from the outset that a line, a little line of
mutation of the family, can begin obliquely, by a detour as it
were. It all begins on a *lesser* line: a line of criticism or attack
against wet nurses and the staff of servants. And already at
this level there is intersection, since the criticism is not directed from the same standpoint as concerns the rich and the
poor. With respect to the poor, what is denounced is a bad

public economy that leads them to abandon their own children, to desert the rural areas and burden the state with unwarranted responsibilities. As to the rich, it is a bad private economy or hygiene that prompts them to entrust house servants with the education of the child confined in narrow rooms. Hence there already exists a kind of hybridization of public and private, which will play with the difference between rich and poor, city and country, in order to trace out the first line.

But at once there is a second line. Not only does the family tend to detach itself from its domestic setting, but marital values tend to break loose from familial values properly speaking and assume a certain autonomy. Marriages will still be regulated by family hierarchies, of course; but now it is less a matter of preserving the order of families than of preparing people for married life, so that this order is given a new code. Preparation for marriage as an end, rather than preservation of the family by means of marriage; a concern for descent more than a pride in ancestry. It is as if the wife and the child, being drawn into the bankruptcy of the old family code, were to find in conjugality the elements of a new, strictly "social" code. The theme of the big sister-little mother comes into being. The social will be centered on conjugality, its apprenticeship, its exercise, and its duties, more than on the family, its innateness, and its prerogatives. But here, too, this mutation will have different repercussions among the rich and among the poor, seeing that the marital duty of the poor wife will cause her to turn back toward her husband and children (to prevent the husband from going to the cabaret, etc.), whereas that of the rich wife will give her expansive control functions and a role of "missionary" in the field of charitable work.

A third line is traced, in that the conjugal family itself tends to work free, in part, from the paternal or marital authority of the head of the family. Divorce, the spread of abortion for married women, and the possibility of loss of paternal authority are the most noteworthy points on this line. But in a deeper sense, what is compromised is the subjectivity that the family finds in its responsible "head," in his ability to govern it, and the objectivity that it derives from an entire network of dependences and complementarities that make it governable. On the one hand, it becomes necessary to find new subjective enticements. Here Donzelot shows the role of *the appeal to saving,* which became the linchpin of a new mechanism of assistance (hence the difference between the old form of charity and the new philanthropy, where aid must be conceived of as an investment). On the other hand, it was necessary that the network of old dependences be replaced by direct interventions whereby *the industrial system* itself would remedy defects for which it would make the family responsible (thus the legislation concerning child labor, where the system is meant to defend the child against his own family: a second aspect of philanthropy). Thus, in the first case, the state tends to free itself of excessive burdens by bringing into play private investment and the incitement to saving; whereas in the second case, the state is obliged to intervene directly by making the industrial sphere into an arena for "civilizing mores." Consequently, the family can be simultaneously the object of liberal praise, as a locus of saving, and the object of social—even socialist—criticism, as an agent of exploitation (protect the wife and the child); simultaneously the occasion of an unburdening of the liberal state and the target or charge of the interventionist state: not an ideological quarrel, but two poles of one strategy on the same line. It is here that the hybridization of the two sectors—the public and the private—takes on a positive value in order to form the social.

And then a fourth line, which produces a new alliance of medicine and the state. Through the action of very diverse factors (such as the development of compulsory schooling, the regimen of the soldier, the breaking loose of marital values with a new emphasis on descent, population control) "hygiene" becomes public at the same time that psychiatry moves out of the private sector. There is still a hybridization, however, inasmuch as medicine keeps a liberal and private complexion (*the contract*), while the state intervenes of necessity through public and statutory actions (*tutelage*).[1] But the proportion of these elements is variable; the oppositions and tensions persist (for example, between judicial power and the psychiatric "jurisdiction"). Moreover, these nuptials of medicine and the state take on a different appearance not only according to the joint policy that is pursued (eugenics, Malthusianism, planning) but according to the nature of the state that is expected to carry out this policy. Donzelot has written extraordinary pages on the adventure of Paul Robin and anarchist groups who bear witness to a "leftism" of that period, with agitation in factories, support of strikes, propaganda for a neo-Malthusianism, and where, in spite of everything, anarchism operates via the promotion of a strong state. As in the abovementioned instances, it is along the same line that the points of authoritarianism, the points of reform, the points of resistance and revolution, come face to face around this new stake, "the social," where medicine combines with the state to foster "hygiene," in several, sometimes opposing, ways that invest and reorganize the family. One learns many disconcerting things—about the Parents' School, the beginnings of Family Planning—through reading Donzelot. One is surprised to find that the political divisions are not exactly what one imagined them to be. All this points up a more general problem: the political analysis of statements—how a statement refers to a politics, and how its meaning changes singularly from one politics to another.

There is yet another line: that of psychoanalysis. Donzelot accords it great importance, in keeping with an original hypothesis. There is currently a manifest interest in arriving at a real history of psychoanalysis that will break with personalist anecdotes about Freud, his disciples and dissidents, or with ideological questions, in order to define more adequately the problems of organization. For if the general history of psy-

---

1. Regarding the formation of a "biopolitics," or a power that proposes to manage life, cf. Michel Foucault, *The History of Sexuality* (New York: Pantheon Books, 1978), 1:139 ff. And regarding contract-tutelage relations in this connection, see Robert Castel, *L'Ordre psychiatrique* (Paris: Éditions de Minuit, 1977).

choanalysis has remained under the personalist stamp up to now, even at the level of the formation of the psychoanalytic associations, this is because we have remained captive to a ready-made schema: psychoanalysis originated in private (contractual) relations, formed private practices, and only tardily moved out of this private sphere in order to encroach upon a public sector (I.M.P.'s, clinics, sectorization, education). On the contrary, Donzelot believes that in a certain way psychoanalysis established itself very quickly in a hybrid—public and private—milieu, and that this was one of the primary reasons for its success. Psychoanalysis was introduced belatedly in France, no doubt; but it was precisely in semipublic sectors like Family Planning that it was to gain support, in connection with problems of the type "How to avoid unwanted children." This hypothesis will have to be tested in other countries. At the least it allows us to break with the summary dualism of "Freud the liberal/Reich the Marxist dissident" in order to delimit a political and social field of psychoanalysis within which the ruptures and oppositions developed.

But in Donzelot's hypothesis, where does psychoanalysis get this power to invest directly a mixed social sector, *the* social, and trace a new line within it? It is not that the psychoanalyst is himself a social worker, of the sort produced by the other lines. On the contrary, many things set him apart from the social worker: he doesn't come to your home, he doesn't verify the things you say, he doesn't call upon any constraint. But we must start again from the preceding situation: there were still many tensions between the judicial order and the psychiatric order (inadequacy of the psychiatric grid, too crude a notion of degenerescence, and so forth), many oppositions between the requirements of the state and the criteria of psychiatry.[2]) In short, rules of equivalence and translatability were lacking. It was as if psychoanalysis noted this lack of

2. For example, in the case of deliriums, the civil or penal authorities reproached psychiatry both for considering people mad who were not "really" insane (as in the case of Judge Schreber) and for not detecting soon enough people who were mad without appearing to be (as in monomanias or deliriums of passion).

equivalence and proposed to substitute a new system of *flota-tion* by creating the theoretical and practical concepts needed for this new state of affairs—exactly as in economy, where a currency is said to be floating when its value is no longer determined by reference to a fixed standard but in relation to the price of a hybrid variable market. Which obviously does not rule out regulatory mechanisms of a new type (the "serpent" that marks the maximum and minimum of currency flotation). Whence the importance of the comparison Donzelot makes between Freud and Keynes, which is much more than a metaphor. In particular, the quite specific role of money in psychoanalysis need no longer be interpreted according to old liberal forms, or inept symbolic forms, but assumes the value of a veritable psychoanalytic "serpent." Now, *how was psychoanalysis able to ensure this utterly special flotation that psychiatry could not accomplish?* According to Donzelot, the essential role of psychoanalysis was to cause public norms and private principles, expertises and confessions, tests and memories, to float, with the help of a whole set of displacements, condensations, and symbolizations linked to the parental images and psychical agencies that psychoanalysis brings to bear. It is as if the relationships between public and private, state and family, law and medicine, and so forth had long been pegged to a standard—that is, to a system of law that determined relationships and parities, albeit with wide margins of flexibility and variation. But *the* social comes into being with a system of flotation, in which norms replace the law, regulatory and corrective mechanisms replace the standard.[3] Freud and Keynes together. Psychoanalysis talks a great deal about law, but to no avail: it belongs to a different regime. Not that it is the last word in the social sector: if the social is indeed constituted by this system of regulated flotation, psychoanalysis is merely one mechanism among many others, and not the most powerful; but it has impregnated

3. Regarding this difference between norm and law, see Foucault, *History of Sexuality,* 1:143ff.

them all, even if it is bound to disappear or dissolve into them.

From the "lesser" line to the line of flotation, going by way of all the other lines (marital, philanthropic, hygienist, industrial), Donzelot has mapped out the social, its emergence, and its expansion. He has shown us the birth of the modern Hybrid: how desires and powers, the new requirements of control, but also the new possibilities of resistance and liberation, come to be organized, laid out opposite one another along these lines. "Having a room of one's own" is a desire, but also a control. Inversely, a regulatory mechanism is haunted by everything that overruns it and already causes it to split apart from within. That Donzelot leaves the reader the task of concluding provisionally is not a sign of indifference, but rather announces the direction of his forthcoming work in the field he has staked out.

Gilles Deleuze

Preface to the English Edition

In order to make the reading of a book like this one easier for a public far removed from its milieu of origin, one might wish to situate its contribution within that wider frame of reference. However, for this I am doubtless not sufficiently acquainted with the work that has been done on the subject in the United States or elsewhere, and perhaps it is just as well. What I propose to do instead is to explain the local conditions in which this book was produced, to point out the targets it aimed at and the polemics it engaged in or opened. In a word, I will try to extrovert its context, with the hope that this will allow "foreign" readers to identify the angle by which they can enter into the text, the part that is likely to interest them.

When it was conceived, this piece of work was addressed to three main interlocutors, three forms of discourse whose contents, to say nothing of their implications, leave too many questions hanging, or reply with certainties too repetitious to be credible. I am referring to Marxists, feminists, and psychoanalysts. Three forms of discourse that are quite heterogeneous and varied in themselves, certainly, but that constitute—by their points of dispute, their interested alliances, or their well-ordered antagonisms—the major configuration of theoretical research in France, the schema to which all reflection has had to adapt, not in order to be produced, of course, but to be understood.

The choice of the family as an object of study was therefore a strategic one, since the family is the concrete locus where these discourses implicitly converge. For someone who felt the need to appeal to a different form of intelligibility of our present, its analysis would constitute a seemingly minor part of the whole, but by effectively examining it one is able to confront, on a precise point, the functioning of "advanced liberal" societies with the mythical representations that sustain these hegemonic discourses.

For Marxists, the family is an apparatus indispensable to the bourgeois order. This is owing to its function as an anchorage point for private property and its function of reproduction of the ruling ideology, for which purpose alone its authority is recognized and mandated. Hence, the evolution of mores (the term commonly applied to the introduction of divorce, the advancement of women, and the child-protection laws) can only be interpreted as a crisis of the bourgeois family, the irruption of a movement that comes into contradiction with the reproductive requirements of the bourgeois order.

To this, one can object that the family has indeed been a direct agent of the established order, but much more so under the *ancien régime* than since the coming to power of the bourgeoisie after the French Revolution of 1789. Under the *ancien régime*, there was a continuity between public power and familial power, or in any case, an implicit homology. The dependence in which family members found themselves with respect to their head was not substantially different from that of the family with respect to the men or agencies above it. Moreover, the head of the family received aid and protection for maintaining his power over his own—witness the *lettres de cachet de famille*—precisely insofar as this power was in keeping with the requirements of the public order.

This position of the family would gradually disappear in the nineteenth century, not through the effect of a crisis in the bourgeois order, but as a consequence of transformations brought about by individuals or groupings who were entirely representative of the new, so-called bourgeois, order.

First there was a transformation of the family from the inside, as it were, resulting from the propagation within it of medical, educative, and relational norms whose over-all aim was to preserve children from the old customs, which were considered deadly. But here it can already be noted that what occurred was not a single imposition of a bourgeois model on the other classes. For the propagation of these norms was carried out via two completely different channels. On the one hand, we see a bourgeois pole take form, where the family willingly seizes on medical instructions and uses them to free children from the allegedly stifling grip of domestic servants and social promiscuities, constructing around the child an educative model that I have termed "protected liberation." On the other hand, the working-class family is reorganized on the basis of a set of institutional constraints and stimulations that also make the child the center of the family, to be sure, but according to procedures much more deserving of the term "supervised freedom."

The family was also transformed in its exterior status by the modification of family law. By the terms of the new law, the ancient and monolithic authority of the father gave place to a dual regime, which took the form of a simple alternative: either the system of *tutelage,* or that of the *contract.* The former is for social categories that combine a difficulty in supplying their own needs with resistances to the new medical and educative norms. In essence, tutelage means that these families will be stripped of all effective rights and brought into a relation of dependence *vis-à-vis* welfare and educative agents. The contractual system—for the others—corresponds to an accelerated liberalization of relations, both within and outside the family. Here, norms are joined—harmoniously, in principle—to a liberal law that fluidifies the family. They are points of support for the never-ending search for more workable relational combinations, that is, those offering a maximum of chances for advancement. In this sense, they bring into play both familial ambition and the divisions, conflicts, and rivalries that exist inside the family, all of which sets in motion an upward dynamic (real or imagined, but effective in any case) operating between the working-class family pole and the bourgeois pole.

So we can neither speak of the family as an ideological apparatus of the state nor put its modernization down to a lack of coherence in advanced liberal societies. Doubtless it is tied, decisively, to the present order, but not in the form of a direct dependence with respect to the "bourgeois state," or in that of a pure and simple subjection to the imperatives of the transmission of fortunes. Before and instead of considerations of this sort, we would do better to take account of its largely successful inscription within a new form of sociality, of which it appears to be both queen and prisoner.

For feminists, this history seems of slight importance when weighed against a patriarchal domination seen as essentially unchanged across the centuries, a more than millenary oppression from which only a few heroic figures of magnificent women in revolt have emerged. Thus beside, or rather beneath, the capital-letter history made by and for men, there would seem to be another history, immobile and profound, linking the pyres where witches were burned alive to modern-day psychoanalytic couches for hysterics. Of course, it is probable that every category that undertakes a struggle to change its condition feels the need to fabricate a version of history that nurtures its combat, a historical mythology that justifies its conviction. It is perhaps not necessary, however, for it to conceal the elements that have done the most to alter its condition—all the more so when it has been in part the willing agent of this alteration.

In point of fact, this transformation of the family was not effected without the active participation of women. In working-class and bourgeois strata alike—albeit by quite different means and with different results—women were the main point of support for all the actions that were directed toward a reformulation of family life. For example, the woman was chosen by the medical and teaching professions to work in partnership with them in order to disseminate their principles, to win adherence to the new norms, within the home. This is not to deny the resistances of women to this domestic instrumentalization of their persons—for example, their resistance to the reduction of their mastery in the ancient techniques of the body in exchange for the role of devoted auxiliaries of men doctors. But this is providing we recognize the extent of the revaluation of power relations between man and woman inside the family, which was the positive consequence for the latter. It is on condition that we perceive in this increase of woman's domestic power not only the support of all the "social" professions that would give her a new access to public life but also the springboard she needed for the recognition of her political rights. How are we to assess the importance of militant feminism in the nineteenth century if we ignore its alliance with social philanthropy? And if, as this process comes to an end, we can with good reason consider that despite the equalization of men and women under the law, the question whether women have gained enough by it has not been settled, are we sure that this is the most fundamental question?

As to psychoanalysis, opening a discussion is even more complicated, owing to the multifold uses to which it has lent itself. Uses that make it possible, in principle, for the psychoanalyst to take refuge behind his pure and simple practice. In the Freudo-Marxism of Reich and Marcuse, we have seen psychoanalysis serve as a crutch for a faltering Marxism. Or inversely, as the object of a denunciation of its function as the twentieth century's dominant ideology through the interplay of resemblances between the employer and the wage laborer, as described by Marx, and the psychoanalytic contract, with its grotesque justifications of the role of money, the one-sidedness of the risks run in the undertaking. Because of the pre-eminence it concedes to the masculine sex, the Freudian theory of sexuality has been seen as the locus of the most accomplished representation of phallocentrism, the pseudo-scientific justification of patriarchalism and sexual racism. But despite all this, psychoanalysis can appear as the only discourse on human psychism that was capable of placing an obstacle in the way of the racist and fascist representations that were generated by a psychiatry obsessed with eugenics.

So the question to ask of psychoanalysis does not bear directly on its political significance, but precisely as most analysts demand, on its practical significance. This does not mean that the remarks we make will necessarily be of a sort to please them. Yet if we are allowed to brush aside the customary naïve remonstrances regarding the success of a doctrine, we can raise the following questions:

1. What made the field of relational and social problems in which psychoanalysis had to deploy so amenable to it?
2. By what means was it made operative?
3. What were the effective properties of the psychoanalytic discourse which enabled it to prevail over the knowledges [*savoirs*] with which it was competing?

The answer I submit comes down to this: While law, medicine, psychiatry, and religion did provide techniques for managing conflictual relations and maladjustments, virtually all of these techniques implied heavy-handed solutions involving direct constraint and hence a high cost in terms of resistance to their application. In contrast, psychoanalysis supplies—directly or indirectly—responses of a regulatory and noncoercive type. Thus, through the role it assigns to parental images in the formation of the individual and consequently in that of his or her existential or social failures, psychoanalysis makes it possible to displace the question of responsibility into the "imaginary order." Concurrently, through its practice and the counseling that derives from that practice, it introduces the possibility of a nondegrading corrective action and a principle of autonomous resolution of conflicts. In this sense, we can suggest that between familial values and social norms, it establishes a principle whereby values and norms are made to float in relation to one another, enabling the individual to circulate back and forth between them, to play them off against each other—provided, of course, he or she is willing to venture into this interchange at the risk of not remaining locked within it!

Two remarks seem appropriate at this point:

It may have been noted that the nature of the arguments we have employed rules out everything that might belong to dogmatic methods of disqualification. Our aim is not to denounce the factitiousness of other discourses but to induce them, so far as possible, to take into consideration what they have allowed themselves to overlook.

We were not the first in this undertaking. As regards the family in France, the now classic works of Philippe Ariès and, more recently, of Jean-Louis Flandrin have profiled its history in a manner that owes nothing to dogmatic treatments of the subject. They did this by attempting, in accordance with the historian's logic, to recapture the old reality of family life, the slow mutations that must have affected it in its actual experience, in its own self-representations. They have thus isolated a vast domain of mentalities and their evolution. But here we have to point out, not a divergence perhaps, but in any case a difference between them and us (this "we" is not the royal one, of course; it refers to a team formed on the periphery of Michel Foucault and Gilles Deleuze). For, to our way of thinking, the disadvantage of this fascinating and meticulous restitution of the familial past is in the haphazard nature of this separating-out of mentalities, in the fuzziness it allows to settle in between this domain and that of economic and political transformations; and consequently, in the excessive leeway it gives pre-existing theoretical machineries to appropriate that kind of investigation for themselves or simply to ignore it.

The method we have employed tries to avoid this danger by positing the family, not as a point of departure, as a manifest reality, but as a moving resultant, an uncertain form whose intelligibility can only come from studying the system of relations it maintains with the sociopolitical level. This requires us to detect all the political mediations that exist between the two registers, to identify the lines of transformation that are situated in that space of intersections.

Following these lines of transformation, we see the contours of a form of sociality gradually taking shape, one that will furnish a tangible surface, an effective plane for understanding the present-day family, its variations, its fragility and its strength, its incentives and its inertia. We thereby gain a clearer idea of the destiny of the family form in liberal societies. But on the other hand, precisely the problem of this new form of sociality, in which the liberalized family form becomes operative, is brought to the fore. In showing the emergence of "the social" as a concrete space of intelligibility of the family, it is the social that suddenly looms as a strange abstraction. As if the enigma had only shifted elsewhere.

How, then, did such a figure come to be constituted in our societies? For "the social" is not society understood as the set of material and moral conditions that characterize a form of consolidation. It would appear to be rather the set of means which allow social life to escape material pressures and po-litico-moral uncertainties; the entire range of methods which make the members of a society relatively safe from the effects of economic fluctuations by providing a certain security—which give their existence possibilities of relations that are flexible enough, and internal stakes that are convincing enough, to avert the dislocation that divergences of interests and beliefs would entail. And perhaps the most surprising thing is the status that "the social" has thus won in our heads, as something we take for granted. A strange aquarium that has become, in a very brief period of time, the reality princi-ple of our societies, the *raison d'être* of development, the proof that it has engendered, notwithstanding wars and pollution, a greater humanization. Thus it is the yardstick by which politi-cal discourses will measure or oppose one another, but also the basis on which they will try to start afresh when its re-alization has effaced the charm of old promises.

It is the genealogy of this figure—the social—that I would like to outline in a forthcoming volume. This implies shifting the center of interest from the family to the question of labor, a shift we are already invited to make by a certain number of similarities in the processes. There is the simultaneity between the laws that reorganized family life in Western Europe at the end of the nineteenth century and those pertaining to labor (divorce and child-protection laws on the one hand; laws con-cerning unions and those protecting work in case of illness, accident, old age, and shutdown, on the other). In other words, the same interplay between the rise of protective norms and the development of contractualization. Another necessary shift: that of the political and territorial scale taken into account. It was at an international level, on the scale of conflicts between the great strategies of the contemporary period, that the social would appear and be shaped and re-shaped until it corresponded to its current texture. But the same method will be used: studying the relationships between technologies of power and strategies, observing the interplay between these levels of materiality, looking for a guiding thread for understanding the place gradually taken by the social within the strategic configurations that succeeded one another from the beginning of the nineteenth century to the present.

To attempt to answer this question:

—How did we pass from a usage of "the social" understood as the problem of poverty, the problem of others, to its current definition in terms of a general solidarity and the production of a life-style; what enabled it to be made into a showcase of development, whose defense comes before all else, something to be offered to the world at whatever cost?

J.D.
March 1979

The Policing of Families

1.

Introduction

What more needs to be furnished by way of introduction? A summary? Directions for use? A straightforward statement? A piece of literary bravura? Not having the feeling of presenting a clearly determined and easily identifiable product, I shall take the risk rather of showing something of the design of the work, the basic impressions, characteristic procedures, and demonstrational pattern that guided its construction.

To start with, there was, certainly, the perception of the family in a series of disparate scenes. The heterogeneity of these visions, the difficulty of articulating them, of blending them into a common entity without effacing their singularities, no doubt provided the impetus to advance, the principle of dissatisfaction that motivated further research. I will evoke three of these scenes. First, that of the juvenile court, where the mode of appearance before the court implies the placing of the child and his family in a setting of notables, social technicians, and magistrates: an image of encirclement through the establishment of a direct communication between social imperatives and family behavior, ratifying a relationship of force prejudicial to the family. Second, that of a film such as *Family Life:* a working-class family installed in a comfortable house; a daughter who tries to leave, who rejects the values of work, saving, the familialization of sexuality; and parents who cannot, will not allow it, who drive her slowly to a state of schizophrenia. This time the image is of suffocation coming from the family itself, from an activity which tends to consume everything that would escape the familial contraction of the investments of desire. I could just as easily have mentioned *The Child* by Jules Vallès, *Death on the Installment Plan* by Céline, or the books of David Cooper. Third, the image of the bourgeois home. The home begins where the children are let out from school. There are those who go home all by themselves and those who are waited for at school. The first have the street, the vacant lot, the shop windows and cellars, while the others have yards, jungle gyms, afternoon snacks, and educative parents. Here the image is no longer of encirclement, but of preservation. Not suffocation, but liberation within a protected space.

Starting from these concrete images, how does one explain the singular position of the family in Western societies? A vexatious position, to be sure, judging by the obsessive questioning to which are subjected the least metamorphoses that affect it. It has become an essential ritual of our societies to scrutinize the countenance of the family at regular intervals in order to decipher our destiny, glimpsing in the death of the family an impending return to barbarism, the letting go of our reasons for living; or indeed, in order to reassure ourselves at the sight of its inexhaustible capacity for survival. Far removed from the immediate rationality of political discourse, it appears to constitute the other pole of our societies, their darker side, an enigmatic figure to which oracles are drawn in order to peer into the depths where it moves and read the inflections of our collective unconscious, the encoded message of our civilization. A cardinal positon, very different from the place it held in the societies of the *ancien régime,* where it was stronger juridically but submerged in vast organic entities— and just as different from the minimal place allotted to it by the "communist" societies, so that it appears as a correlative figure of parliamentary democracy.

What link is there between the extreme disparity of visions that we obtain of the family and the singular social value that is attributed to it? What relationships exist? How can we go from the former to the latter? And first of all, what means are available to us for attempting this operation?

To begin with, there is political history in its conventional version: the history of events, organizations, ideas. During the nineteenth century, political historiography could distinguish opposing sides in terms of their conceptions of the family. The family constituted a clear dividing line between the defenders of the established order and those who contested it, between the capitalist camp and the socialist camp, with a few exceptions, the most noteworthy of which was Proudhonism. Who sided with the family? Mainly conservatives who favored the restoration of an established order centering around the family, a return to an idealized former regime; but also liberals who saw the family as the protector of private property, of the bourgeois ethic of accumulation, as well as the guarantor of a barrier against the encroachments of the state. Those who attacked the family, the scientific or utopian socialists, did so against those very functions ascribed to it by the ruling classes. Its disappearance was programmed for a dawning socialism, and its partial breakup, its crises, were considered so many signs heralding the latter's arrival. At the beginning of the twentieth century, however, this clear disposition of forces and issues quickly became blurred. The family continued to be denounced for its hypocrisy and egocentrism, but the destruction of the family was no longer on the agenda except where the anarchist minorities were concerned. On the contrary, in the mass organizations the family became the buttress at the foot of which all criticism stopped, the point of support from which demands were launched for the defense and improvement of the standard of living.

This is the point at which the history of mentalities enters the field. Breaking with the foregoing political reading, it points to the existence of a system of transformations specific to sensibilities and manners, to the organization of everyday existence. In its view, the modern sense of the family emerged in the bourgeois and aristocratic strata of the *ancien régime,* then spread in concentric circles to all social classes, reaching the proletariat at the end of the nineteenth century. But what might be the reasons for the lower classes having adhered to bourgeois morality, for their having complied with the familialist injunctions of those who ruled them? Can it be maintained that family life became a universal value solely by the attractive force of its bourgeois model? And what entitles us to affirm that the sense of the family that exists in the lower classes is of the same nature as that existing in the other social strata, that it obeys the same constitutive logic, that it embraces the same values, the same expectations, that it has the same effects?

As we pursue in this fashion the two major forms of history at our disposal, the problem raised by the cortical position of the family remains in its entirety. The one form exhausts itself with defining the family by the one-sidedness of a function of reproduction of the established order, of a narrowly political determination. The other endows the family with a specific being, but at the cost of reducing it to the unicity of a model whose variations are only distantly tied in with the economic evaluation of societies. Hence there is nothing in either form that would enable us to specify the place of the family here and now.

The work of Michel Foucault has succeeded in identifying—between the empty gesture of the voluntary and the inscrutable efficiency of the involuntary—a field of practices that can be considered directly responsible for the transformations we are trying to analyze, avoiding the endless cleavage between politics and psychology by taking account of what he calls the biopolitical dimension: the proliferation of political technologies that invested the body, health, modes of subsistence and lodging—the entire space of existence in European countries from the eighteenth century onward. All the techniques that found their unifying pole in what, at the outset, was called *policing*: not understood in the limiting, repressive sense we give the term today, but according to a much broader meaning that encompassed all the methods for developing the quality of the population and the strength of the nation. "The purpose of policing is to ensure the good fortune of the state through the wisdom of its regulations, and to augment its forces and its power to the limits of its capability. The science of policing consists, therefore, in regulating everything that relates to the present condition of society, in strengthening and improving it, in seeing that all things contribute to the welfare of the members that compose it. The aim of policing is to make everything that composes the state serve to strengthen and increase its power, and likewise serve the public welfare."[1]

I have in mind a plan of description that I hope will permit us to escape both the epic register—that narrative loftiness where the inscription of a meaning in history proceeds through the recounting of manichean confrontations—and the one characterized by the passive contemplation of in-depth mutations. On the basis of this twofold rejection of the lofty and the profound, we shall attempt a history of the social surface. This will involve identifying lines of transformation fine enough to account for the singularities assigned to family roles in the different types of figures noted earlier, but perceiving those roles as the strategic resultant of these diverse forces. This form of history is not without rigor: it has recourse to theory only insofar as theory generates the possibility of another narration of events; it unfolds this narration only to the extent that the latter casts light on the components of an enigmatic setup, the workings of the familial mechanism in its relations with the existing social organization.

This first object, the family, will thus be seen to fade into the background, overshadowed by another, the social, in relation to which the family is both queen and prisoner. By and large, the procedures of transformation of the family are also those which implant the forms of modern integration that give our societies their particularly well-policed character. And the celebrated crisis of the family, setting the stage for its liberation, would appear then not so much inherently con-

1. Johann von Justi, *Éléments généraux de police* (1768).

trary to the present social order as a condition of possibility of that order's emergence. Neither destroyed nor piously preserved, the family is an agency whose incongruity with respect to social requirements can be reduced, or made functional, through the establishment of a procedure that brings about a "floating" of social norms and family values, just as there is established, concurrently, a functional circularity between the social and the economic: Freud and Keynes together.

A critique of political reason is overdue; the need for it is evident. I would like to contribute to such a critique by showing concretely how sieve-like concepts such as "crisis" or "contradiction" are inadequate. Inadequate because they make it possible to neglect crucial transformations by referring them to the terms of a simple but outmoded debate; they blur the positivity of these transformations and obscure their efficacy. And because they lead one in the end to mistake for decisive breaks, for surfaces of confrontation (whether real or merely logical), what is in fact the emergence of new techniques of regulation. People doggedly persist in seeing the approach of the final struggle every time a new rule of the social game makes its appearance. It is rather by using these new mechanisms as our yardstick, testing our analysis against the recent figures which surfaced at the end of the last century, that we must gauge the current resistances, the conflicts and lines of escape which sometimes reinforce these new rules of the game and at other times undermine them.

Stated simply, my objective here is little more than to militate for a usage of history different from that of speaking in its behalf or of taking refuge in its meanders. It is time for us to ask history to tell us who we are instead of beating its sides once more in order to extract a final drop of prophetism, or using it as a surface on which to engrave, in philosophical letters, the maxims of an arrogant disdain.

2.

The Preservation of Children

In the middle of the eighteenth century, an abundant literature began to flourish on the theme of the preservation of children. At first it was the work of physicians like Essartz (*Traité de l'éducation corporelle des enfants en bas âge, ou, réflexion pratique sur les moyens de procurer une meilleure constitution aux citoyens,* 1760), Brouzet (*Essai sur l'éducation. médicinale des enfants et sur leurs maladies,* 1757), Raulin (*De la conservation des enfants,* 1767), Leroy (*Recherches sur les habillements des femmes et des enfants,* 1772), Buchan (*Médecine domestique,* 1775), Verdier Heurtin (*Discours sur l'allaitement et l'éducation physique des enfants,* 1804); to say nothing of the celebrated works of Tissot on the subject of onanism and his *Avis au peuple sur sa santé* (1761). Joining this medical procession were administrators like Prost de Royer, lieutenant-general of police at Lyons, or Chamousset (*Mémoire politique sur les enfants*), and military leaders like Bousmard and even Robespierre were also to be found in their ranks. They all questioned the educative customs of their century, with three privileged targets: the practice of foundling hospitals, the rearing of children by domestic nurses, and the "artificial" education of rich children. These three techniques were accused of engendering, through their circular linkage, both the impoverishment of the nation and the etiolation of its elite.

9

The administration of foundling children was reproached for the appalling mortality rates of the minors in its care: ninety percent of these "forces" died before having been "made useful to the state," in spite of the great cost incurred by the state in their upkeep during childhood and adolescence. All these dissertations took pains to demonstrate the advisability rather of saving these bastard children for eventual service in national endeavors such as colonization, the militia, and the navy, for which they would be perfectly suited owing to their lack of constricting family ties. "Being without parents, with no other support than that obtained for them by wise government, they hold to nothing, and have nothing to lose. Could death itself appear as something to be feared by such men as these, whom nothing seems to attach to life, and who could be accustomed to danger at an early age? It should not be difficult to make people look upon death and danger with indifference when they are brought up without these sentiments and are not distracted by any mutual tenderness. They will be equally well suited to serve as sailors, to supplement the militia, or to populate colonies."[1] The author was thinking in particular of the colonization of Louisiana, where his brother had invested all his capital.

But what exactly was the origin of this high mortality rate? It resulted from the administration's difficulty in finding nurses for the children, and from the ill will and incompetence of these nurses. And here the special problem of foundlings took its place within the more general problem of nursing infants. The reliance on nurses from the country was the prevailing custom in the population of the cities. Women depended on them, either because they were too taken up with their own work (as wives of merchants and artisans) or because they were rich enough to be able to avoid the thankless task of breast-feeding. The villages in the immediate environs of the cities supplied nurses to the rich, and the poor had to search for theirs much farther away. The distance involved

1. Chamousset, *Mémoire politique sur les enfants. Oeuvres complètes* (1787), 2 vols.

and the absence of contact between nurses and parents other than that necessitated by intermediary difficulties (with the recruiters of nurses) meant that the placing of children with nurses was often a means of disguising desertion and an object of shady schemes. The nurses found it hard to collect their pay, despite the prison sentences meted out by the courts to fathers who were anything but prompt in fulfilling this obligation (so much so that one of the first philanthropic organizations set out to raise money for the freeing of fathers detained as a result of this infraction). Thus, in order to compensate for the risk, the poorer nurses would take on several infants at the same time. This was where the recruiters came in. They would make inquiries about all the women who were likely to furnish a child, whom they would deliver to the nurse on payment of a commission, sometimes arranging, with the nurse's complicity, to defraud the mother of an infant who had died in transit by continuing to draw money in its name. Under these conditions, the death rate of children entrusted to nurses was huge: around two-thirds for nurses living at a distance and one-fourth for those nearby.

The wealthy could buy themselves the exclusive services of a nurse but rarely her good will, and doctors suddenly discovered in the behavior of nurses the explanation for many of the defects that afflicted the children of rich parents. In the words of Buchan: "One is sometimes surprised to see the children of upright and virtuous parents display, from their earliest years, a fundamental baseness and malice. We can be certain that it is from their nurses that these children derive all their vices. They would have been decent if their mothers had nursed them."[2] Ballexserd was also of the opinion that bad habits could be transmitted by lactation, "especially if, desiccated by work, overcome with fatigue, the nurse offers the infant a steaming breast from whence there barely trickles a milk that is sour and inflamed." There were two very simple reasons for the spitefulness of nurses: self-interest and hatred. For exam-

2. William Buchan, *Médecine domestique* (1775).

ple, "the use of swaddling bands was instituted when mothers, refusing to nurse their infants, put them in the hands of vile slaves who in no wise sought to foster the growth of forces that might one day overwhelm them. The slave, being by nature the enemy of the master, was perforce that of the son as well; these nurses had only feelings of fear for the latter, and they gladly adopted these bands that allowed them to abandon the child without their facing any of the risks that might betray their negligence."[3] The education of children of the rich suffered from being left up to house servants who treated them to a mixture of constraints and liberties unsuited to their development, as was shown by the use of swaddling clothes. It was still the custom to rely on servants for all the practical tasks that were necessary for a certain corporal education of rich children, one that trained them exclusively in pleasure and in dress; witness the use of corsets for adolescents, a practice denounced by doctors at least as much as the swaddling of babies. The corset was an assemblage of whalebone stays laced tightly around the trunk in such a way as to make the waist slender. Applied with force to the chest and stomach, it obliged the body gradually to take on the desired shape, the price of this aesthetic molding being the litany of troubles caused by the compression it imposed. For the girls this was coupled with the debilitating confinement to which they were subjected up to the age of their first excursion into the world at large, an enfeebling seclusion that often rendered them unfit for the duties of motherhood and thus perpetuated the need for servants.

At the poorest extreme of the social body, what was denounced was the irrationality of the administration of foundling hospitals, the meager benefits the state derived from the rearing of a population that rarely attained an age at which it could repay the costs it had occasioned; in short, what was denounced was the lack of a *social economy*. At its wealthiest extreme, criticism was aimed at the organization of the body

---

3. Alphonse Leroy, *Recherches sur les habillements des femmes et des enfants* (1772).

with a view to the strictly wasteful use of it through the refinement of methods that made the body into a pure pleasure principle; in other words, what was lacking was an *economy of the body*.

The force of these discourses urging the preservation of children derived no doubt from the connection they set up between the medical domain and the social domain, between the theory of fluids on which eighteenth-century medicine was based and the economic theory of the physiocrats. Their whole militant power resulted from the relation they were able to bring into play between the production of wealth and the treatment of the body. The two theories effected a parallel reversal: for the physiocrats, in the relationship between wealth and the state; for the medical theorists, in the relationship between the body and the soul. Before the physiocrats, wealth was produced to provide for the munificence of states. It was their sumptuary activity, the multiplication and refinement of the needs of the central authority, that was conducive to production. Hence wealth was in the manifest power that permitted levies by the state for the benefit of a minority. With the physiocrats, the state was no longer the end of production, but its means: it was the responsibility of the state to govern social relations, in such a manner as to intensify this production to a maximum by restricting consumption. The mechanical theory of the body which formed the basis of eighteenth-century medicine consisted in a similar reversal of the respective positions of the soul and the body from the standpoint of perfection. "Of all the beings God has created, man is without question the most nearly perfect. He contains within him that particle of divine spirit, the soul, which the Sovereign Creator gave him for regulating his conduct and moderating his passions. In fashioning souls and uniting them to creatures, God gives them all the same perfections. How then does it happen that there are not two of the same character? Whence comes this absence of perfection that is found in most individuals? If these diversities issue from the soul, it must be that the soul changes with every change in the weather, a notion that lacks good sense. What, then, is the origin of this fact?" The question was raised by Nicolas Malouin in the opening passage of a work, *Le Traité des solides et des fluides* (1712), which might also have served as an inaugural statement for all of eighteenth-century medicine. Between this guiding principle that was the soul and the extreme variability of results, one must envisage the solidity of a mechanism whose variations and dysfunctions could offer the keys to the manifestations of the human race. What was it that could upset this mechanics, this assemblage of "fibers" (muscles) that made up the human body? External factors such as the air and all the deleterious principles it conveyed; but also the relative ease of circulation of fluids, their retention or excessive dissipation which, through the process of their thickening or abatement, caused repercussions on the firmness of the solids (the fibers). This was the case with the retention of mother's milk: finding its natural exit blocked, it "precipitates itself without distinction over all the parts according to the number of obstacles they place in its path, causing them to suffer manifold ills."[4] And likewise with the dissipation of sperm through onanism, of that "essential oil whose loss leaves the other humors feeble and stale," producing the maladies everyone knew of.[5] Once a certain threshold had been crossed in this deterioration, the movements of the fibers escaped completely the control of the soul. And besides, "what is coitus, if not a little epilepsy?"[6] It was necessary, therefore, to place the soul in command of the circulation of flows, the haunting fear being their escape, movement for its own sake, convulsion, viewed as a failure of the soul. It was no longer the body that must, by its stigmata or its purity, testify to the loftiness of the soul, to its detachment; it was the soul that was in turn called upon to account for the imperfections of bodies and conducts, to apply itself to their management through a healthy regulation of flows.

4. Joseph Raulin, *Traité des affections vaporeuses du sexe* (1758).
5. S.-A.-D. Tissot, *De l'onanisme* (Lausanne, 1760).
6. Ibid.

The correspondence between the economy of social flows and the economy of body flows was not simply metaphorical. The physiocratic school pitted ground rent, the serious nature of agricultural production, against the illusions of sumptuary production. Similarly, all of eighteenth-century medicine could be ordered around the following question: How was it that the peasants, and particularly their children, who had a far more arduous life and a diet less rich than the bourgeois and the nobles, were nonetheless in better health? The answer: Because they were not subjected to the same aesthetic constraints; instead of submitting to the artifices of dress and confinement, they enjoyed the beneficial effects of regular exercise; instead of surrendering to the passions, they were compelled by their labor to lead a regular existence.

But what was responsible for the movement of rural production toward the crowded cities? What caused the disaffection with peasant ways in favor of the unwholesome pleasures of the city? Was there a practical link between, on the one hand, the wasteful use of bodies, both in the scant value they were accorded (abandoned children) and in the refinement of methods that marked them out exclusively for pleasure, and on the other hand, that economy of expenditure and prestige on which the cities so dubiously prided themselves? Yes, there was a guiding thread; the trouble lay with those hapless beings against whom the entire social and medical thought of the eighteenth century raised its voice: the house servants. It was through them that the saturation of the cities and the disaffection of the countryside were related. Men rushed off to become house servants because the position afforded them exemption from service in the militia. Instead of remaining on their lands and supervising production in person, the nobles and newly arrived bourgeois moved to the city, where they found no other way to display their wealth than to surround themselves with the very men who constituted the living forces of production, whom they attracted by wearing fancy clothes and high-sounding titles. These urban servants would then try to live above their means. They would contract marriages and have children whom their circumstances did not allow them to rear, and so they would leave these children in the care of the state. As a result, the poor women of the rural areas, no longer able to find anyone to marry, would offer themselves to the mortiferous industry of child nursing, or else resign themselves to coming to the city as servants; once there, dazzled by the lives of their mistresses, who were totally absorbed in entertainment and finery, they would be dying to follow their example whatever the cost might be. Whence the growing procession of indecent and corrupting prostitutes. The evil circuit of domesticity led relentlessly to the indolence of the ladies and to the insolence of the prostitutes.

Preserving children came to mean, on the one hand, putting an end to the misdeeds of domestic servants, creating new conditions of education that would be capable of counteracting the harmful effects suffered by the children entrusted to them, and on the other hand, attaching to the education of their children all those individuals who tended to abandon them to the care of the state or to the murderous business of the nurses. If the cause of the evil was everywhere the same, the remedies were different precisely according to whether it was a question of the rich or the poor. The eighteenth century is extolled for its revalorization of educative tasks, and it is said that the image of childhood underwent a change in that period. No doubt, but it is also true that what was set into place then was a reorganized educative behavior which revolved around two very distinct poles, resulting from two quite different strategies. The first was centered on the spread of household medicine, that is, a set of knowledges and techniques designed to enable the bourgeois classes to rescue their children from the negative influence of servants and to place them under the parents' observation. The second aimed at the consolidation, under the label of "social economy," of all the forms of direction of the life of the poor, so as to diminish the social cost of their reproduction and obtain an optimum number of workers at minimum public expense: in short, what is customarily termed philanthropy.

From the last third of the eighteenth century to the end of
the nineteenth, doctors put together a series of works concerning the rearing, education, and medical care of children
of bourgeois families. After the classical texts of the eighteenth century, by the likes of Tissot, Buchan, and Raulin,
one notes a continuous series of publications on the art of
bringing up young children, along with guidebooks and dictionaries of hygiene for the use of families.[7] Medical treatises
in the eighteenth century had expounded a medical doctrine
and offered medical advice at the same time. In the nineteenth century, the medical texts addressed to families
changed their tone and limited themselves to giving prescrip-
tive advice. This was for two, doubtless convergent, reasons.
After Lavoisier, the mechanical conception of the body was
no longer tenable; the perfect congruence between medical
doctrine and educative ethic disappeared along with it. Doctors no longer had a homogeneous discourse at their disposal,
but rather a knowledge [*un savoir*] that was rapidly changing;
and they were obliged for tactical reasons to separate the
category of hygienic precepts from that of the diffusion of a
knowledge, especially as they began to fear the effects of a
hasty vulgarization of medical analyses that would lead
everyone to act as impromptu doctors, with all the mistakes
this could involve, and more serious still, a resulting loss of
power by the medical profession. Hence the search for a relationship between medicine and the family that would make it
possible to get around these two difficulties. The establishment of a family medicine, directly anchoring medicine in the
family molecule, was the best means of foiling the tempta-

---

7. A few of the most important of these: Richard, *Essai sur l'éducation physique des
enfants du premier âge* (1829); Pierre Maigne, *Choix d'une nourrice* (1836); Alfred
Donne, *Conseils aux mères sur la manière d'élever leurs nouveaux-nés ou de l'éducation
physique des enfants du premier âge* (1842); François Servais, *Hygiène de l'enfance ou
guide des mères de famille* (1850); Eugène Bouchut, *Hygiène de la première enfance:
Guide des mères pour l'allaitement, le sevrage et le choix de la nourrice* (1869); Francis
Devay, *Traité d'hygiène spéciale des familles;* Jean-Baptiste Fonssagrives, *De la régénération physique de l'espèce humaine par l'hygiène de la famille et en particulier du rôle
de la mère dans l'éducation physique des enfants* (1867); *Dictionnaire de la santé ou
répertoire d'hygiène pratique à l'usage des familles et des écoles* (1876).

tions of charlatans and uncertified doctors. And within the family itself, the privileged alliance between doctor and mother would serve to reproduce the distance, originating in the hospitals, between men of learning and the level of execution of precepts that was assigned to women. In 1876, the hygienist Fonssagrives introduced his *Dictionnaire de la santé* with two major notes of warning: "I would caution those persons who might look in this dictionary for the means of practicing medicine to their detriment, or to that of others, that they will find nothing of the kind therein. I propose solely to teach them to look after their health amid the perils that threaten it, not to concern themselves with the health of others; to comprehend fully what medicine can do and what it cannot; to secure themselves against the deadly effects of routine and prejudice; to establish their relations with their physician in a manner that is reasonable and beneficial for all. Secondly, my purpose here is to teach women the art of *domestic nursing*. Hired *attendants* are to true nurses what professional nursemaids are to mothers: a necessity, and nothing more. It is my ambition to make women into accomplished nurses who are understanding of all things, but who understand most of all that their role is there with the sick, and that it is as exalted as it is helpful. The role of the mother and that of the doctor are, and must remain, clearly distinct. The one prepares and facilitates the other; they are, or rather they should be, complementary to each other in the interest of the patient. The doctor prescribes, the mother executes."

This organic link between doctor and family was to have profound repercussions on family life, leading to its reorganization in at least three directions: (1) the closing up of the family against the negative influences of the older educative milieu, against the methods and prejudices of domestic servants, against all the effects of social promiscuities; (2) the making of a privileged alliance with the mother, favoring the advancement of women by virtue of this recognition of their educative usefulness; (3) the utilization of the family by the doctor against all the old structures of education, religious discipline, and the practice of the boarding school.

Up to the middle of the eighteenth century, medicine took little interest in children and women. Considered simply as reproducing machines, women had their own medicine, scorned by the School of Medicine and forming a tradition whose trace remains in the expression "old wives' remedies." Childbirth, the maladies of women giving birth, and children's illnesses were the responsibility of the "old wives," a corporation that was on the same footing as the servants and nursemaids who partook of its knowledge and put it into practice. The conquest of this market by the medical profession therefore implied the destruction of the dominant influence of the old wives, a long struggle against their practices, which were deemed worthless and pernicious. The main points of confrontation were, of course, maternal breast-feeding and the clothing of children. The works of the eighteenth and nineteenth centuries repeat the same praises of maternal nursing, lavish the same pieces of advice on the choice of a good nursemaid, and tirelessly denounce the practice of swaddling babies and the use of corsets. But they also open a multitude of combat fronts on the question of children's games (celebration of the educational game), on the stories told to them (criticism of ghost stories and of the traumas they cause), on the daily routine, on the creation of a space specifically reserved for children, on the notion of observation (in favor of a discreet but ubiquitous mother's gaze). All these little focuses of struggle were organized around a strategical objective: insofar as possible, to free the child of all constraints, of everything that might interfere with his freedom of movement, with the exercise of his body, so as to facilitate to the maximum the growth of his forces; to protect him fully from contacts that might cause him harm (physical danger) or corrupt him (moral dangers, from ghost stories to sexual deviation) and so divert him from the straight line of his development. Hence the close supervision of servants, the transformation of the family dwelling into a space programmed in such a way as to foster the playfulness of the child, the easy control of his movements. Through the action of this domestic medicine, the bourgeois family gradually came to resemble a hothouse insulated against outside influences. This change in the government of children was necessary not only for their hygiene but for the treatment of their illness as well. The education practiced by servants was based on the principle of the least effort for them; also on the principle of their greatest pleasure, as, for example, in the sexual games they would play with the children. Consequently, it produced children who were malformed and capricious, spoiled in both senses of the word, a veritable prey to all illnesses, and the more difficult to heal in that they would not submissively follow the treatment one tried to apply to them. Hence the doctor's need for an ally in place: the mother, the only one capable, on a daily basis, of containing the obscurantism of the servants and of imposing her will on the child.

This was an alliance profitable to both parties: with the mother's help, the doctor prevailed against the stubborn hegemony of that popular medicine of the old wives; and on the other hand, owing to the increased importance of maternal functions, he conceded a new power to the bourgeois woman in the domestic sphere. It became evident as early as the end of the eighteenth century that this alliance was capable of shaking paternal authority. In 1785, the Academy of Berlin offered the following questions for competitive discussion: (1) In a state of nature, what are the foundations and limits of paternal authority? (2) Is there a difference between the rights of the mother and those of the father? (3) To what degree can the laws extend or restrict this authority? Among the award-winning replies, that of Peuchet, the author of the *Encyclopédie méthodique,* took a position clearly in favor of a revaluation of the powers of the mother: "If the grounds for the power that parents hold with respect to their children during their age of weakness and ignorance reside for the most part in the obligation they are under to attend to the welfare and preservation of these fragile beings, there is no question that the extent of this power grows in proportion to the duties one has to fulfill in their behalf. Owing to her position as mother, nurse, and protectress, the woman is prescribed duties that are unknown to men, and consequently she has a more positive right to obedience. The best reason for asserting that the mother has a more genuine right to the submission of her children is that she has greater need of it."[8]

By augmenting the civil authority of the mother, the doctor furnished her with a social status. It was this promotion of the woman as mother, educator, and medical auxiliary that was to serve as a point of support for the main feminist currents of the nineteenth century.[9]

The defects of the education of young children in the private sphere had their equivalents in the public sphere. Fonssagrives used the same emphases to denounce the dangers that public education brought to bear on the health of children, invoking the same principles as those employed to proscribe the old customs of the swaddling band and the corset. Were not these reflected in the monastic rigor and inflexibility of the *lycées* and convents? Did not the overcrowding, the poor ventilation, and the lack of exercise echo the confinement of children in the narrowest rooms of the family dwelling? Were not the promiscuity of the dormitory and the threat of contagion from the corrupt habits it bred of the same order as the risk of depravation of children by unscrupulous servants and seemingly innocent games? Doctors cautioned families against the boarding school, the conventual rules of the *lycées,* the overexertion of the programs of instruction, against that "homicidal education," as it was called;[10] they inspired a crusade that would result in the formation of the first associations of parents of schoolchildren at the end of the nineteenth century. And accompanying this crusade, the principle

8. Jacques Peuchet, *Encyclopédie méthodique* (1792), category 111–112, the article "Enfant, police et municipalité."

9. See Ernest Legouvé, *Histoire morale de la femme* (1849); Julie Daubié, *La Femme pauvre au XIXe siècle* (1866); Léon Richer, *La Femme libre* (1877).

10. Victor de Laprade, *L'Éducation homicide* (1866).

of a mixed education involving the family and the school, where the parents would prepare the child to accept scholastic discipline, but at the same time would see to it that good conditions of public education were maintained. This called for improving the health standards of the boarding schools, doing away with the vestiges of corporal punishment, eliminating the physical dangers that might threaten their children (such as broken glass lining the tops of the walls), developing gymnastic exercises, keeping watch over the approaches to the *lycées,* over the newspaper kiosks, the bars, and the exhibitionists and prostitutes who hung about in such places. The idea was to establish the same proportion of physical liberation and moral protection in public education as existed in private education.

Of course all this applied only to families who were well-off, those who had servants, those in which the wives could devote themselves to the organization of the household, who could pay for their children's studies at the *lycée,* and those, finally, who had enough education themselves to benefit from these kinds of texts. The intervention in the affairs of working-class families went through other channels than the circulation of books and the establishment of an organic alliance between the family and medicine. In the first place, the illiteracy rate among these families was substantial up to the end of the nineteenth century; secondly, people of the lower classes could not afford a family doctor; but most important, the problems they presented were entirely unlike those discussed above. Seemingly, what was at issue was a similar concern to ensure the preservation of children, to spread the same hygienic precepts; but as regards *social economy,* the operations that were undertaken were completely different in nature from those conducted under the auspices of domestic medicine, and they produced results that were virtually opposite. The aim was no longer to free children from awkward constraints but to call a halt to the liberties that were being taken (abandonment in foundling hospitals, the disguised abandonment of putting children out to nurse), to control unauthorized associations (the growth of concubinage that accompanied urbanization in the first half of the nineteenth century), to block lines of escape (the vagabondage of individuals, of children in particular). In this case, it was no longer a question of enacting discreet protective measures but of establishing direct surveillance.

A study needs to be made concerning the parallel histories of convents for the perservation and correction of young girls, supervised brothels for prostitutes, and foundling hospitals. These three institutions arose and declined within approximately the same time span. In the seventeenth century, convents were induced by the Counter-Reformation to take in unmarried women in order to train them for missionary, relief, and educative work. At the same time, Vincent de Paul set out to centralize the disposition of abandoned children, to give the state the final responsibility for their care, as opposed to their use by the corporation of beggars, who would often resort to mutilations in order to make them into objects of pity. The repression of prostitutes also dates from this period. After having been confined since the Middle Ages to special districts, they saw themselves gradually banished from the streets. At the end of the eighteenth century and in the first half of the nineteenth, the police itself organized the system of brothels, searching out prostitutes who worked on their own and forcing them into dens that were under the direct control of the police. At the end of the nineteenth century, these three practices were simultaneously discredited: Public Assistance was organized against the automatic abandonment of illegitimate children in foundling hospitals; the workrooms and convents of preservation were the object of all sorts of financial and moral scandals; and the vice police that organized prostitution were vociferously attacked for the arbitrary nature of their arrests and for their function as a parallel police. Hence a single historical curve unifies these three types of procedures, suggesting their function of transition between the old family regime and the new.

The setting up of these practices of collection and segregation is understandable only in relation to the axioms that governed the old system of alliances and filiations: the determining of those—male and female—on whom would devolve the perpetuation of the patrimony; the possibility for them alone to marry, the others remaining in their charge; the discrimination between the legitimate offspring of sexual unions and the illegitimate offspring. The regime of alliances, therefore, did not seek to coincide with sexual practices, but was based rather on a calculated distance from them. It was necessary to preserve the persons intended for profitable alliances from any union that was not consistent with this purpose; it was also necessary to divert those without the means from any familial aspirations. All this implied a separation between the sexual and the familial, a divergence that produced illegalities which were more or less tolerated, and also generated endless conflicts and the loss of "useful" forces. As regards the family, this discrepancy between the regime of alliances and the sexual domain constituted a permanent threat to the peace of households through the seductive, fraudulent practices it engendered and which the law treatises did their best to codify.[11] From the standpoint of the state, individuals who were rejected by the law of alliances became a source of danger through their vagabondage and indigence; they were also a loss in that they constituted unemployed forces. When the convents of preservation came into existence, along with brothels and foundling hospitals, their explicit purpose was to reconcile the interest of families and the interest of the state, to bring harmony to families through the moralization of behavior, and to consolidate the force of the state through the treatment of the inevitable casualties of this family regime: the unmarried men and women and the abandoned children. The growth of the police in the eighteenth century relied on the power of the family, promising it peace and happiness while extending police authority over the family's rebels and

11. Eugène Fournel, *Traité de séduction* (1781).

castoffs. Hence the central apparatus proclaimed itself to be in the service of families. An author like Rétif de la Bretonne could even imagine that the development of this machinery represented a means of solving, once and for all, the problem posed by the divergence between the family and sexuality. In *Le Pornographe, ou Idées d'un honnête homme sur un projet de règlement pour les prostituées propre à prévenir les malheurs qu'occasionne le publicisme des femmes* (1769), he proposes an institution that would combine the advantages of the convent, the brothel, and the foundling hospital. It would be a place where all the young women not intended by their families for marriage could go. In this conventlike edifice, the most beautiful of the young women would be reserved for the satisfaction of clients who could eventually marry them. The others, together with the older women, would busy themselves with the education of the children produced by these unions and would thus place "in the service of the state a nursery of subjects who would not be a direct burden upon it (since the clients would pay) and over which it would have an unlimited power, since paternal rights and the rights of the sovereign would be combined."

But this harmony between the order of families and the order of the state was more the result of a tactical collusion than that of a strategical alliance. For the one and the other were not scandalized by the same thing. What troubled families was adulterine children, rebellious adolescents, women of ill repute—everything that might be prejudicial to their honor, reputation, or standing. By contrast, what worried the state was the squandering of vital forces, the unused or useless individuals. So, between these two types of objectives there was indeed a temporary convergence on the principle of the concentration of the family's undesirable members; but whereas for families this concentration served the purpose of exclusion, for the state it was valuable as a means of checking the costly practices of the family, as a starting point for a policy of conservation and utilization of individuals. Functioning as a surface of absorption for the undesirables of the family order, the general hospitals, convents, and foundling hospitals served at the same time as a strategical base for a whole series of corrective interventions in family life. These assembly points for society's misfortunes, miseries, and failures facilitated the mobilization of philanthropic energies, providing it with a point of support, serving as a laboratory for observing working-class behavior, as a launching ramp for tactics designed to counter the socially negative effects of this behavior and to reorganize the working-class family in terms of socio-economic urgencies.

Nothing better exemplifies this reversal in the relationship between state and family than the history of the foundling hospitals. The concern to combine a respect for life with a respect for family honor brought about—in the middle of the eighteenth century—the invention of an ingenious technical device: the *turret*. This was a revolving cylinder with an opening on one side of its revolving surface; its closed side faced the street. An outside bell was placed nearby. When a woman wanted to abandon a newborn child, she merely had to alert the person on duty by ringing the bell, and straightway the cylinder, revolving on its axis, would present its open side to the exterior; it would then receive the infant and, continuing its motion, convey the child inside the hospital. In this way the donor would not have been seen by any of the house staff. And this was the objective: to break, cleanly and without scandal, the original link identifying these individuals as the offspring of objectionable alliances, to cleanse social relations of progeny not in conformity with the law of the family, with its ambitions and its reputation.

The first turret went into operation in Rouen in 1758. It was aimed at eliminating the ancient practice of abandonment on the porches of churches, private residences, and convents, where the infants had ample time to die before anyone took charge of them. In 1811, the turret system was generalized in the framework of the reorganization of the hospitals, and 269 of them were counted in that year. They were to be gradually done away with. From 1826 to 1853, 165 turrets were closed, and the last one disappeared in 1860. The appearance and disappearance of the turret corresponded to a substantial increase in the number of abandoned children, followed by a reduction and stabilization. At the time of its establishment, the foundling hospital of Saint Vincent de Paul sheltered 312 children; in 1740, 3,150; in 1784, 40,000; in 1826, 118,000; in 1833, 131,000; in 1859, 76,500. From this, one gets an idea of the importance of the debates on keeping or discontinuing the turrets. All the defenders of the juridical strength of the family were supporters of the turret: men such as Lamartine, A. de Melun, and Le Play. They acclaimed its function of redeeming sexual waywardness, it being a kind of confessional that recorded the results of error and absolved it at the same time. In order to mitigate the danger of too large a number of abandonments, they suggested giving added weight to the juridical status of the family by restoring paternity inquiry procedures that had fallen into disuse since the Revolution, by instituting a tax on single life, and by clearly separating the class of individuals who were inscribed in the family context from bastard children who could be reserved for external tasks such as colonization or substitute for legitimate sons in militia duty. Those who were hostile to the turret were the proponents of enlightened philanthropy, men like Chaptal, La Rochefoucauld-Liancourt, and Ducpétiaux, who spoke for the rationalization of public assistance, for the expansion of adoption, and hence for the primacy of the conservation of individuals over the preservation of the rights of blood relations.

What made the decision swing in favor of the latter was the discovery of a popular use of the turret that had nothing to do with its primary purpose, which was simply to relieve families of those objects of social scandal, their adulterine children. As early as the end of the eighteenth century, the administrations of foundling hospitals began to suspect their institutions of being the object of a fraudulent maneuver. In *L'Administration des finances de la France,* Necker allowed that "this praiseworthy institution has doubtless prevented beings meriting compassion from becoming victims of the unnatural feelings of their parents," but "by slow degrees people have got used to seeing the foundling hospitals as public houses in which the sovereign would deem it just to feed and care for the poorest of his subject's children; and as this notion has gained currency, it has loosened the ties of duty and parental love among the people."[12] Puzzled by this staggering rise in the number of abandonments, the administrators multiplied their commissions of inquiry in order to determine the causes. First, they discovered a substantial number of legitimate children among the abandoned, all the more as, owing to a decreasing infant mortality rate in the foundling hospitals, the scruples of parents were disappearing. But even more serious in the eyes of the managers, not only were legitimate families deserting their children because of extreme poverty, but some who were capable of rearing them were also undertaking to have them nurtured by the state by getting themselves assigned to foster their own children. "Since the legislation regularizing the condition of foundling children by allocating a salary to nursemaids, a new sort of abandonment has suddenly arisen and assumed extraordinary proportions in a brief space of time. Now the mother who brings a newborn child to the turret of a hospital has not the least intention of abandoning it; if she separates herself from it, this is in order to reclaim it a few days later with the complicity of go-betweens. When the hospitals were burdened with a large number of infants, they soon realized the impossibility of providing the proper care for them within their walls. Nurses in the countryside became indispensable. They were entrusted with the children, and a salary was allocated for this service. Carriers would bring the newborn from the hospital to the women who were to nurse them, and serious irregularities ensued. It occurred to these girls and women of the country that they had much to gain by abandoning their infants; if, through their understanding with the carriers, they could resume pos-

---

12. Jacques Necker, *De l'administration des finances de la France* (1821), vol. 4 of his *Oeuvres complètes.*

session of their infants a few days later, they would thus ensure themselves the enjoyment of several months of fosterage and later a pension. The fraud defied all the inquiries. When the mother was hindered by special considerations and dared not bring up her child at home, neighbors would take official charge of the infant."[13]

Drawing inferences from these inquiries, the minister of the interior, De Corbière, circulated a memorandum in 1827 calling for the movement of children to another department, so as to prevent mothers from receiving pay for nursing infants they had themselves deposited in the turret, or from visiting their infants at the homes of unrelated nurses to whose care they had been committed. He was assuming that to deprive mothers of the sight of their children would dissuade them from their plan of abandonment. The result was more on the negative side. Of 32,000 children transported in this way from 1827 to 1837, 8,000 were reclaimed by their mothers, who only brought them back again a short time later when the measure was rescinded, and almost all the others perished from the effects of this brutal transplantation. In 1837, De Gasparin officially recognized the failure of this policy in a report to the king in which he put forward the idea of replacing the hospital sanctuary, with all its drawbacks, by a system of aid to mothers at home. This would amount to paying the mother the monthly wages formerly paid by the hospital to a nurse who was, in principle, unrelated. It also meant replacing the turret system with that of the open office. The secrecy as to origins which the turret made possible lent itself to all kinds of deceptive schemes and caused the administration to lose the initiative. By organizing admission offices on an open-door basis instead of on that of a blind reception, it was possible on the one hand to discourage abandonment and on the other to assign aid based on an administrative investigation of the mother's situation.

This reversal was rich in consequences: by the decision to

13. J.-F. Terme and J.-B. Monfalcon, *Histoire des enfants trouvés* (1837).

furnish financial and medical assistance not only to the poorest women but also to the most immoral, a mechanism was activated that implied the generalization of these allowances to all other categories of mothers to avoid accusations of subsidizing vice. Thus, what might have been allotted to an underage mother to encourage her to keep her child became a right that was all the more justifiable for the widow burdened with children, then for the mother of a large family, then for the woman worker who must not be discouraged from reproducing. Family allowances thus came into being at the end of the nineteenth century, at the meeting point of a welfare practice that gradually widened the circle of those under its jurisdiction and an employer's practice of paternalism that was happy to unburden itself, on a national level, of an administration that reaped it as many troubles as benefits.

What also resulted was the extension of medical control over the rearing of children from working-class families. The first societies for the protection of children appeared in Paris in 1865 (founded by A. Meyer), then in Lyons. They sought to ensure the medical inspection of children placed with nurses, but also to perfect systems of education, methods of hygiene, and the supervision of children of the lower classes. In their publications they kept, for example, a column with the heading "crimes and accidents" in which were cited all the facts pointing to bad treatment, all the misdemeanors of "nonsupervision" committed by parents. These societies got support from the patronage committees that had already sprung up in connection with the supervision of children in the hospitals. More important, they argued from the fact that, in the poorer classes, the children who received the best medical treatment were those who depended on Public Assistance. This argument would be taken up again by Théophile Roussel in setting forth the conditions of application of his Law of 1874 on the supervision of wet nurses: "Notwithstanding the disinterested counsel of physicians and enlightened persons, the force of habit, the brutish stubbornness of the peasants, and the foolish advice of the midwives maintain practices that are fatal to children whose health needs are poorly attended to; let it suffice for me to add one characteristic detail: the fact is that the only children who are properly cared for in the poor departments, with a mortality rate as low as 6 percent, are those belonging to underage mothers who have managed to obtain monthly assistance from the department and who are specially supervised by an inspector from the prefecture whom they fear and whose advice they heed."[14]

The image was thus formed of the mother of the working-class family. She was more nurse than mother, actually, since she owed her origin to the model of the state-certified wet nurse. From this model she took the dual dimension of her status: collective remuneration and medical-state supervision. Because of this nursing aspect, the link attaching her to her child would long remain questionable, arousing suspicions of laxity, abandonment, self-interestedness, or hopeless incompetence: the legacy of an encounter between the working-class woman and state assistance, in which the positive aspect in the eyes of her protectors would always be more the result of a conjunction and a forced dependence of the mother on the child than that of a desired procreation. Abandoned children were called *enfants de la patrie*. So that they might be reared without too great a loss and at the least expense, they were returned to their mothers, making the latter, then by extension all working-class mothers, into "state-approved nurses," according to Lakanal's phrase.

The campaigns for the restoration of marriage in the poorer classes originated in this same concern to combat the unverifiable inflation of the costs of assistance. When, after having exhausted the considerations of higher morality and religion that the subject required in those days, the licensed observers of the working class (Villermé, Frégier, Blanqui, Reybaud, Jules Simon, Leroy-Beaulieu) came around to the

14. Théophile Roussel, *Rapport sur l'application de la loi de 1874* (1884).

real basis of their fears, the point at issue was always the threat to the public budget posed by this mass of illegitimate children, destined to vagrancy and death at an early age. Since the end of the eighteenth century, a multitude of philanthropic and religious associations had made it their goal to come to the aid of the poorer classes, to moralize their behavior and facilitate their education by concentrating their efforts toward the restoration of family life, the first form and the most economical formula of mutual aid. In 1850, the Academy of Moral and Political Sciences passed a resolution supporting the Société de Saint-François-Régis, an association that promoted civil and religious marriage among the poor; the words of this text could hardly have been more explicit: "Men placed at the head of business and government know how urgent it is to diminish and restrict not only the costs of policing and judicial action occasioned by the excesses that the depraved classes indulge in, but also all the expenses for the almshouses and hospitals that result from the mutual abandonment of fathers, wives, and children who should have helped one another as members of the same family, but who, not being united by any social tie, become strangers to one another. The task at hand is not only a social necessity and a highly moral endeavor; it is also an excellent piece of business, an obvious and immense saving for the state, the departments, and the municipalities. When the man and woman of the people live in disorder, they often have neither hearth nor home. They are only at ease where vice and crime reign free. But on the contrary, once a man and a woman of the people, illicitly joined together, are married, they desert the filthy rooms that were their only refuge and set up their home. Their foremost concern is to withdraw their children from the hospitals in which they had placed them. These married fathers and mothers establish a family, that is, a center where the children are fed, clothed, and protected; they send these children to school and place them in apprenticeship."[15]

15. Resolution of the Academy of Moral and Political Sciences, published in the *Annales de la charité*, vol. 2 (1847).

Restoring marriage, in the first phase at least, was the role of the protective societies. These societies differed in their philanthropic choices: they included such representatives of Enlightenment philanthropy as had survived the Revolutionary period (Société philanthropique; Société de la charité maternelle, founded in 1784; Société de la morale chrétienne, Société pour l'instruction élémentaire), but also religious charities inspired or reanimated by the spirit of the Restoration (Société Saint-Vincent-de-Paul, Frères des Écoles chrétiennes, Société de Saint-François-Régis, and so on). The differences did not keep them from operating as a combine with a system of mutual relays. For example, the Société de la charité maternelle, whose objective was to prevent legitimate families from abandoning their children by supplying them with material and financial subsidies, would refer the illegitimate families who came to it to the Société de Saint-François-Régis, making the marriage contract a condition for benefitting from its aid.[16] The Frères des Écoles chrétiennes practiced the same blackmail with regard to the education of poor children. For its part, the Société de Saint-François-Régis, founded in 1826, facilitated the transfer of administrative records (the extent of migrations made it difficult for the poor to obtain papers verifying their civil status), provided for the registry of documents free of charge, and obtained a gradual reduction of the juridical conditions for marriage (for instance, a lowering of the legal age for marriage for men and women). This might explain the expansion of the society and others like it: Société du mariage civil, Oeuvre des mariages indigents, Secrétariat du peuple, Secrétariat des familles. From 1826 to 1846, the Société de Saint-François-Régis attended to 13,798 households "living in disorder" and thus brought 27,596 individuals back to "religion and morality"; in the same space of time, 11,000 children received the blessings of legitimation.[17]

16. Regarding the Société de la charité maternelle, see F. Gille, *La Société de la charité maternelle de Paris* (1887).
17. Jules Gossin, *La Société de Saint-François-Régis* (1844); in addition, see the *Manuel de la Société de Saint-François-Régis* (1851), by the same author.

But these numbers were small given the extent of concubinage in the working-class strata, a figure that varied, according to the area considered, between one-third and one-half of couples. Observers like Louis Reybaud, Jules Simon, Leroy-Beaulieu, and Julie Daubié noted, starting in the middle of the century, that negligence and the difficulty of obtaining the necessary papers were factors, certainly, but only superficial ones: the very quality of these marriages was a problem. "It is all very well to regularize situations, to give rights to the woman," wrote Jules Simon, "but what happens to the family once the marriage is concluded? Does the husband give up the cabaret in order to live within the family? Does he take to saving money? Does he put his wife in a condition to take care of the children and the household? Not at all; respectable people have gone out of their way to smooth over all the difficulties of marriage; they have caused his papers and those of his future wife to be furnished, obtained all the necessary authorizations, seen to all the expenses, so that he only has to say a few words and enter his name in a register. He lets himself be led through the ceremony and then goes on living as before."[18] Contracted with specific advantages in mind, these marriages were valuable only insofar as they were necessary for obtaining those advantages; they did not make for the desired transformation of the working-class way of life. They were less a contract between a man and a woman than a contract between them and the protective societies. What was the reason, then, for the ill favor with which family life was regarded by the workers?

The protective societies furnished the explanation by calling attention to the difficulties they encountered. They had no trouble making themselves understood among the women, but with the men, things were different. "The husband-to-be takes this step only grudgingly; the woman has to drag him. So, if the reception he gets is not superabundantly cordial, all is lost. Glad of the least pretext, the man withdraws in a

18. Jules Simon, *L'Ouvrière* (1861), p. 285.

huff."[19] Why this reluctance? It seems that for the worker, marriage was associated with the acquisition of an *état,* a "station"—a shop, a market stall, a trade, a piece of property—to which the dowry would contribute. By means of the dowry, the woman provided a contribution that was meant to make up for the cost of her keep and that of her children. The importance of this phenomenon was such that under the Second Empire, the army still prohibited soldiers from marrying women without dowries as well as from legitimizing their natural children.[20] Through the dowry, the woman bought her special position. Whether it was a question of her marrying or entering a convent, every recognized position implied this starting capital. A woman without a dowry remained out of the running, under the domestic control of her family or of whoever might want to use her. Traditionally, this dowry was furnished by the family, the municipal corporation, or the trade association; but the disappearance or reduction of the role of these agencies, along with industry's drawing off of workers of both sexes, who were thus detached from their territorial and family moorings, led to the concentration of a large number of women who were too poor to command a dowry and who consequently were open to "adventures."

What might take the place of this starting capital that they could no longer supply? It could not be a sum of money, as they were too numerous; so it would have to be their labor, their domestic labor, requalified, given added value, raised to the level of a trade. This solution offered three advantages. First, it would allow a social expense to be replaced by an additional quantity of unpaid labor. It would also allow elements of hygiene to be introduced into working-class life in the areas of child rearing and nutrition, and would make possible a regularization of behavior, the lack of which explained the frequency of premature deaths, illness, and insubordination (for what was at the root of this physical decay and moral independence if not the habit of living in furnished

19. Gossin, *La Société de Saint-François-Régis.*
20. Daubié, *La Femme pauvre.*

rooms, taking one's meals at the wine seller's, in brief, prefer-
ring the life of society and the cabaret?). Finally, this would
make it possible to have the man controlled by the woman,
since she would provide him with the benefits of her domestic
activity only to the extent that he deserved them. In place of
the contract she had formerly entered into with him, which,
through the dowry, afforded him the possibility of an *exterior*
autonomy, of a social position by virtue of the profession or
trade—*état*—he held, she would now make him dependent on
an *interior* that would be her exclusive domain, something she
could give but also take back at any time. In the Second
Empire, the works of Jules Simon began to spread the word
of this great discovery: woman, the housewife and attentive
mother, was man's salvation, the privileged instrument for
civilizing the working class. It sufficed merely to shape her to
this use, to furnish her with the necessary instruction, to instill
in her the elements of a tactics of devotion, in order for her to
stamp out the spirit of independence in the working man.

This was not a matter of discourse but of active alliances
and effective operations. The second half of the nineteenth
century was marked by a decisive alliance between promotional feminism and moralizing philanthropy, in the dual
struggle first against brothels, prostitution, and the vice police, then against convents and the backward education of
women.

Re-establishing family life in the working class thus implied
completely altering the ground rules, the failure of which was
becoming increasingly apparent.

On the one hand, there were women who were delivered
over willy-nilly to the industrial process. The jobs they found
within it were the least skilled and the lowest paid. With the
wages they received, they were able to feed themselves, just
barely, but taking care of their children was a serious problem. Especially as the men, if they were not actually displaced
from their jobs by women, were at least under a greater risk
of unemployment, and in any case were the victims of a process of disqualification of labor that caused them to lose both

their rights over women and children and, by the same token, their responsibilities. So there was nothing surprising in the fact that the men tended to desert the factory and send the women and children in their place, living off them and letting their health and their strength go to ruin. In the long run, this ill-considered exploitation of women's labor posed a menace to the productive forces of the nation. It was a party to the destruction of the family that was being carried out through an odious abuse of patriarchal power. It was not surprising either that women workers in this situation often turned to prostitution, thus performing their "fifth quarter" of work, according to an expression noted by Villermé. The vice police, who methodically sought out all women they regarded as suspect, only ratified this situation instead of remedying it. They even made it worse: by forcing every woman presumed to practice prostitution into a brothel, they claimed to be preserving public morals, when in fact they were condemning these unfortunate souls to an irreversible destiny.

On the other hand, there were women who tried to protect their contractual ability through the acquisition of a dowry and to preserve their honor by joining a religious workroom or industrial convent. The substantial proliferation of religious communities of women in the middle of the nineteenth century was due to this continuing role of the dowry. The *ouvroirs* were women's workshops organized by religious congregations that sought to pursue their mission of preservation by putting their pensioners to work, thus compensating for the spoliation they had suffered during the Revolutionary period. They benefitted from tax exemptions, and they numbered anywhere from a dozen to three or four hundred girls, all engaged in different kinds of manual work, mainly in the textile industry. In the middle of the Second Empire, the population of these workrooms was estimated at 80,000, and their numbers increased up to the end of the nineteenth century.[21] Entry into an *ouvroir* was already a privilege, requiring

21. See Mounier, *De l'organization du travail manuel des jeunes filles* (1869), and Paul Gemähling, *Travailleurs au rabais* (1910).

that the family go through certain official religious channels and often demanding the payment of a small sum of money. The formula of the convent-factory—comprising a mixed management: part industrial, part religious—had been developed for the poorest women, particularly in the textile-manufacturing regions. Starting from a Lyonese model, the formula prospered, producing three celebrated firms at Jujurieux, La Séauve, and Tarare. It featured conventual rules, a time schedule entirely taken up with religious exercises and industrial labor, a supervision that was assigned to the Sisters of Saint Joseph and the Sisters of Saint Vincent de Paul, and remuneration by yearly contract. Everything was calculated to appeal to the poorer families, to whom it offered the assurance of the moral preservation of their daughters, the opportunity to collect a lump sum when they entered or left, and, for the women themselves, the hope of marriage with the help of these wages, which were held in trust as in the case of domestic servants.

Between these two formulas for maintaining good morals, the moralizing philanthropists and the promotional feminists denounced, rather bluntly, the existence of a sort of vicious circle that did more to foster and reproduce the physical and moral decline of the poor population than to deter it. The distance is not great between a book like *La Femme pauvre au XIXᵉ siècle,* by Julie Daubié, the eminent feminist of the Second Empire, and *Le Travail des femmes* of Leroy-Beaulieu, the noted economist and philanthropist.[22] The two were in agreement when it came to denouncing the shortcomings of the cloistral organizations. The denunciations focused first on their supposed negative effect on revenues. In 1849, at Lyons, Macon, and Saint-Étienne, religious communities were violently attacked and forced to close by unemployed women workers, who sacked several convents, breaking and burning the looms.[23] This was explained by the fact that the conventual organizations came between labor power and the market, using their fiscal exemptions and their communal regime to

22. Pierre-Paul Leroy-Beaulieu, *Le Travail des femmes au XIXᵉ siècle* (1873).
23. Jules Tixerant, *Le Féminisme à l'époque de 1848* (1908).

offer prices lower than those resulting from "free" labor, thus causing wages to be lowered and consequently inciting free women to immoral conduct. Moreover, they monopolized the jobs that would best suit women (such as welfare work and teaching), so that the woman without a dowry was obliged either to become a nun if she wished to pursue these occupations, or to become a prostitute if she accepted a free trade. The two books also denounced the incongruous nature of conventual education. Daubié pointed out that women who spent their youth in convent-factories in the hope of preserving their chances for marriage were rejected by male workers who did not want to marry "those nuns" once they left these factories. Leroy-Beaulieu decried "hothouse education," boarding schools which trained young women for "semi-artisanal trades" that were already overcongested, and did not prepare "the young woman's mind through a substantial instruction that would energetically shape her personality. Every woman, and especially the woman of the people who is exposed to more struggles and perils, has to have will power and strength of character. An education that does not awaken these faculties misses its goal." Hence the logic of *preservation for marriage* must give place to that of *preparation for family life*: develop domestic training; make it possible for the young woman, the widow, and occasionally the wife to have direct access to remunerative work; open up specific careers to women in order to prepare them effectively for the family; take steps to prevent women workers from falling into prostitution; and finally, reduce the rivalry between men and women by making the social careers of women a natural extension of their domestic activities.

The effectiveness of this familialist strategy was due no doubt to the way it linked masculine and feminine pursuits, progressively attacking the old situation in which, as Gemähling expressed it, the woman competed with the man and the child competed with the woman, resulting in the demoralization of the family. The entry of women into the labor market was not thereby blocked, but adjusted to fit a plan that introduced a principle of advancement into the feminine career, one that came through the acquisition of a domestic proficiency. The industrial labor of girls, single women, and poor wives was recognized as an occasional necessity, but not as their normal lot in life. If the man were to improve his situation through stability and professional merit, the woman would be able to remain at home and make use of abilities that would turn it into a true interior domain. And then, in the course of things, she might prepare herself for one of the administrative, educative, or assistance professions that corresponded best to her natural aptitudes. This inflection that was introduced into the feminine career gave men back the impression, if not the reality, of their former patriarchal power by guaranteeing them the primary responsibility in providing for the home, and placed women in the position of constant watchfulness over the men, since wives would have an interest in the regularity of their husbands' professional and hence social life, as their own chances of betterment depended on it.

The strategy of familializing the popular strata in the second half of the nineteenth century rested mainly on the woman, therefore, and added a number of tools and allies for her to use: primary education, instruction in domestic hygiene, the establishment of workers' garden plots, and Sunday holidays (a family holiday, in contrast to the Monday holiday, which was traditionally taken up with drinking sessions). But the main instrument she received was "social" housing. In practice, the woman was brought out of the convent so that she would bring the man out of the cabaret; for this she was given a weapon—housing—and told how to use it: keep strangers out so as to bring the husband and especially the children in.

The social housing that emerged at the end of the nineteenth century, its major form being the *habitations à bon marché** (H.B.M., ancestors of the present-day H.L.M.†), was the result of numerous studies of the working class carried out

* Low-cost dwellings [Translator's note].
†*Habitations à loyer modéré* = low-rent housing.

in the course of the century; the result too of experimentation and international exchanges (beginning in the Second Empire, the world fairs devoted a portion of their activities to this question). A dual objective gradually comes into focus.

First, the new housing had to make a breakthrough between the formula of the hovel and that of the barracks. The hovel was the outcome of the rural and artisanal custom in which the family dwelling was regarded as a hiding place, a retreat hidden from view, where the family amassed their valuables like an animal its kill, making it into a little fortress they could hide in by day and go out of at night. If the hygienists were obsessed by this image of the working-class accommodation, this was certainly not because it expressed a primitive conception of existence: aside from the problems of heating and protection, the lack of openings in the worker's house was not unrelated to the practice inherited from the *ancien régime* whereby taxes were calculated upon the number of doors and windows. Moreover, the clutter and accumulation often corresponded to a professional usage; the famous caves of Lille, well known for their unhealthiness, were occupied by worker families who found that the humidity afforded the best conditions for conserving their materials. In their struggle against the unsanitariness and immorality of these hovels and caves, the hygienists were also struggling against a conception of the dwelling as a refuge, a place of defense and autonomy. For them it was a question of replacing autarchic power with labor power, of making housing into a sanitary space and no longer a "military" space, of ridding it of everything that made for secret alliances and dubious combinations. And for that, the least details had to be taken into account: for example, the suspicious custom of covering the interior walls of the dwellings with equivocal engravings. "One must be strict and show no leniency in proscribing excessive decorations, obscene or degrading images, in order to replace them with flowers about the house."[24]

The formula of the barracks presented equal dangers, in

24. C.-E. Pilat and A. Gosselet, *Catéchisme d'hygiène à l'usage des enfants* (1850).

that it brought together a large number of individuals under the same conditions, where the cohabitation of single persons and families led to a lowering of moral standards and, more important, made it impossible to enforce regulations. Furthermore, those responsible for maintaining order saw these gigantic aggregates as constituting an invitation to riot. The solution consisted in granting housing based on conditions of eligibility that guaranteed the morality of the occupants under penalty of repossession. The housing developments that were constructed from 1850 on, the *cités Napoléon* in Paris and Lille, and those of Mulhouse, answered this requirement. They were testing grounds for ideas of paternalistic and philanthropic employers. Taillefer, the physician for the *cité Napoléon* in Paris, announced that it would be "the grave of the riot," supporting his contention by recalling the behavior of the members of "his" housing project during the events of December 2, when the insurgents came to harangue them: "After a few friendly words on my behalf, they all withdrew to their respective quarters and the troublemakers were obliged to leave."[25] The worker's adherence to public order was ensured by his desire to keep his lodging; and if he was lacking in this regard, his wife would take charge of the matter, as Reybaud remarked with reference to the workers of the Cunin-Gridaine factory at Sedan, where it had become the custom for the wife to "come and ask forgiveness for the failings of her husband."

Research concerning the interior arrangement of this housing was aimed explicitly at furthering this function of mutual surveillance. Hence the formulation of a second objective: to design a housing unit small enough so that no "outsider" would be able to live in it, yet large enough for the parents to have a space separate from their children, so that they might watch over them in their occupations without being observed in their own intimate play. The practice of taking in one or more "lodgers" was very frequent in the working-class milieu.

25. A. Taillefer, *Des cités ouvrières et de leur nécessité comme hygiène et tranquillité publique* (1850).

This custom, which was linked to the old family organization of production—wherein apprentices and sometimes journeymen were housed with the family—and also to the high rents being charged, made the family space a social one as well, a relay in the daily rounds rather than the enclave of surveillance and peace that observers like Blanqui and Reybaud had in view.[26] The architect Harou-Romain, who specialized in both prison buildings and social housing, proclaimed this apparent concern for economy to be the cause of the immorality and lack of hygiene of the working-class milieu, since it resulted in the concentration of children, boys and girls together, and sometimes the parents, in the same room.[27] To remedy the situation, the workers' housing development of Mulhouse prohibited all subleasing, and in Belgium, Ducpétiaux advocated setting apart a room inside the lodging with an independent entry. Exit the outsider, leaving the family space to be redistributed between parents and children.

The objective was to reduce the "social" part of the lodging in favor of spaces set aside for the parents and for the children. The bedroom was to become its virtual center, one that would not be seen by the children. According to Fonssagrives, it was "the little capital of the peaceable kingdom of the household." What was needed for the children was "a room adjoining that of the parents, which would deprive secret observation of the oppressive aspect it might have were it more apparent, while preserving its effectiveness." This separation of the sexes and ages within workers' lodgings ran so counter to the old forms of aggregation that it mobilized the philanthropists throughout the century. One can get

26. Adolphe Blanqui, who was commissioned by the Academy of Moral and Political Sciences to report on "the state of the working classes after the fearsome revolutionary movement of 1848" (*L'État des classes ouvrières après le formidable mouvement révolutionnaire de 1848*), related that it was in the areas where the workshop had not yielded to manufacturing that unhealthy conditions and lack of discipline were greatest; for it was here that "pauperism and utopias kept house together" and roving children became the prey of agitators. He was thinking in particular of the silk weavers of Lyons. Reybaud would take up the subject again fifteen years later.
27. Nicolas Harou-Romain, "Projet d'association financière pour l'amélioration des habitations des ouvriers de Bruxelles," *Annales de la charité,* 1847 and 1848.

an idea of the seriousness of the issue from the following exchange, drawn from the debates of the Congrès d'hygiène publique de Bruxelles in 1851, on the question of "the internal distribution of houses." Ebrington: "The separation of the sexes is indispensable for morality and decency. A minister said to me: 'I have done all that I could, but the common bedroom has gotten the better of me.'" Ducpétiaux: "In cases where this separation is not possible, can't we achieve the same effect by suspending bedding from the ceiling for the children?" Gourlier: "One would have to separate the hammocks from the rest of the room by a kind of curtain; but it would be there one day and be taken down the next." Ramón de la Sagra: "Would you prefer hammocks, or a bed where parents and children are all brought together?" Gourlier: "Supposing that this separation were not achieved, then our efforts would come to nothing. The children would see the parents from their hammocks, and thus the requirements of decency would not be satisfied."

Islands of unhealthiness, elements in a system of defense, a shelter for animal relations: these were the working-class dwellings, the furnished rooms of Paris, the caves of Lille, and the hovels of Lyons. The right equation for social housing was sought in the solution to these three nuisances. The problem was to organize a space large enough to be hygienic, small enough so that only the family could live in it, and distributed in such a way that the parents could monitor their children. Housing had to become a factor that complemented the school in the supervision of children: its mobile elements had to be excluded so that the children might be immobilized within it. The search for intimacy and the domestic jurisdiction that was proposed to the working-class woman were the means to make this dwelling acceptable, and even attractive, in the transition from a schema that was tied to production and social life to a conception based on separation and surveillance. If the husband preferred the outside, the lights of the cabaret, and the children the street, with its spectacles and its promiscuity, this would be the fault of the wife and mother.

The advent of the modern family, recentered on the primacy of the educative function, was not, therefore, the result of the slow propagation of the same familial model through all the social strata, following the logic of their greater or lesser resistance to modernity. There were at least two distinct channels for promoting this educational concern, and the differences between the political effects they brought about were sufficiently great for them to be given the form of a reverse symmetry.

There was a recentering of the family on itself in both series, but the process did not have the same meaning in each of the two channels. The bourgeois family was constituted by means of a *tactical constriction* of its members aimed at suppressing or controlling an internal enemy, the domestic servants. This cohesion gave it an added power that enhanced its social position and enabled it to return to the social field with the force it needed in order to exercise certain controls and champion various reforms. The woman's alliance with the doctor reinforced her internal authority and mediated the external power of the family. The working-class family, on the other hand, was forged on the basis of a *turning back* [*rabattement*] of each of its members onto the others in a circular relation of vigilance against the temptations from outside, the cabaret and the street. It carried out new educative tasks at the cost of a loss of its coextensiveness with the social field; it was dispossessed of everything that situated it in a field of exterior forces. Being isolated, it was now exposed to the surveillance of its deviations from the norm.

More significant was the difference between the tactical positions in which the bourgeois woman and the working-class woman now found themselves. Owing to the revalorization of educative tasks, a new continuity was established for the bourgeois woman between her family activities and her social activities. She discovered a new missionary domain in which to operate; a new professional sphere was opened, consisting in the spread of the new welfare and educational norms. She could be at once the support for a transfer of the inheritance within the family and the *instrument of cultural diffusion on the outside*. The proletarian woman had a job to do that was by nature antagonistic to her status as mother. For her, cultural diffusion was out of the question: her mission was rather to see to a *social retraction of her husband and children*. On her, on the regularity she imposed, depended the transfer of an inheritance that almost always remained outside the family, the "social inheritance"—as the jurists expressed it—which was beyond the family's control and which the worker could not make use of in his lifetime, since he only obtained it through his own deterioration and demise. "Whereas the transfer of the inheritance of the bourgeois family is effected by testament or *ab intestat,* for the inheritance of the worker's family it is no longer a question of transfer by testament; and with respect to succession *ab intestat;* it is no longer determined in a uniform manner, but depends on the laws and regulations adopted by the various institutions whose object is the creation of this inheritance for the worker. As we have said, the question of the freedom to make a will is not raised here, because the different institutions of providence do not propose to form an inheritance that the worker might dispose of as he wishes, but to protect his family, who without the aid of the aforementioned institutions would be a displaced family, dependent on Public Assistance. Lastly, whereas in the bourgeois family the heir carries on the personality of the deceased, at the same time receiving all his goods and assuming the burden of his debts, in the working-class family the person of the heir is entirely independent of the personality of the deceased; all his rights come down to the collection of a fixed sum determined in advance, and he is in no way responsible for debts."[28]

28. P. Aivarez, *De l'influence de la politique, de l'économie, et du social sur la famille* (1899).

What of childhood? In the first instance, the solicitude of which it was the object took the form of a *protected liberation,* a freeing of children from vulgar fears and constraints. The bourgeois family drew a sanitary cordon around the child which delimited his sphere of development: inside this perimeter the growth of his body and mind would be encouraged by enlisting all the contributions of psychopedagogy in its service, and controlled by means of a discreet observation. In the second instance, it would be more exact to define the pedagogical model as that of *supervised freedom.* The problem in regard to the working-class child was not so much the weight of obsolescent constraints as excessive freedom—being left to the street—and the techniques employed consisted in limiting this freedom, in shepherding the child back to spaces where he could be more closely watched: the school or the family dwelling.

3.

Government Through the Family

Under the *ancien régime,* the family was both a subject and an object of government. It was a subject by virtue of the internal distribution of its powers: the wife, the children, and the other member of the household (relatives, servants, apprentices) were answerable to the head of the family. Through him, the family was inscribed within groups with a common adherence, whether in the form of *networks of solidarity,* as in the case of the corporations and village communities, or *blocks of dependence* of the feudal or religious type, or, more often, both at once. The family thus constituted a *plexus* of dependent relations that were indissociably private and public, a social linkage that organized individuals around the possession of an *état* (at the same time a trade or profession, a privilege, and a status) which was granted and recognized by larger social groupings. Hence it was the smallest political organization possible. Set directly within social relations of dependence, it was integrally affected by the system of obligations, honors, favors, and disfavors that actuated social relations in general. But if the family was caught up in this way, it was also an active participant in the give-and-take of social ties, goods, and actions through the strategies of matrimonial alliances and clientelist allegiances that kept society embroiled in a sort of permanent civil war. The inordi-

48

nate recourse to the judiciary in this period bears witness to the degree of turmoil.

This direct insertion of the family into the political sphere of the *ancien régime* had two consequences for the exercise of social power. With regard to the central apparatuses, the head of the family was *accountable* for its members. In exchange for the protection and recognition of the state, he had to guarantee the faithfulness to public order of those who were part of that order; he also had to supply a fee in taxes, labor (*corvées*), and men (militia). Consequently, the fact of not belonging to a family, and hence the lack of a sociopolitical guarantor, posed a problem for public order. This was the category of people without ties, without hearth or home, of beggars and vagabonds who, being in no way connected to the social machinery, acted as disturbers in this system of protections and obligations. There was no one to supply their needs, but neither was there anyone to hold them within the bounds of order. They were dependent on charity, on alms, a gift that honored the giver because he could not expect reciprocation, but did nothing to integrate the receiver and so maintained this floating population. Or else they depended on the public administration, which kept them in general hospitals or confined in poorhouses for the sole purpose of putting them socially out of action, of bringing an end to the scandal constituted by the spectacle and behavior of these uncontrolled elements.

In compensation for his responsibility toward the authorities that bound him, the head of the family had virtually a *discretionary* power over those around him. He could make use of them for all the operations that were intended to further his *état;* he could determine the children's careers, decide how the family members would be employed and which alliances would be contracted. He could also punish them if they did not live up to their obligations toward the family, and for this he could get the support of the public authority that owed him aid and protection in his endeavor. The notorious *lettres de cachet de famille* derived their significance from this regulated exchange of obligations and protections between the public agencies and family authority, playing alternately on the menace to public order constituted by an individual who had broken with religion and morality, and on the threat to the family interest posed by the disobedient acts of one of its members. The petitions calling for the confinement of girls whose unseemly behavior gave rise to the fear of public disorder and defamatory consequences for their families conformed to the same logic as those requesting the internment of a boy who had run away with a young lady of inferior rank to his. The disorders of the first threatened the family through the discredit they would bring upon it, since such behavior would signify that it was unable to contain its members within the prescribed limits and hence would underscore the unreliability of the family in meeting its obligations. The escapade of the second would cause just as much harm to the family by nullifying matrimonial plans. The mechanism was the same in both instances: to ensure public order, the state relied on the family for direct support, trading indiscriminately on its fear of discredit and its private ambitions. All this took place according to a very simple scheme of collaboration, with the state saying to families; "You will keep your people within the rules conforming to our requirements, in return for which you can use them as you see fit, and if they go against your injunctions, we will furnish you with the support necessary to bring them back to order."

This apparently faultless mechanism was to become progressively inadequate as the eighteenth century wore on, revealing the seeds of a twofold conflict at the heart of this collaboration between the administration and families. First, the family was finding it harder to contain its members by ensuring their upkeep. The barriers that held individuals within organic groupings were slowly crumbling. The separation between the "proud" poor (those who refrained from asking publicly for help through fear of dishonor) and the imploring beggars who shamelessly displayed their miseries and their sores was tending to disappear, and the end of the eighteenth century saw a substantial increase in the number of poor people demanding assistance. Moreover, the beggars were gradually transforming themselves into dangerous vagabonds who roamed through the countryside levying a tax—partly by appealing to pity, partly by extortion (the threat of violence, arson, and so forth)—in competition with that of the state. Organized into bands, they practiced pillage and sowed disorder.

Secondly, family authority and the practice of *lettres de cachet* were vigorously called into question by the victims themselves. Complaints against the letters grew steadily up to 1789, and the history of the civil tribunals under the Revolution reveals, together with proceedings for the recognition of paternity, a large number of claims for damages by reason of arbitrary confinement.[1] The administration itself stiffened in the face of these demands and set out systematically to verify their validity. The construction of general hospitals corresponded in part to the express desire to furnish poor families with a means of coercion against their undisciplined members. The administrators soon suspected families of using these enclosures more for getting rid of their crippled and disabled than for giving a salutary and momentary lesson to the refractory members of the social order.

These two lines of deconstruction of the old government of families converged in the taking of the Bastille. Led by the *petit peuple* and indigents of Paris—in other words, by those whom the socio-familial apparatus could not keep in check, whom it was no longer able to feed and maintain—this action was the outcome of a muted summons to the state, calling on it to take charge of its citizens, to become the agency responsible for the satisfaction of their needs. At the same time, it constituted the symbolic destruction *par excellence* of family arbitrariness in its collusion with royal sovereignty, for it was there that a large proportion of the individuals detained through the procedure of *lettres de cachet* were confined. This

1. Cf. A. Douarche, *Les tribunaux civils à Paris sous la Révolution,* 2 vols. (1905-1907).

twofold abolition formed the material for many dreams projecting, on the basis of this *tabula rasa* of the old entanglement of state and family powers, a future state that would organize the citizens' welfare, dispensing assistance, work, education, and health to everyone without regard to outmoded family adherences. But it also engendered the opposite vision: the nightmare of a totalitarian state, one that might guarantee the satisfaction of everyone's needs, but at the cost of a leveling of fortunes and an authoritarian corseting of society. Thus the family was cast into the center of the most significant political debate, since the very definition of the state was at issue. On one side were the socialists, the "statists," who, being negators of the family, were accused of totalitarianism. On the other side were the partisans of a liberal definition of the state who would let society organize itself around the private property of the family and so were accused of conservatism.

At any rate, this was how the problem of the family was classically formulated, in the language of a reassuring manicheism opposing the defenders of the established order and the family to the collectivist revolutionaries. The least one can say about this schema, however, is that it does not offer much of a hold for grasping either the present configuration of the family or the nature of the attachment that individuals of liberal societies have conceived for it. It does not explain why this fondness for the family is associated with a feeling for liberty, or how the defense of the family can be effectively undertaken in the name of safeguarding people's sphere of autonomy. If today's family were simply an agent for transmitting bourgeois power, and consequently entirely under the control of the "bourgeois" state, why would individuals, and particularly those who are not members of the ruling classes, invest so much in family life? To assert that this is the result of an ideological impregnation comes down to saying, in less delicate language, that these individuals are imbeciles, and amounts to a not too skillful masking of an interpretative weakness. Nor does it explain why the modern family organized its ties in so supple a manner, so contrary to the old juridical rigidity. If the family were solely a means for the bourgeoisie to cling to the defense of the established order, why would it let the juridical framework that sanctions its power grow so lax? To say that this is a contradiction be-tween liberal ideology and the interests of the bourgeoisie implies that a reform can only be a lie or a wish, but never a positive solution to a problem.

In other words, the question is not so much one of knowing what the family is used for in a liberal economy geared to private property as one of understanding why such a setup works, how the family came to constitute an effective way of warding off the dangers that hung over a liberal definition of the state when the poor revolted, demanding that it be made into the reorganizing principle of society, and when individ-uals rose up against the arbitrariness of familial power, threatening to level this fragile but crucial bulwark standing in the way of a collective and state administration of citizens. The problem, then, was that of the family's transformation rather than its preservation. If it had only been a matter of preserving it against the winds of change, against the assault of the hungry and the revolt of the oppressed, its history would be that of a pure and simple defense of the privileges it sanctioned, and its visage that of an undisguised domination of one class over another. The fact that the discourses de-nouncing social privilege and class domination had to dissoci-ate themselves gradually from the critique of the family; that demands slowly came to be based on the defense and im-provement of family living conditions of the "disadvan-taged"; that the family became at the same time the point where criticism of the established order stopped and the point of support for demands for more social equality: all this is sufficient invitation to regard the family and its transforma-tions as a positive form of solution to the problems posed by a liberal definition of the state rather than as a negative ele-ment of resistance to social change.

Now what could have threatened a liberal definition of the state at the turn of the nineteenth century? Two things. First, the problem of pauperism, the abrupt rise of those waves of indigents who, demanding more subsidies from the state, had urged the latter, at the height of the Revolutionary period, to become the agency for reorganizing the social body on the basis of the right of the poor to welfare, work, and education. Secondly, the appearance of divisions with respect to living conditions and mores that ran so deep within the social body that they risked generating cataclysmic conflicts, thus posing a challenge to the very principle of a liberal society. The face-to-face encounter of a bourgeois minority and a barbarian populace that haunted the cities more than it inhabited them raised the specter of their destruction.

In the questions placed in competition by the academies in the first half of the nineteenth century—that is, at a time when the academies and learned societies had a larger part in intellectual life than the universities, closer connections with political life, and a role of adviser and declared inspirer of government inquiries into the working class which were often financed by these same academies—the same two lines of inquiry kept recurring: (1) How could the problem of pauperism and indigence be solved while averting the danger represented by discourses that made the augmentation of the prerogatives of the state the only means of achieving this end, to the detriment of the free economic process (Malthus, Gérando, Villermé)? (2) How was one to reorganize the laboring classes in a disciplinary way when the ancient ties of fellowship and vassalage no longer attached them to the social order, these ties persisting here and there in forms that served much more as points of resistance to the new order (the corporations, the Lyons silk weavers), and disappearing elsewhere in favor of a total loss of responsibility by the population, which was becoming weak and uncontrollable owing to the prevalent morbidity and the emergence of industrial cities (De La Farelle, Frégier, Cherbuliez)? The problem was especially delicate because it could not be solved simply by repression as under the *ancien régime,* since the liberal economy required the setting up of procedures for preserving and shaping the population. In the eighteenth century, the promotion of these necessary public services and facilities went hand in hand—in the pre-Revolutionary discourse of the Enlightenment philosophers—with a calling in question of the political order. Once the iron grip of the ancient power of sovereignty had been broken, the alliance of the working classes and the bourgeoisie collapsed, since the political interest of the former was in the maintenance of a conjunction between the reorganization of the state and the development of public services, while the interest of the latter obviously lay in the dissociation of the two, the only means of maintaining their acquired positions and the latitude needed for the functioning of a liberal economy. So the two major questions that were discussed can be lumped into one: How was it possible to ensure the development of practices of preservation and formation of the population while at the same time detaching it from any directly political role and yet applying to it a mission of domination, pacification, and social integration?

The answer: By means of philanthropy. Philanthropy in this case is not be understood as a naïvely apolitical term signifying a private intervention in the sphere of so-called social problems, but must be considered as a deliberately depoliticizing strategy for establishing public services and facilities at a sensitive point midway between private initiative and the state. When one examines the centers around which philanthropic activity was to organize itself in the nineteenth century, one finds that they were all characterized by the search for a calculated distance between the functions of the liberal state and the spread of techniques of welfare and administration of the population. First, there was an *assistance pole,* which depended on this liberal definition of the state in order to refer to the private sphere the demands that were directed to the state, and formulated in terms of the right to work and assistance. Hence this was a pole that used the state as a *formal means* for transmitting certain guidelines and precepts of behavior, for turning a question of political right into a question of economic morality: since there is no legally constituted social hierarchy, since the state is no longer the apex of a pyramid of feudal oppressions, and since we are all formally equal where it is concerned, you cannot rightfully demand that it take charge of your welfare, but neither do you have any grounds for refusing our advice, for it is different from the orders you once obeyed. Rather than a right to assistance from the state, whose increased role would disturb the workings of a society freed from its shackles—the main impediment being the state itself—we will give you the means to be self-sufficient by teaching you the virtues of saving; and for our part, we are at least entitled to a disapproving scrutiny of the demands for aid that you might still put forward, since they would constitute a flagrant indication of a breach of morality.

Secondly, there was a *medical-hygienist pole,* whose aim was not to check a demand that would inflate the role of the state but rather to employ the state as a direct instrument, as a *material means* for averting the risks of a destruction of society through the physical and moral weakening of the population, through the appearance of struggles, of conflicts that would thrust the sword of political violence into the free play of social relations and thus threaten to annihilate the very thing the state is pledged to protect. "The medical tendency is the necessary counterpart to the industrial tendency, for the influence the latter has exerted on health is beyond question, in that it is bound to have multiplied the number of dangers to which manufacturing populations are generally much more exposed than agricultural peoples. However, if the causes of unhealthiness have multiplied with the extension of the arts of industry, it must be admitted that the improved study of the sciences whence these causes directly issued offers means of preventing and combatting them which were unknown in former times: this is the lance of Achilles that heals the wounds it inflicts."[2] This programmatic text of the movement of hygienist philanthropists makes the direction they intended their action to take quite clear. Their func-

2. *Annales d'hygiène publique et de médecine légale,* preface to vol. 1 (1827).

tion was to prompt state intervention only where the liberalization of economic society risked inverting into its opposite. The group of measures relating to public and private hygiene, to the education and protection of individuals, would have their effect primarily at the level of the problems that might be posed for the economy by the broadened management of the population it employed—problems of conservation, but also problems of integration; and these measures would radiate out from the industrial sphere, making it into the point of application and the basis for the civilizing of mores, the integration of citizens. It was in this spirit of preservation of liberal society through the positive adaptation of individuals to its regime, and solely on those grounds, that the hygienists would urge the state to intervene in the sphere of private law by applying the norm.

Thus the context was found in which to place the necessary construction of public services and facilities without their undermining the liberal definition of the state. It remains to be explained why the scheme was successful. Was it effected through a brutal imposition? Clearly not. It can already be noted that these two axes of the philanthropic strategy replaced the ancient techniques of sovereign power with new forms of positive power: effective advice rather than humiliating charity, the preserving norm rather than destructive repression. But this was not all. For if people were not arbitrarily administered by a capricious power that alternated between the carrot and the stick, this was because the new deployments contained a money of exchange; they were one of the terms of an everyday alternative, the other being a worse situation. If the discourse on the morality of saving was able to function, this was not primarily because workers were compelled to deposit a portion of their meager resources in savings accounts (even if this was the case in some paternalistic firms) but because this saving enabled them to achieve a greater *family autonomy* in relation to the blocks of dependence or networks of solidarity that continued to exist after a fashion. If the *hygienist norms* pertaining to the rearing, labor, and education of children were able to take effect, this was because they offered children, and correlatively women, the possibility of increased autonomy within the family in opposition to *patriarchal authority.*

In other words, this philanthropic strategy was effective because it reflected back to the family the two lines of decomposition that emanated from the family, joining them into a new synthesis meant to solve the problems of the political order. In one sense, the family became, through saving, a *point of support* for reabsorbing individuals for whom it had been inclined to relinquish responsibility, calling upon the state instead as the agency politically responsible for their subsistence and well-being. In another sense, through a consideration of the complaints of individuals against its arbitrariness, the family became a *target;* by taking account of their complaints, they could be made agents for conveying the norms of the state into the private sphere. Hence we can attempt to understand the liberalization and valorization of the family that occurred at the end of the nineteenth century, not as the triumph of modernity, the profound mutation of sensibilities, but as the strategic result of the coupling of these two philanthropic strategies.

A. Moralization

Under the *ancien régime,* there existed three types of assistance to the poor: the general hospitals and almshouses for vagabonds; individual alms for beggars; and charitable societies, organized around parish churches, for the "proud poor." All three were considered ineffective, more apt to maintain and even cause the spread of poverty than to eliminate it.

Why was this? Because they all conspired to distort the way poverty was perceived.

The almshouses and general hospitals only hid vagrants and bona fide indigents from public view by offering them a shelter that either rewarded their laziness or caused them to flee and thus reinforced beggary. Confining indigents was a false solution to the problem of poverty, for organizing spaces where work and sustenance were guaranteed risked making them attractive, drawing in all those who had some difficulty providing for their needs and leading to a further loosening of the primary ties that ought to contain them. But if these enclosed spaces were made repellent by their repressive character, it would become impossible to attract to them the elements that needed controlling, and these would wander off in search of another solution, thereby becoming more dangerous. In both instances, the intervention falsified the problem, artificially increasing the number of poor to be helped, or drastically reducing the scope of its action.

Individual alms fell into the same traps. These too could contribute to multiplying indigents by playing into the hands of false indigents. Beggars employed a whole array of spectacular tricks to take advantage of private alms, including false infirmities, lying spiels, and various other deceptions. For example, in the seventeenth century, children were used by beggars who deliberately deformed and mutilated them after buying them more or less directly in the charity houses that existed before Saint Vincent de Paul became active, or from that association of vagabonds who specialized in teratological surgery, the *comprachicos* (literally, buy-children). Charity that was kindled by such methods as these could reach the point of conferring on the person being aided a better situation than that of the independent worker, and thereby influence the latter to become a mendicant in turn, disguising his situation in the hope of transforming it through a favor elicited in this fashion. Charity could also have harmful effects on true indigents, on those who disguised neither their miseries nor their resources, for it encouraged lack of foresight, that "fatal security" which resulted from the certainty of being assisted in case of need when one had a protector. But conversely, this inscription of alms in the register of solicitation discouraged those who were perhaps most deserving, owing to the tediousness, subtlety, servility, and deception these proceedings implied. Everything pushed the person who was resigned to beggary into making a profession of it: the necessity of pandering to the rich by exaggerating the importance of their gift through the ritual humility of the transaction, but also the gift itself, which could turn out to be more profitable than many professions.

Inversely, assistance to the proud poor was a protection of these who had a trade, an "honest" occupation, and whose problem was in concealing their poverty so as not to lose their good standing. "We shall consider the proud poor to be those who have honest responsibilities and occupations, those who have operated in the past or are at present operating a shop as merchants or artisans belonging to a trade association, and those who have some reason to be ashamed to ask publicly for relief owing to their profession or their birth."[3] The members of the charitable societies were bourgeois, merchants, and employers who, within the bounds of the parish, came to the aid of those who were attached to this territory by virtue of an *état* and so were tied to it by obligation. By the same token, all those who did not attend church services, couples who lived in furnished rooms, elements who were too mobile (one had to have been living for at least six months in one place), and also workers who made theatrical costumes or persons who maintained lodgings of doubtful morality, were excluded from assistance. The charitable society was an instrument of corporatist and territorial preservation, and it also acted as a morals police for the parish. This is why a demand for assistance had to be accompanied by a certificate of confession signed by the priest. The inquiry conducted by the society consisted in questioning the parents on religious matters, in verifying that they attended services and that their children were sent to the charity schools and to catechism, and in consulting their neighbors as to their devotion and their morals. In short, an examination of the outward signs of morality and respectability which did not take stock of real

3. Paul Cahen, *Les Idées charitables au XVII⁰ et XVIII⁰ siècles à Paris* (1900).

needs, an assistance which modeled itself after the blocks of dependence and networks of solidarity, and could not contain what escaped them on principle.

The problems of assistance that arose out of this distorted perception of poverty, which by turns urged it to display itself and helped it to mask itself, which encouraged it through public relief and turned it back toward private charity by repressing its public manifestations, created a situation in which governments were obliged in the end to choose between an institutionalization of charity which sanctioned aid as a right, or a violent repression of the poor when their misery incited them to insurrection. "The time is past when one could to a certain extent dispense with taking account of the state of affairs in the lower classes and rely on the expedient of crushing them if need be when they were stirred up; now these classes think, reason, speak, and act. It is undeniably much wiser and more prudent to think of taking legislative measures, some of which would be for the protection of morals and the prevention of a new wave of abandonments, while others would tend to make all these abandoned beings genuinely useful and to qualify them to fill an active role in society."[4] The possibility and the advisability of a repression of the poor as a solution to the problems they posed diminished, therefore, with their entry onto the political stage. But the other aspect of the old attitude toward poverty, public and private charity, became all the more delicate as a result. If there was no longer any question of repressing poverty as systematically as before, did it follow that one must acknowledge a legitimate right of the poor, the indigent, to assistance by public agencies? To go in this way from optional charity to "legal charity," as Malthus put it, was it not in fact to risk carrying all poverty over into pauperism, "poverty being the state in which an individual has the option of supplying his needs from a public fund legally set aside for that purpose"?[5]

4. François-Emmanuel Fodéré, *Essai sur la pauvreté des nations* (1825), p. 556.
5. Chalmers, a disciple of Malthus, quoted in Joseph-Marie Gérando, *Traité de la bienfaisance publique*, vol. 1 (1839).

This would be a dangerous procedure, as it would make the state the agency responsible for satisfying the needs of citizens, the representative of the poor before the rich, the agent of a leveling of fortunes, and the destroyer of that margin of liberalism whose very mission—in view of its liberation from the old arbitrary functions—it was to guarantee.

All the discourses of the economists and philanthropists positioned themselves around the question of assistance framed in this way. First, there were the socialists, with Godwin in England and the utopians in France, who advocated the abolition of private property and the family in favor of a state administration of needs. Second, there were the Christian political economists, rallying men like Bigot de Morogues, Huerne de Pommeuse, and the viscount de Villeneuve-Bargemont, and other members of the Société des établissements charitables, founded in 1828. All were partisans of a revamping of the old type of charity, a restoration of the ties of obedience that had once united the rich and the poor. Starting from the idea that the development of the economy, far from eliminating misery, rendered it more appalling in many areas, they saw this situation as offering a new chance for the old allegiances. "Charity establishes relations and ties of affection between the classes, institutes a salutary and benign hierarchy, and is not based on the general rules which public charity requires, but which repel or aggravate so many miseries. We have no intention of attacking society at its roots, in the conditions that are inseparable from its existence; we will not proffer vain and dangerous words regarding labor and indigence; we will not indulge in chimerical illusions; we do not wish to enlist the poor and unfortunate in the service of political passions, nor to exploit their miseries with a view to making revolutions. It belongs solely to religion to address severe reproaches and solemn threats to the rich, because at the same time it teaches gentleness and resignation to the poor."[6] And finally, there was a

6. This profession of faith figures in the preamble to the first issue (1884) of the *Annales de la charité,* the journal of the Société d'économie charitable.

third group, the social economists, with Droz, Sismondi, Gérando, Michel Chevalier, Dunoyer, De La Farelle, the duke
of La Rochefoucauld-Liancourt, Guizot, Villermé, Dupin,
and others. This group was organized into societies that continued the old philanthropic spirit of the eighteenth century
under protective names, taking into account the climate of
the Restoration: Société de la morale chrétienne, Société pour
l'instruction élémentaire, and so on. The reference discourse
for all these people, even if they insisted on marking their
differences from it somewhat, was that of Malthus.[7] Malthus
was both the first to counter the socialists—he conceived his
most famous work as a reply to William Godwin's *Inquiry
concerning Political Justice and its Influence on General Virtue
and Happiness* (1793)—without intoning once more the old
chant of charity and without playing on the yearning for the
old dependences.

It was this last group that gained acceptance for its propos-
als on the question of assistance and eventually got them in-
corporated into most of the procedures of transformation of
the social body. This achievement was due primarily to the
force of their argumentation. De La Farelle explained that,
contrary to the Christian economists, who wrongly privileged
the relationship between rich and poor, they favored taking
the great majority of citizens into consideration. For what
were the very rich and the very poor groups of society if not
minorities? Was it possible to reflect on the foundations of
our society on the basis of these two categories alone? That
would be to disregard the masses of petty rural property own-
ers, craftsmen, and shopkeepers, by far the most numerous
and the most interesting group by virtue of their efforts to
produce everything while ensuring their independence. De La
Farelle added that they upheld the family, which the socialists were bent, consciously or not, on destroying by transfer-
ring its power to the state, whereas in fact it was the best
point of support for holding individuals to the practice of

7. Thomas Robert Malthus, *An Essay on the Principal of Population* (1798).

hard work and for preserving their will to independence.[8] And the philanthropists should let it be understood that it was precisely the old system of clientelist and charitable obediences that could pave the way for socialism. Did not the habit of counting on a protector to solve their problems create the guilty insouciance of the poor population? And when this protection was not forthcoming, were they not left with the feeling in their minds that something was owed them? Did one not see them turn this arbitrary gift, freely given, into a right—a right to work, a right to assistance—which they imperiously demanded? Taking the opposite view to that of the charitable line of reasoning became the only way to forestall the advent of a state charity that would ruin fortunes, and so was the best means of defending the public order.

It should be added that this argumentation was able to convince the propertied classes to the extent that it relied on the promotion of a new political technique whereby need was made to operate as a means of social integration and no longer as a cause of insurrection. What was wrong with the old practice of assistance? Everything: the nature of what was dispensed to the poor (material gifts), the criteria of expediency (which distorted the perception of poverty), and the modes of allocation (which ended with the alternative of repression or legal charity). It was all this that the philanthropists proposed to change by making the incitement to saving the mainspring of the new deployment of assistance, using it to brace the family against the socialist and statist temptations, and relying on it to counter the old forms of solidarity and dependence, pitting the family, as a possibility of autonomy, against these old forms.

The first task of the philanthropists, therefore, was to change the nature of the welfare system in order to make it serve those who were in need of help, and no one else. In theory, what needed to be given was advice rather than handouts, "to establish between these proverbial lower classes and

8. François-Félix de La Farelle, *Du progrés social* (1839), and *Plan d'une réorganization disciplinaire des classes laborieuses* (1842).

the higher classes relations that are not those of giving, buying, and commanding on the one side, or those of receiving, selling, and obeying on the other. . . . Nothing is rarer than to exert an influence on the poor that is not the result of fear or expectation, and yet this is the thing that is absolutely necessary. So it is a matter of persuading them that they are entirely free to refuse what we are asking of them. This will not be easy. The uneducated proletarian will take our request as a command to be obeyed. If he is an independent sort, he will resent what he perceives as an interference in his affairs and will think he sees an aristocratic pretension in the advice given to him. Advice is the act that evinces the most equality since it follows at the same time from the desire to influence in the one who gives it and from the perfect freedom of the one who receives it. Wherever the exercise of political rights is lacking, it is difficult to get the poor man to understand that the advantages of the rich man give the latter no material power, but rather a legitimate moral influence. "[9] The danger, then, was the old relation of dependence between the rich and poor, the expectation of a gift or an order, the alternative of charity or repression. The answer lay in the attribution of political rights, the necessary precondition enabling the relations between social classes to change from dependence to "legitimate influence."

Why advice? First, because it cost the haves nothing, and second, because it prevented the have-nots from acquiring bad habits. Of course the philanthropic societies dispensed material aid, but this was always in order to employ it as a vehicle of their "legitimate moral influence." The Société philanthropique de Paris extended its patronage to the mutual-aid societies that wished to benefit from its financial support, providing they observed a certain number of rules relating to how these other societies were run. Among other preoccupations, it was motivated by the concern to struggle against the habit of subscribers of using up what remained

9. Charles Dupin, *L'Ouvrière* (1828).

from the yearly allotments in community festivals, whereas by saving they could gradually do without the donations of private benevolence. The logic of saving was always the same: reduce the organic, festive, transfamilial forms of solidarity so as to eliminate the risk of dependence as well as the parallel risk of insurrection.

In the same spirit, it was necessary to change the criteria for granting aid; the order of priorities had to reflect this concern to reinforce family autonomy. Children came before the elderly, for "beyond childhood, there was the whole period of maturity, while most indigent old people have lived in their maturity as men undeserving of help in their old age."[10] And women before men, for by aiding them one was also aiding their children. In the middle of the eighteenth century, a charitable association had been formed to come to the aid of fathers imprisoned because they had been unable to pay the costs of nursing their children. It would obtain their release by paying the arrears, but then everything would begin again. In 1787, the Société de la charité maternelle was founded, with the stated objective of aiding poor mothers on condition that they pledge to nurse their children themselves, or bottle-feed them at home if they were unable to breast-feed them.

In general, philanthropy differed from charity in the choice of its objects, based on this concern for pragmatism: advice instead of gifts, because it cost nothing; assistance to children rather than to old people, and to women rather than men, because such a policy would pay off, in the long run at least, by averting a future expense. Charity was alien to this kind of investment; it could only be kindled by the fires of extreme misery, by the sight of spectacular suffering, and then only for the feeling of inflated importance accruing to the giver through the immediate solace his charity brought to the sufferer. The exemplariness of the gift was in opposition to the gratuitousness of counseling, in that it was an exchange that

10. Ibid.

presupposed two symbolically contrary and not abstractly equivalent poles. In Guizart's view, charity "admits of the greatest devotion, no doubt, because it always presents itself to the mind in vivid and personified features, while philanthropy, which contemplates the evils it combats, or the well-being it procures, from a broader perspective, is less aided by the emotions of sympathy and pity. A priest goes down into dungeons and lavishes consolations there. But when the philanthropist occupies himself with prisons, it is in order to study them, to determine their goal and bring to bear all that the sciences and the arts offer in the way of means of achieving that goal; and the improvements of which his work consists, far from ending with him, are sooner or later transformed into institutions."[11] A competition was established during the nineteenth century between charity and philanthropy, and it was the latter that benefitted from it. In 1899, the *Annales de la charité* was rechristened *Revue philanthropique*. This was at the end of a process of disqualification of the relation between rich and poor expressed in terms of a symbolic exchange: I will give you my misery so that you may give me your goodness; I will give you my nature, my physical strength, so that you may display your culture and put it to use; and so on. It was doubtless no accident that the last manifestations of the charitable spirit were localized on people with incurable afflictions, on the bitter vestiges of the domain of misery, suffering, and horror. A striking testimony to this withdrawal was furnished by the Oeuvre du Calvaire, which was awarded a prize at the Universal Exposition of 1900. The only people who could be admitted for charitable aid were young, poor, and preferably foreign women guaranteed to be suffering from incurable cancer and having running sores that needed dressing. The "free dressers," as the Ladies of Calvary called themselves, were widows bearing some of the great names in politics, the army, and the world of letters;

11. L. de Guizart, *Rapport sur les travaux de la Société de la morale chrétienne pendant l'année 1823-1824*, pp. 22-23.

their donation bought them the right to treat the patients in this last charitable "preserve": "Our incurables are happy and they will tell you so."[12]

Since it was a matter of giving advice, of not giving material aid except insofar as it would make for the penetration of these pieces of advice, the displacement of the old form of charity in favor of philanthropic benevolence was to rely for the most part on the perfection of new modes for allocating assistance, on the search for a procedure that would make it possible both to discriminate between "artificial indigence" and "genuine poverty," and to incorporate into social assistance the demand for its elimination. The invention of this technique was the work of the baron de Gérando, who conceived his *Manuel du visiteur du pauvre* in 1820 in reply to a question of the Academy of Lyons: "Indicate the means of recognizing genuine indigence and making alms useful to givers and receivers alike." "While the recommendation to visit the poor before offering them relief and during the time that they are receiving it is not a new idea, the proper way to go about visiting them has not been well laid out, at least not to my knowledge. I know personally of numerous examples that show this method in action, and it is precisely this happy experience that I wish to gather up, summarize, exhibit, and turn to further advantage."[13] The objective of this examination, its characteristic novelty, was to make the granting of assistance conditional on a painstaking investigation of needs by delving into the life of the poor recipient. An inspection that was necessary in order to uncover the artifices of poverty: for example, a mother surrounded by infants begs for your help, but do the children belong to her? Has she not borrowed them for the occasion from the actual mother? An invalid entreats you, but is his infirmity real? In order to distinguish between genuine poverty and artificial indigence, it is preferable to probe into the life of the poor rather than being moved by the sight of ragged clothing and open sores. You

12. *Memoire de l'Oeuvre des dames du Calvaire à l'Exposition universelle de 1900.*
13. Joseph-Marie Gérando, *Manuel du visiteur du pauvre* (1820).

will see, for instance, how in these cases the price of a remedy can be changed into a good meal.

An inspection that was also necessary for judging the advisability of assistance: an old man appeals to you, tells you he's been forsaken, but what of his family? Are they not able to feed him? Is he not speculating in the degradation to which they have condemned him? Aren't you becoming an accessory to this conspiracy that breaks the bonds of nature?

Supplying relief to those whose poverty did not conceal any ruse was not enough. This relief must also serve some purpose; it must also contribute to a rehabilitation of the family. This was why, in every request for aid, one had to locate and bring to light the moral fault that more or less directly determined it: that portion of neglectfulness, laziness, and dissolution that every instance of misery contained. In this new policy, *morality was systematically linked to the economic factor,* involving a continuous surveillance of the family, a full penetration into the details of family life. Gérando put together a model booklet where the resources of the family were to be recorded on one side and the use to which they were put on the other, with an eye to the family's moral standards. It is worth noting that this booklet corresponds—excepting a few details—to the present-day reports of welfare caseworkers. With regard to the old form of charity, the transformation was considerable. Charity either sanctioned an individual's loss of autonomy or maintained him short of beggary on the basis of criteria of externally manifested associations, including the practice of religion, and family respectability. The new benevolence projected a line inside family life, distinguishing, on the basis of criteria inherent in the family setup, between the possibility of autonomy through saving and that of relief payments in conjunction with a supercilious tutelage. The autonomization of the family with respect to the old allegiances and networks of solidarity was accompanied by a displacement of morality from the level of public relations to the private relationship with the economic sphere. In short, a technology of needs was established which made the family into the cornerstone of autonomy, based on the following alternative: control its needs or be controlled by them.

B. Normalization

In 1848, Adolphe Blanqui was commissioned by the Academy of Moral and Political Sciences to travel through the chief manufacturing regions of France and determine the exact situation of the working classes as a contribution to "the re-establishment of the moral order which has been gravely disturbed by the consequences of the revolutionary movement that took effect at the beginning of the year." At the end of his investigation, he suggested "the existence of a veritable law of moral progress of the population." "Among the leading factors that contribute to the promotion of this progress, we must place the just proportion between the number of inhabitants and the riches allotted for their nourishment, the certainties of work, the greater steadiness of wages, the greater latitude accorded to the education of children, the habits of temperance, order, and economy." Conversely, wherever the concentration of the population was extreme, where the dwellings were unhealthy, where promiscuity favored the contagion of example, where the work was uncertain, and where children were left to their own devices, it was "pauperism and utopias" that flourished. "Too often seduced by the temporary elevation of wages, the field workers have been rushing into the cities." Once arrived, they proliferated and reproduced till the day when a crisis brought wages down, driving the whole mass to desperation and down the path of revolt. In the cities of the South, where the workers lived in healthy quarters, no revolts had occurred and one never encountered "those scrofulous, stunted, rickety children, roaming about in bands, such as one sees in some cities of the North." It was "in wretched lodgings that the dissolution of the family and all its woes begin." It was in cities like

Lyons and Saint-Étienne that the real centers of antisocial doctrines had been established, doctrines that had weakened the moral fiber of the working classes. These were the cities where the workers labored in workshops belonging to sedentary overseers who subcontracted from the manufacturers and employed nomadic workmen on a daily or weekly basis. As a jobber, the Lyonese worker did not have the advantage of a regular wage, but he did enjoy an extreme moral independence: "He decides how his time and his will are to employed; he has only his own needs and requirements to take into account." This independence and nomadism created promiscuity among the individuals of the working classes and favored the easy spread of revolt. "In Saint-Étienne, they live in groups organized almost militarily, and they are as well disciplined for their collective defense as they are poorly disciplined for work." In Lyons, all the shop foremen provided housing for their journeymen. This execrable custom too often engendered a promiscuity that was fatal to morals and no less favorable to bad influences. One was obliged to take this factor into account in order to explain those unexpected uprisings that had made the working populace of the cities descend on the public squares so many times as if responding to some common signal or military cue.

This configuration of relations within the working class had the most disastrous consequences for children. "Once he has become an apprentice, the child is practically left to himself, at a time when he needs the most anxious and devoted supervision. Hence there exists, in Lyons and Paris alike, a class that is halfway between childhood and maturity, having neither the naïveté of the one nor the reason of the other, a class that will, if we do not take heed of the situation, serve for a long time as the base for recruiting the disturbers of the social order." Lastly, if one considered the areas where factories and small workshop industry existed side by side, one noted that children were either required by their parents in order to protect the maintenance of their *état,* living in conditions (poor diet, scanty clothing, and so on) that implied their death at an early age, or else "like their mothers, they were cynically sent to work in factories in spite of their age."

Thus, whatever aspect of the problem of the working class was taken up, and irrespective of the region considered, the key question was always that of the adult-child relationship. Either because children were produced with no thought to their number, or because they were exploited in their work by their parents, directly or indirectly. "So long as society will not begin this reform at the base, that is, through an untiring vigilance over childhood education, our manufacturing cities will be constant centers of immorality, disorder, and sedition." The enemy of civilization, the cause of the dangers of political confrontations that were destructive of the social order, perhaps did not originate in the economic sphere; was it not created rather by the arbitrary authority of the family, which authorized the latter to reproduce itself without any concern for the future of its offspring, which allowed it to keep them in the nets of mechanisms of solidarity that were inimical to progress, and legitimated the state of semi-abandonment in which they found themselves, along with the precocious exploitation of their forces? Between the development of industry and that of pauperism, revolts, and revolutions, many people, including socialists and members of the Christian Political Economy group in particular, saw a relationship of cause and effect. But, said the hygienist philanthropists, wasn't this a "fallacy of concomitance," to use the words of Louis Reybaud? There were abuses, no doubt—the premature and overly harsh work of women and children, conditions of public and private hygiene that seriously threatened the health of the population—but these abuses could be corrected by decreeing norms that would protect children, health, and education. And this could be done right in the workplaces more easily than elsewhere. The Law of 1841 regulating child labor was being applied in the factories but was not respected in the small workshops. Wasn't factory discipline the best way to spread these norms, to bring about the pacification of the population through the greater regularity of wages it made possible, together with the settling of the population, the easy verification of sanitary conditions, the regulated distribution of educative counseling? Rather than from industry, did the danger not come from the population which resisted their efforts, which sank deeper into more and more barbarous and unhealthy ways of life? Assistance-oriented philanthropy had tried to evade a political challenge to the state by redirecting energies toward the role of the family, which it hoped to strengthen and autonomize through the doctrine of savings. Hygienist philanthropy evaded a political challenge to the economic order by transforming it into a challenge to family authority by way of the norm.

But what means was to be used to spread this norm throughout the social body? How was one to generalize its observance, win appreciation for its advantages, faced with these stubborn holdouts from the *ancien régime?* Through schooling, obviously. And yet, wasn't it just as dangerous to impose compulsory school attendance? Wasn't this to risk interfering with the free process of liberalism that should be safeguarded at any price? Wouldn't it begin a process of destruction of the family whose support was counted on in order to cope with collectivist threats? From the Guizot Law (1833) to the Jules Ferry Law (1882), these were the terms in which the question of schooling was discussed in all the academic and political circles. This theoretical problem came to be annexed to Malthusian teachings, which were employed by the hygienist philanthropists against the more liberal and traditionalist faction. The best example of this was in the exchange of articles between Gustave de Molinari and Frédéric Passy following the Congress of Benevolence of Brussels, which had resolved, at its Frankfort meeting in 1857, in favor of compulsory education, probably the first time such a body had taken that position.[14]

Passy strongly objected to the proposal, in the name of the private nature of the marriage contract: the child and society

14. F. Passy and G. de Molinari, *De l'enseignement obligatoire* (1859).

were not present at the signing of the latter, he argued. Understood in this way, the family had an external responsibility toward society, not an internal one. It was an association, not a contract of bondage. In this sense, relations between parents and children belonged to the sphere of benevolence, not that of legal charity. Its responsibility was moral, not juridical. The family constituted its own government, accountable for the social effects of its members, not its private behavior. The situation of the child in relation to its father was like that of the poor in relation to the rich. To refuse him an education was a moral offense, not a juridical one. "In the worst instance, the child will be in certain respects as if he were left to himself. So it is with the poor person whom you would refuse the aid he demands out of dire necessity, or the sick person on the verge of perishing, whom you implore in vain to go seek out a doctor who might save him. They are justified in reproaching you for your cruelty, but they have no right to say that you are harming their lives."

To counter Passy, Molinari had to demonstrate that the educational obligation was indeed a debt, hence a phenomenon that was integral to the laws of the economy, and that this obligation was not a preliminary to socialism, but on the contrary a means of averting it. The obligation to provide an education was a claimable debt whose nonpayment could be penalized, not a gambling debt as Passy implied, for if it were not respected, there would exist no curbs on the excitation of the senses, no social contract or market society would be possible. "Let us suppose that instead of imposing the necessary sacrifices on themselves in order to bring up their children, parents behaved like American slave breeders with their pickaninnies. They would profit in the short term, but society would suffer because of the exceptional sacrifices it would be forced to make in order to protect itself and them against the brutality of men who, brought up like slaves, would not have learned anything of the duties and obligations that freedom imposes, or again, in order to come to the aid of these formless and inert generations that are the residue of the bankruptcies and attritions of paternity. We would see more children born than there would be resources available to make men out of them; and, as a last consequence, not only would infant mortality reach shameful and unheard-of proportions, but a part of the resources of the lower classes being assigned in an unproductive, sterile manner to the rearing of these beings whom the lack of care or the application to a hasty and exhausting labor would harvest before their time, the survivors would receive only an insufficient culture; the dead would devour the substance of the living."

In other words, either procreation was to be considered as being accompanied by an "advance on capital," made by the family, as a claimable debt, or it was to be considered as outside any social contract, in which case an "attritional paternity" was created, resulting in "the unrestrained and abusive exploitation of child labor which relegates our society to that state of barbarism in which the head of the family relies on the weakest of his underlings to take charge of his subsistence." A still worse alternative was to side with the supporters of the turret, that reward for improvidence, that asylum for the bankruptcies of paternity, which was the true purveyor of communism since it made the state responsible for the irresponsibility of citizens. This was where Malthus came in. His solution, the moral constraint that would forbid marriage for those who did not have the means to ensure the survival of their offspring, was very alluring. But it had one drawback, making it conducive to all the repressive techniques: it was incapable of preventing the incidence of a large percentage of illegalities, of illegitimate births that filled the turrets and foundling hospitals. Malthus was aware that these hospitals might have constituted a *de facto* solution to the problem of pauperism, through the very high mortality rate of their pensioners—indeed, he said this himself. But this solution was no longer viable since medical progress had brought about an increase in the number of foundling children from the mere fact of their improved chances of survival. So another means had to be found, and schooling was this means.

A providential solution, since it did not rule out marriage, but brought into its internal life both an element of constraint— by making it impossible for parents to count on a sizable direct gain from their children's labor—and the benefit of what was taught in the schools, hygienic and behavioral norms that were favorable to well-being. Through schooling, it was possible at the same time to limit the lack of planning in reproduction and to allow for more planning in the organization of life, exploiting the chief stimulus to human activity, which, as Malthus would say, was much more the fear of need than need itself.

But if schooling was the solution to this sum of problems that threatened the political order, how was it to be imposed? By decreeing free schooling for everyone? This would not be sufficient, as was discovered in England in the first half of the nineteenth century, when superb establishments were constructed for the poor. These were distinct from the "schools of adventure," as the paying schools, of very uneven value, were curiously called, but it was not long before well-to-do families preferred to place their children in the poor schools, since they were designed according to rigorous norms and furnished a unified program of instruction. At the same time, the poor children were gradually deserting these schools, which were intended for them but which they were able to attend only a part of the day, in the evening, when they were dulled by factory work and scarcely able to follow the instructions. So they found themselves in parish schools again, or nowhere at all. In France itself, there existed a possibility of free schooling for poor children, but since the Guizot Law, it required the enrollment of the parents in indigent lists, which was resented as a humiliating procedure, leading the poorest ones to seek the favors of the Frères des Écoles chrétiennes, who did not oblige them to pay, or else to keep their children at home. Free education alone was not the solution, therefore. Should a single system of compulsory education be decreed, then? No, such a proposal seriously clashed with liberal logic. So why not reverse the tactics? Use exemption from payment to attract families that were imbricated in the blocks of dependence and use compulsoriness against those who lived marginally in the dubious vestiges of the old networks of solidarity.

In the course of the first two-thirds of the nineteenth century, the congregationist schools, particularly those of the Frères des Écoles chrétiennes, held a key place in education. The schoolteachers who owed their positions to the Guizot Law were everywhere put on short allowance owing to this surge of religious education, whose enrollment rose from 220,000 children in 1847 to 500,000 in 1860.[15] But what was the cause of this success? Obviously, the patronage that surrounded its deployment. One had only to see the mobilization of notables that occurred when prizes were distributed by these schools. The soldiers, national guardsmen, firemen, plus the presence of civil, military, and religious authorities, made it all too clear that enrollment in these schools would be looked on favorably by the notables. And further, their financing was assured by the "Catholic party," which collected huge sums from all those who wanted to maintain the ancient religious hold over individuals, or re-establish it, rather, in order to constitute an army of reaction, bringing the poor back into the bosom of the Church through the free educative services they rendered and the assorted protective measures they were able to extend. There was a political danger, therefore. The disadvantages of this congregationist setup were especially glaring in light of the kind of education it gave to girls. In complicity with the patriarchal system, it neglected their instruction, or else, when it did attend to the latter, this was in order to train them for its own missionary ends. A dangerous negligence at a time when the realization was growing that it was through women and the education dispensed to them that the norms of a healthy, regular, and disciplined conduct would be able to pass into domestic life. Hence, in order to reach these young women, to spread the

15. Louis-Arsène Meunier, *Lutte du principe clérical et du principe laïc* (1861).

norms, and bring out their advantages, public education had to be made competitive with that of the congregations by being offered free of charge.

As for the old networks of solidarity, and the population of pariahs that were their dislocated products, "these families who people the suburbs of our great cities, the crests of our mountains, the environs of our forests, our seaports, mines, and factories, these entire races of bohemians, gypsies, or Egyptians who have preserved the customs of the barbarians in our midst, all these populations who have been weakened, dulled, and demoralized by the habits of vice and vagabond-age"—as regards these populations with their tendency to drift, the social mission of the teacher would be to place the child at odds with patriarchal authority, not in order to wrest him away from his family and disorganize it a bit more, but "to cause civilization to penetrate into the home through him." Was it not because of the irresponsibility with which they lived, the latitude they had to abandon, train, or exploit their children, that the men of this uncertain class might at any moment "desert the countryside for the cities, the small towns for the large? Do they have to worry about the possible consequences of their imprudent actions, except as concerns themselves?"[16]

From the 1840s to the end of the nineteenth century, a slew of bills were enacted decreeing standards for protecting children, laws concerning child labor (1840–1841), unsanitary housing (1850),[17] the contract of apprenticeship (1851), the use of children by merchants and peddlers (1874), the supervision of wet nurses (1874), compulsory education (1881) and so on. To understand the strategic significance of this movement of normalization of the adult-child relationship, we have to recognize that the object of these measures was hygienic and political in nature, the two facets being indissociable. Doubtless they were aimed at remedying the state of aban-

16. Ibid.
17. See Jourdain, *Discussion à l'Assemblée nationale législative de la loi de 1850 sur l'assainissement des logements* (1879).

donment in which the children of the laboring classes were apt to find themselves, but, just as important if not more so, they also sought to reduce the sociopolitical capacity of these strata by breaking the initiatory ties that existed between children and adults, the autarchic transmission of skills, the freedom of movement and of agitation that resulted from the loosening of ancient communal constraints.

In the philanthropist's violent diatribes against the vagabondage of children these three elements are encountered time and again: abandonment (physical downfall), appropriation (exploitation), and dangerousness (Gavroche*). Three themes that were reduced to the theme of corruption. Sexual corruption: "These little vagrants, who in England are called 'Arab boys,' congregate at night in the suburbs of Paris. What goes on at these meetings of both sexes, the kinds of obscene remarks that are exchanged during the hours of waiting, the liaisons that are formed, and the demoralizing influences that are brought to bear in this corrupting milieu are truly frightening. The sight of these faces of poor girls who have forgotten how to blush is altogether a saddening spectacle."[18] Economic corruption: their parents brought them up at little cost by sending them to beg and pillage, by renting them out to itinerant workers—like the famous Savoyard chimney sweepers—or by placing them as apprentices to be rid of them, without regard to their living conditions. Political corruption: "One day, the little vagabond will enlist with the avengers of Flaurens, or else he will have a share in orgies and massacre in the Commune." Georges Bonjean, one of the most active members of this movement for the protection of children and the author of *Enfants révoltés et parents coupables* (1895), was the son of a magistrate executed by the Communards.

---

18. Othenin d'Haussonville, *Le Vagabondage des enfants et les écoles industrielles* (1878).
* Hugo's irrepressible Paris gamin of *Les Misérables,* who dies heroically at the barricades in the revolution of 1832. [Translator's note]

In order to understand what this fear was about, it is helpful to read a little-known work like *Les Mémoires et aventures d'un prolétaire,* by Norbert Truquin. A résumé of the life of one of those vagabond workers, it was published in 1884, that is, at a time when the agitation of the philanthropic class on the theme of the safeguarding and social control of children was at its peak. It is the narration of an experience rather than a reasoned discourse. Truquin's father is a small-scale contractor who tries his hand at manufacturing, commerce, and agriculture, all without success. Following one of his failures, he places his seven-year-old son with a poverty-stricken wool comber, where he has to work ten hours a day for a little food and many slaps in the face. When his boss dies three years later, Truquin is reduced to begging till two prostitutes take him in, bring him back to health, and use him as an errand boy. When they are put into prison, a former soldier of the Empire takes charge of him and sends him off to harvest grapes in Champagne. He falls ill and goes to the hospital, but soon leaves in order to work on the construction of a canal, then in a brickyard. In 1848, he is in Paris and participates in the uprising. There he finds his father again, who had been running a wineshop until the closing of the national workshops deprived him of his customers. Norbert invites his father to leave with him for Algeria, where, to hear the government recruiters, a man could hope to remain his own master. They arrive there but are soon disappointed by the conditions of colonization, and Norbert Truquin decides to go back to France. Upon his return, he works for a while in the construction of earthworks, and then in weaving in Lyons. He gets married, and with his wife's savings, he pays the first installments on three looms and tries to establish a small workshop. But the irregularity of orders, combined with the hostility of the manufacturers and dealers consequent upon his political initiatives, bring him to the brink of disaster. In 1871, he is arrested for attempting to organize a defense of the city against the Prussians. In 1872, he embarks for Argentina but suffers further disappointments there and returns to rejoin his family. In 1878, he leaves again for Argentina, with his wife and children this time, and crosses into Paraguay, where he manages to install himself and his family. He dies there in 1887.

In view of this trajectory, one understands how the philanthropic struggle against the abandonment and exploitation of children was also a struggle against these popular enclaves that allowed for autonomous ties between the generations, and consequently, against what resulted politically: a population broken loose from its territorial moorings but still preserving the weight of its origins, which made it a moving force that was unpredictable and uncontrollable. Of course Truquin, like the philanthropists, draws up a severe indictment of the excesses that are permitted and absolute parental authority. When he goes to Algeria, his father appeals to the police to oblige him to come back and work for him. He rebels against the legislation that requires a child to supply the needs of the father, whereas, all the while he was wandering about and begging, no gendarme intervened to compel his father to feed him. On another occasion, he alludes to an old woman who obliged her children to beg for her. But on the other hand, there were the people who took him in, the two prostitutes, the old soldier, and an artisan from Champagne. With them, one discovers the other aspect of the adult-child relation existing at the time, the reciprocity implied by mutal utilization, the initiation of children through their social circulation, the custom of placing them in other families. Hence the interest of the testimony he furnishes regarding theose drifting social species, the populations of petty tradesmen and seasonal laborers, and the masses who went from the countryside to the factories and from the factories to the colonies, the soldiers without generals, the prostitutes without registration cards—all the categories he is bound to encounter and connect with one another precisely because of the freedom he enjoys. The social territory he marks out in this way has nothing marginal about it, at least not yet, since it is the old world of labor that has gradually been twisted out of shape through the efforts to resist the spread of factory discipline. A compression: women, children, apprentices, workers, and foremen live cramped together around their occupations in domestic workshops. But a dislocation as well: the old customs shatter, leaving workers and apprentices free to lodge in furnished rooms, eat in cheap restaurants, stop work and start up again as they please, change occupations, cities, countries. These were the "preindustrial" masses who produced the great revolts of the nineteenth century; they created the working-class theory of association, a recurrent theme of Truquin. It was their political defeat that was sounded by the crushing of the Commune.

C. Contract and Tutelage

At the end of the nineteenth century, we note the emergence of a third philanthropic pole, which made the first two converge on the question of childhood by combining what might threaten the latter (children in danger) and what might make it threatening (dangerous children) into the same target. On the one hand, there were the societies that grew out of the concern to replace private initiative with that of the state in the administration of morally abandoned children, or vagabonds, and delinquents, children who had rebelled against parental authority and were placed in correctional institutions through parental action. Under this heading, we can place, for example, all the protective associations for children and adolescents that multiplied under the Second Empire with the Law of 1851, inviting private initiative to take control of delinquent minors in establishments designed to moralize them and instill healthy work habits. In the last third of the century, the most prominent of these societies were the Société pour l'enfance abandonnée et coupable, created by Georges Bonjean in 1879, the Patronage de l'enfance et de l'adolescence, founded by Henri Rollet (the first juvenile judge in France), and the Union française pour le sauvetage de l'enfance, directed by Jules Simon. On the other hand, beginning in 1857, there was a proliferation of societies for the protection of children that anticipated and then accompanied the application of the Roussel Law on the supervision of wet nurses, and which, at one go, undertook to introduce modern methods of child rearing and education in working-class families.

Taken as a whole, these societies eventually found themselves confronted with an unbreachable point of resistance; namely, parental authority, whether they operated by placing minors in establishments of their own invention or in families of their choosing, or by intervening directly in the children's families. It was impossible to go and verify the quality of the children's education in a suspect family if the family was opposed, if it refused entry into that inviolable sanctuary, the home. The charitable organizations that carried out the placements also complained of the uncomfortable situation in which they found themselves with respect to the families, who might at any moment use their sovereignty to interrupt the educative activity of the centers and call their children back home. Or worse, indulge in "the following odious calculation: these parents who had considered their children as too many mouths to feed or as things to be exploited, would freely abandon them to societies willing to take charge of their upbringing. But when they deemed them to be old enough, they would reclaim them in order to exploit them, delivering them over to vagrancy and prostitution."[19]

It was to satisfy these groups that the laws of 1889, 1898, and 1912 were to organize a gradual transfer of sovereignty from the "morally deficient" family to the body of philanthropic notables, magistrates, and children's doctors. The Law of 1889 determined that "fathers and mothers who, through their habitual drunkenness, their notorious and scan-

19. Passage from a brochure of the Union pour le sauvetage de l'enfance (1885).

dalous misconduct, or through ill treatment, compromise the safety, health, or morality of their children" would face the loss of parental authority. This was the ultimate weapon, so much so that it soon proved to be difficult to wield. In reality, it did not offer any way of dealing with the great mass of parents who were more incompetent than unfit and whose weakness and negligence, more than anything else, were the cause of their children's vagabondage; parents whom "a blind resistance and sentimental scruples led to refuse their consent to the charitable societies." So there came the Law of 1898, which granted the judge the power to assign guardianship over a child either to Public Assistance or to a person from a charitable society, in all cases of "offenses or crimes committed by or against children." This completely altered the relationship which the organizations could have with families, for on the one hand, in the interest of monitoring and preventing crimes *against* children, they were able to organize a lawful system of denunciation in the surroundings, and they were authorized to verify the allegations. On the other hand, they could penetrate into families from the angle of violations committed *by* children, in accordance with a procedure set up at the beginning of the 1890s that made them the mediators between families and the judiciary.

The difficulty in which the state found itself, faced with the breadth of the problem, stemmed from its blockage by the following alternative. Either quasi-prisons were to be constructed for these little vagrants, where they could be confined until they reached adulthood, which came down to inflicting punishment on a minor whose only crime was to have been deserted by his parents, a punishment that was often harsher than that inflicted on delinquents, who were subject to payment of a fine. This was a contradiction in the legal sphere, therefore, which upset the arithmetic of crime on which the law had rested since the adoption of the Napoleonic Code. Or else they were to be given the advantage of a genuine professional training. But the problem with this was that it would encourage working-class families to abandon their children without a second thought, since they could be sure that the latter would benefit from an education that the parents themselves were incapable of providing. In order to mitigate these drawbacks, the collaboration of the judiciary and the philanthropic organizations devised a system that prefigured present-day parole procedures and educative assistance administered to delinquent minors "on the outside." The system had three phases: first, the minor was judged and thus became the responsibility of the penal administration; second, the latter consigned him to a protective society, which—third—returned him to his family while keeping checks on their supervision of the minor. If something was not to the society's liking, it could reclaim the youth and place him in one of its centers, and if he was rebellious there, it could send him off to prison. Hence the main recourse was no longer a crude dumping ground for all the wayward members of the family, all those it could not and would not contain, but rather a sort of annex, a last prop serving a system of referral to the family and a surveillance of it. Leaning on one another for support, the state norm and philanthropic moralization obliged the family to retain and supervise its children if it did not wish to become an object of surveillance and disciplinary measures in its own right.

This junction of the hygienic norm and the economic ethic also worked to the benefit of the other side of the state-family relationship, inasmuch as the family had demanded the support of the state in order to reinforce its authority over its recalcitrant members ever since the end of the *ancien régime.* The Napoleonic Code had maintained part of the old power of the family, formerly based on the procedure of the *lettres de cachet de famille.* Article 375 of the Civil Code stipulated that every father whose child afforded "compelling grounds for dissatisfaction . . . can cause him to be imprisoned for a period of one month if he is less than sixteen years of age, and for a period of six months if he is older." A piece of legislation, then, which extended the principle of dual justice, that of the state and that of the family, but only by combining them in practice into a single mode of application: the form of the prison. This combined use of prison for a function of prevention (the preservation of family honor) and for a function of punishment (implying public and not private retribution and *de facto* dishonor to the family) was to account for a slow disqualification of this procedure. In the last third of the nineteenth century, magistrates and philanthropists warred against the measures of parental correction by employing two types of argument.

In the first place, they argued, in the case of "family" children (read: children from comfortably-off families), parental correction was seldom applied because the dishonoring nature of prison, the promiscuity it implied with criminals and with the lowborn, dissuaded parents from using it. They preferred psychiatric confinement as a solution—like Jules Vallès' relatives who, in 1848, feared for the father's career as a result of "the declaration of the rights of children" that Jules had proclaimed in his *lycée.* Or else they dealt directly with convents or with certain private establishments such as the famous Maison paternelle at Mettray, built in 1885 by Demetz. That institution (not to be confused with the reformatory by the same name, which was for poor people) offered comfortably-off families a space of discreet confinement for their offspring where they could continue their studies with the help of professors from the Tours *lycée,* in the strictest anonymity (the students' work was coded) and without prejudicing their social future, since the children could even indulge in fencing, riding, swimming, and so forth. The director of the house was in contact with the headmasters of the *lycées,* who would send him, with the consent of the families concerned, the rebels who were threatened with expulsion. These establishments functioned, therefore, within the educational framework. They were at the same time depositories for family rejects and a last resort for families confronted with the mediocre accomplishments of their children, and in this sense they were more the ancestors of the "diploma mills" of today than reformatories.

So there remained the poor families, and this was what most annoyed the magistrates: they found themselves at the disposal, as it were, of the "most mediocre population"; they were obliged to deliver warrants of parental correction at the latter's behest. Doubtless there were good poor people who appealed to them, but it was often these very people who backed out, owing to "a guilty weakness," when the time came to carry out the order. And further, the magistrates regarded a month in prison, or even six months, as too brief a stay to rid the children of bad tendencies that had taken root. The field was left open to questionable types, "those who have their children confined so as to get rid of them for a month in order to travel or indulge more conveniently in shared fantasies—widowed fathers, for example."[20] "Those too who fight with their children to get them to hand over more of their week's pay."[21] For the majority of people who had recourse to it, "the law on parental correction is nothing short of a democratic Bastille, perhaps more full of abuses than the notorious Bastille that was demolished on July 14, 1789."[22]

The taking of this "democratic Bastille," the wrenching away of this "rather uninteresting fraction" from its privilege, whose use it had scandalously preserved, was carried out juridically on the theme of making men, women, and children equal before the law. The widowed mother, for example, could not lodge a demand for correction without the approval of two members of the husband's family. In view of the dislocation of family ties, this amounted to leaving her powerless. There was also the situation of divorced mothers. Moreover, when a father wanted to put his child in a house of correction, he was not bound to present him to the judge, who thus had to decide solely according to the assertions of the head of the family. Extending the right of correction to the mother created the means for arousing controversy between husband

20. Puybaraud, *Bulletin de la Société générale des prisons,* 1895.
21. Henri Joly, *Revue pénitentiaire,* 1895.
22. Ibid.

and wife and hence of justifying a procedure of verification that implied an investigation involving the child and the neighborhood. This was a means of discouraging abusive demands, since the outcome could turn into the reverse procedure of depletion of parental authority. A means too of widening the possibilities of intervention through the many viewpoints and contradictions of the concerned parties.

Demands coming from these families could thus be referred to the same modes of administration as those resulting from the corrective intervention in families that abandoned their children. Assistance (to the abandoned) and repression (of family rebels) were combined in one and the same preventive activity, whose instrument was the protective societies equipped, thanks to the medical norm and the laws that ensued, with a widened margin of intervention within families, and whose material, the source that nurtured it, would be the family members themselves, in the form of their financial and moral demands, their psychological and educative conflicts: their shortcomings, denounced by the neighbors.

At their point of intersection on childhood, the two strategic lines sketched out a general plan whereby effective procedures would be exchanged, resulting in what I shall call "the social sector" [le social].

On the one hand, the assistance and paternalist movement that had undertaken to ward off the problematic of pauperism by means of private initiative found the basis of a legitimation of its action in the decreeing of hygienic and educative norms, together with the possibility of relieving itself of the problem in favor of an administrative management. It became legitimate to acknowledge the public usefulness of social housing, schools, savings banks, family allowances—of all the services and facilities set up by employers anxious to contain the poor populations, since these instruments of moralization were also necessary to a healthy society. And this did not commit one to a process of increasing the prerogatives of the state, which would be contrary to a liberal definition of the state, since it was only a matter of organizing what was already there, without altering its purpose. On the contrary, this rationalization of the products of philanthropy took the strain off the productive activity of a management sector whose variations, whose unevennesses of supply, were detracting from its effective operation, just as it unburdened the employers of the image of direct domination that resulted from their paternalist ways of establishing the facilities in question. It was not as if the state had taken the initiative, the original and thus political responsibility for these facilities and services. By ensuring their rationalization and generalization *in the last instance,* it only confirmed its function of guarantor of the sound working of liberal societies. The social sector relieved the economic sphere of that portion of poverty it had been obliged to assume, after a fashion, during the nineteenth century, thus removing this last impediment.

On the other hand, the normalization practices that issued from the state received from economico-moral philanthropy a formula for intervention that made it possible to spread these norms according to two distinct lines of transformation.

Where they were not respected, where they were accompanied by poverty and hence by a presumed immorality, the neutralization of patriarchal authority would permit a procedure of tutelage to be established, joining sanitary and educative objectives with methods of economic and moral surveillance. This procedure involved the *reduction* of family autonomy, a reduction that was facilitated by the appearance, in the closing years of the nineteenth century, of a whole series of bridges and connections between Public Assistance, juvenile law, medicine, and psychiatry. By thus bringing together, under the theme of prevention, the formerly separate activities of assistance and repression, the care and custody of children without families and of rebels against the family, one stripped the latter of its long-standing position of interlocutor, one reversed the relationship of collusion between the state and the family, making the family a sphere of direct intervention, a missionary field. At the same time, the private initiative that had been deployed to limit the role of the state could now be put at its service, with its experience in the administration of the poor, in order to apply the norms through an economic tutelage, or else to oversee the economic management of poor families on behalf of those norms that they were not in the habit of respecting. The juncture of this double line announced the social tutelage that was to characterize the gigantic hygienic and moral campaign inaugurated among the poorer classes at the end of the nineteenth century.

On the other hand, where the family showed a capacity for economic autonomy, the spread of these norms could be carried out along the same channels as those by which philanthropy had fostered and encouraged that autonomy, by playing on the same strings. The perfusion of new sanitary, educative, and relational behaviors in the family was to follow the path that was already cleared for it by the savings campaign. The relationship thus established between the family and the school system, between the family and the agencies of relational counseling, like the relation to the savings plan, was one of *enticement*. In this case, private initiative would operate as a means of reinforcing the autonomy of the family and its members against the risk of public intervention. Private initiative relied simultaneously on the desire of families for autonomy and on that of individuals, joining the success of the former to the achievement of the latter in an intensifying recourse to contracts.

The philanthropists never tired of asking workers who lived in cohabitation, "Why don't you get married?" To which they would receive the customary reply: "First give us back divorce, then we'll see."' However insufficient it was to ensure the control of individuals, however inadequate for enabling the perfusion within the family of the new educative and health requirements, the patriarchal institution of the family offered a minimum bulwark, a necessary base for maintaining the social order. The Restoration's abolition of the right of divorce promulgated by the Revolution of 1789 corresponded to the fear of seeing a nucleus of order dissolve as a result of law at a time when its *de facto* erosion was already posing enough problems. All the philanthropists concurred, during the first two-thirds of the century, in seeing the rigidity of marriage as an archaism, but a necessary archaism so long as there was no other basis for the relationship between the social apparatus and the family, an archaism that had to be maintained as it was until it could be disengaged from the social ensembles of which it was a functional component and connected up with the new contrivances such as the savings banks, the school apparatus, and the mechanisms of prevention. From being the plexus of a complex web of relations of dependence and allegiance, the family became the nexus of nerve endings of machinery that was exterior to it. These new mechanisms acted on the family on the basis of a double game that eventually required its juridical conversion. On one hand, they penetrated it directly, turning family members, with the help of the norm, against patriarchal authority, organizing—in the name of the hygienic and educative protection of these members—the depletion of parental authority in general, and placing the family under an economico-moral tutelage. On the other hand, they induced the reorganization of family life, by promoting the new norms as being so many advantages favoring a more complete realization of the family's goal of increased autonomy. They relied on a liberalization of intrafamilial relationships to get the norms accepted. Only five years separated the law on divorce (1884) and the law on the destitution of parental authority (1889). So it is as if the liberality of the contract between conjugal partners was coupled with another, tacit contract with the state: this freedom that presides over your union, the ease with which you are able to contract it outside the old exigencies of families and group adherences, and the liberty you have to break it, we grant to you on condition that you turn it to advantage in order to better ensure your autonomy through the observance of norms that guarantee the social usefulness of the members of your family; or else, losing that autonomy, you will fall back into the register of tutelage.

What was at issue, then, was the transition from a government of families to a government through the family. The family no longer served to identify an interlocutor completely apart from the established powers, a force of the same nature as itself; it became a relay, an obligatory or voluntary support for social imperatives, conforming to a process that did not consist in abolishing the family register but in exacerbating its existing tendencies, in exploiting to the maximum its advantages and drawbacks as perceived by its own members, so as to link together normative requirements and economico-moral behaviors. There were two kinds of couplings, the one negative, the other positive. A negative coupling: the absence of financial autonomy and the demand for assistance functioned as an indicator of an immorality that produced educative and hygienic deficiencies and thus justified an economic tutelage to enforce these norms. But on the other hand, the noncompliance with these health requirements could justify a preventive action whose material would again be the tutelage formula. In the name of the supposed injury inflicted on its members by one or the other of these deficiencies, the family became the object of a direct management. Basing itself on the defense of the interests of the weakest family members (women and children), tutelage made possible a saving and corrective intervention by the state, but at the cost of a near-total dispossession of private rights. A positive coupling: although autonomy was no longer guaranteed, the family could nonetheless preserve and augment it. Preserve it by utilizing its economic capacity, controlling its needs in order to solve, in the private sphere of contractual exchanges, the problems that might arise with regard to the normality of its members; for a comfortably-off family this would be the option of having the problem of a minor handled through psychotherapy, whereas the same minor in a working-class family would bring about increased social pressure on the family. Augment this autonomy by making the appropriation of norms contribute to family success, with the possibility of constituting a thriving milieu, resistant to crises and failures; but also the possibility of seeing better educative and conjugal combinations through free contractuality.

Let us now compare the results of this formation of power relations between the family and the social apparatus and those deriving from the internal reorganization of the family based on the promotion of new educative know-how—that is, the bipolarity of the working-class family and the bourgeois family. It is not hard to see how the tutelage mechanism put into operation at the end of the last century could serve to support and systematize the transition, in the working classes, from the "clannish" family to the family reorganized according to the canons of domestic hygiene—the withdrawal to interior space, the rearing and supervision of children. Similarly, the devices of savings, educational prompting, and relational counseling became operative by connecting the moralized and normalized working-class family to the bourgeois family. Between the powerlessness of the former and the blossoming of the latter, they wove an obsessive web of social promotion which was to furnish the petty bourgeoisie with its characteristic traits, its overinvestment of family life, its sense of economy, its fascination with education, its frantic pursuit of everything that might make it into a good "environment."

Should the family, then, be understood as an agent of reproduction? The formula worked well for the *ancien régime,* where the family commanded favors and obligations precisely as a function of its status in society, and where it was marked by its direct localization within blocks of dependence and networks of solidarity. The placing of the family outside the sociopolitical field, and the possibility of anchoring mechanisms of social integration in the family, are not the result of a chance meeting between the capitalist imperative of maintaining private property and a structure dedicated to producing subjection by means of the Oedipus complex or what have you, but the strategic outcome of a series of interventions that wield family authority more than they rest on it. In this sense, the modern family is not so much an institution as a *mechanism*. It is through the disparity of the familial configurations (the working-class and bourgeois bipolarity), the variances between individual interests and the family interest, that this mechanism operates. Its strength lies in a *social architectonics* whose characteristic feature is always to couple an exterior intervention with conflicts or differences of potential within the family: the protection of poor children which allowed for the destruction of the family as an island of resistance; the privileged alliance of the doctor and the educator with the wife for developing procedures of savings, educational promotion, and so on. The procedures of social control depend much more on the complexity of intrafamilial relationships than on its complexes, more on its craving for betterment than on the defense of its acquisitions (private property, juridical rigidity). A wonderful mechanism, since it enables the social body to deal with marginality through a near-total dispossession of private rights, and to encourage positive integration, the renunciation of the question of political right, through the private pursuit of well-being.

It could even be said that this familial mechanism is effective only to the extent that the family does not reproduce the established order, to the extent that its juridical rigidity or the imposition of state norms do not freeze the aspirations it entertains, the interplay of internal and external pressures and pulls that make of it a locus of possible or imagined transformations. It was only at this cost that relations of dependence could be replaced by relations of promotion, that *claims* procedures could be substituted for networks of solidarity. These are the things that made the family into the essential figure of our societies, into the indispensable correlate of parliamentary democracy. From this fact, one can also see how the problem of the twentieth century was to be, not the defense or abolition of the institution of the family, but the resolution of the questions that arose at the two trouble spots of the juncture between family and society: (1) How to cope successfully with family resistances and individual deviations in the working classes in such a way that the necessary intervention does not generate excessive advantages or overly harsh repression and thus cause the old forms of dependence or organic solidarity to reappear (the tutelary complex); (2) How to achieve the maximum harmony between the principle of family authority, its egoisms and specific aspirations, and the procedures of socialization of its members (the regulation of images).

4.

The Tutelary Complex

A new series of professions has appeared since the end of the nineteenth century, comprising social assistants, specialized educators, and activity directors. They all assemble under a common banner: social work. These occupations are currently in process of full expansion. Rather marginal at the beginning of the century, the social worker is gradually taking over from the teacher in the mission of civilizing the social body, and opinion polls attest that he has inherited the latter's prestige. If social workers are not yet as numerous as teachers, their numbers are swelling at an extremely rapid rate. In the last ten years, they have more than doubled and have now passed the 80,000 mark. Doubtless their unity, their institutional homogeneity, is less great than that of the teaching body. They are not attached to a single institution but rather are appended to the pre-existing apparatuses: the judiciary, public assistance, the education system. Scattered throughout a multiplicity of inscription sites, they are nevertheless unified by their sphere of intervention, which follows the contours of the "less-favored" classes. Within these social strata, they focus on a privileged target, the pathology of children in its dual form: children in danger—those whose upbringing and education leaves something to be desired, and dangerous children, or delinquent minors. All the newness, all the modernity of social work is in this: the increased attention to the problems of children, a consistent revision of the old attitudes of repression or charity, the promotion of a boundless educative solicitude, more concerned with understanding than with the application of judicial punishment, replacing charity's good conscience with the search for effective techniques.

Reading the specialized journals, the publications of the centers of research concerning supervised education, one learns little about social work, but one does discover how it conceives of its own expansion. At the start, there are always the figures on delinquency, the statistics of offenses committed by minors. Experts in criminology study this first layer and detect in the delinquent minors' past, in the organization of families, the signs they have in common, the invariables of their situation, the first symptoms of their bad actions. With the help of these findings, the typical portrait of the future delinquent, the predelinquent, the child in danger of becoming dangerous, can be drawn up. An infrastructure of prevention will then be erected around him, and an educative machinery will be set into motion, a timely action capable of stopping him short of a criminal violation. Not only will he be an object of intervention, but by the same token, he will in turn become an object of knowledge. The family climate, the social context that causes a particular child to become a "risk," will be thoroughly studied. The catalogue of these indications makes it possible to encompass all forms of maladjustment, so as to construct a second circle of prevention. Starting from a desire to reduce appeals to the judiciary and reliance on the penal system, social work would depend on a psychiatric, sociological, and psychoanalytic knowledge for support, hoping to forestall the drama of police action by replacing the secular arm of the law with the extended hand of the educator. And from one stage to the next, this approach—slowed down, alas, by the sluggishness of repressive mentalities, but fortunately guided by the lights of knowledge—ideally would end by abolishing stigmatizing punishment in favor of a careful consideration given to each individual's case. Knowledge would dissolve repressive power by opening the way to a liberating education. But the opposite can just as easily be said, as many people have not hesitated to do, including some individuals from the ranks of the social workers themselves. This sequence of interventions, each one based on the one before, makes all proceed originally from the same judicial definition. Indeed, in this criminological knowledge, which has the form of a nest of Russian dolls, there is an initial model, the judicial one, of which all the others are only enveloping copies. The substitution of the educative for the judicial can also be interpreted as an extension of the judicial, a refinement of its methods, an endless ramification of its powers.

Over the last dozen years or so, we have been accustomed to witnessing a series of regulated jousts, with well-indexed arguments and well-oiled replies, between these two versions of the process of development of social work. These debates are fundamental, no doubt, but they are ultimately sterile, for how can one fail to remark that in order to take place at all, they must prudently remain at a level of abstraction that greatly diminishes their appeal? If, for example, they raise the problem of the family, the formal rigor of the one and the other of these positions becomes untenable and their opposition gratuitous. How can one go on claiming that prevention no longer has anything to do with the exercise of a repressive power when it is judicially mandated in order to penetrate into the family sanctuary, when if necessary it can mobilize a police force to accomplish this? But too, how can one denounce the inflation of procedures of control and prevention without at the same time legitimating another arbitrariness, which is sometimes infinitely more dangerous: that of the family, which, behind the shelter of its walls, can mistreat its children and seriously handicap their future?

The only way to transcend these academic debates is to change questions. We must cease asking, What is social work? Is it a blow to the brutality of centralized judicial sanctions, putting a stop to the latter through local interventions and the mildness of educative techniques, or is it rather the unchecked expansion of the apparatus of the state, which, under the guise of prevention, is extending its grip on citizens to include their private lives, marking minors who have not committed the least offense with a stigmatizing brand? Instead, we should question social work regarding what it actually does, study the system of its transformations in relation to the designation of its effective targets. Cease considering the power-knowledge relationship according to the magical conception that can imagine only relations of contamination or denaturation between the two terms: "those generous human sciences which will lead, by the strength of their views, to the near-disappearance of man's oppression, in favor of a rational administration of things"; and by contrast, "that abominable power which misappropriates knowledge for its own ends and nullifies pure intentions in the interests of a blind and extensive domination." In short, *we must try to understand the socially decisive effect of social work from the standpoint of the strategical disposition of the three agencies that compose it: the judicial, the psychiatric, and the educative.*

1. What is the place of the judicial in the development of these practices of social control?
2. What purpose is served by the psychiatric, situated as it is between the judicial drama and educative practices?
3. What politics of the family is implemented by educative authority?

A. The Setting

Make your way into a courtroom for juveniles. At first glance, you will not notice any appreciable difference between it and an ordinary court. A rostrum in the center of which sits the judge, surrounded by his two assessors, plus, to his left, the prosecutor, and to his right, the clerk. Facing this platform, a series of concentric benches. In the front row, that of the accused, often very long because of frequent court appearances of minors in groups. Directly behind, that of the parents of the accused; then, a little further back, that of the educators and a few seats for the public. The same arrangement, one thinks, but miniaturized. "Family" law court: entry is forbidden to the public, with the exception of persons having a recognized interest in the problems of children, and with the consent of the judge. Moreover, the smallness of the room gives an impression of relative intimacy. Family justice: the presence of the family is provided for; in principle, it is even required. In short, a theatrical deployment that does not differ a great deal from that used for adults, with reduced dimensions due to the age of those who appear therein, and more discreet in character, out of consideration for the persons concerned. It is only by seeing it function that one discovers, behind this intangible appearance, a series of fundamental shifts in judicial practice.

1. *A shift in the content of the thing judged*

Juvenile court calls to mind a board meeting of a corporation for the production and management of maladjusted children, rather than a place of public deliberations and judgments.

In the eyes of the lawmaker, this lightening of the theatricality of the judicial apparatus would have the sole purpose of reducing the distance separating the judge from the minors and of allowing consultation with the parents in arriving at decisions. But these are pious representations—in the new language of agreement—of reasons that are much less "democratic." If we refer back to what was said about the first juvenile courts by their very founders, Benjamin Lindsay, the first juvenile judge in Chicago (1889), and Louis Albanel and Henri Rollet, his like numbers in France, we find that their primary object was to fight against the state of excitement produced in the children by the public character of their court appearance: "The public's absence has excellent results, for the child tends to glory in the interest he arouses and takes pride in seeing his name in the newspapers."[1] Against the popular emotion that the sentencing of children was liable to give rise to. Against the attitude of parents who would either not come, to avoid having the onus of a conviction fall back on them, or would come to wrest their children away from the bars of the apparatus by means of heartrending tales of misery and suffering. In a word, it was Gavroche—the shame of the family, the pride of the people—who had to be killed by forcing the family to appear with him and by eliminating the people.[2]

But only the people, not respectable men and women: since the 1860s, a Seine court had specialized in children's cases and one would see persons of distinction, in search of an interesting occasion, come and sit next to the curious onlookers. When a child who was not yet too marked by vice was about to be sent to a correctional institution for want of a family to reclaim him, one might see one of these respectable figures stand up and kindly offer to take charge of the child. The establishment of the modern juvenile court has carefully reserved a place for these valuable personages. Better still, it has arranged one by making them into the institutional collaborators of the judge. In a first phase, they were still present in the room as attentive and discreet observers, authorized according to their mandate by one of the philanthropic organizations. When the judge had questioned the child and had evaluated the various reports concerning him, the association members would have their cards passed to the judge in the event they wanted to take the child. Rejects were sent to the state houses. This slave-market aspect gradually disappeared through the bipolarization of the philanthropic clan into two categories: the tutelary agencies, who were installed

1. Henri Rollet, preface to Chloé Owings, *Le Tribunal pour enfants* (1922).
2. Regarding this transformation, see Henri Joly, *L'Enfance coupable, combat contre le crime* (1892); Henri Rollet, *Les Enfants en prison* (1892); Édouard Juhliet, "Tribunaux spéciaux pour enfants aux États-Unis" (1914); E. Huguenin, *Les Tribunaux pour enfants en Italie* (1912); Louis Albanel, *Étude statistique sur les enfants en justice* (1897).

on the dais next to the judge as his assessors, and the tutelary bodies' agents of execution, who replaced them in the room and came to give account of their mandators.

It is to Mussolinian Fascism and Pétainist legislation that we owe the inscription of notables in the juridical apparatus. First version: the *benemerito,* defined in the Mussolinian code as "citizens having rendered services in assistance matters and versed in the biological, psychiatric, crimino-anthropological, or pedagogical sciences, motivated by that noble feeling of duty which is one of the foundations of fascism and of the good operation of the juvenile courts."[3] The formula was applied in France at the beginning of the forties, and it remains in effect, following the same principles, to this day. These are voluntary "civilians" who have been recommended by the juvenile judge for approval by the Ministry. The criteria are honorability and an interest in the problems of children. Among the fourteen assessors in the juvenile court of Valenciennes, for example, there are a director of a transportation company, an insurance agent, three high school teachers, a former lawyer, the wife of a corporation president, an attorney, a building contractor, the director of a vocational and educational guidance center, an engineer, a retired Red Cross officer, a superintendent of schools, and a seller of sporting goods. That takes care of honorability. As to interest in the problems of children, apart from the numerous instances in which the indicated professions require it, it is attested to by membership on the board of directors of some public or private body entrusted with young people.

Educators in the courtroom: let us picture the young ones, soberly dressed and sporting beards. As a manifestation of the tutelary agencies in the lives of young people, they need to be close to the minors in age and yet be good conveyors of the gravity of their mandators. The all but systematic wearing of beards serves to introduce a certain hierarchy in faces still capable of expressing spontaneous reactions. Their domain is

3. Pierre de Casabianca, *Guide à l'usage des rapporteurs et délégués près les tribunaux* (1934).

the entry into the world of work and collective discipline, the gaining of the confidence of responsible citizens. In court, they report on the combat they are engaged in against the evasive maneuvers of the adolescent. It can be owing to them that a minor appears before the court: the result of a report on a parole case, the signaling of a flight, a charitable institution's request for a change in the minor's placement from the civil register to the (more intimidating) penal register: faced with too restive a client, the institution dealing with him under the child-protection clause of the Law of 1958 may request his placement under the penal Law of 1945, pertaining to juvenile delinquents. Instead of being in a position of constraint with respect to the child, the institution thus becomes a means of his escaping a stronger constraint: prison. And there is never a lack of peccadillos for effecting this displacement from the assistancial to the judicial. In addition, the educator is there to furnish a statement concerning the means of placement and intervention that are available for a child who falls for the first time into the hands of the law.

Set within this double network of social guardians and technicians, the family appears as though colonized. There are no longer two authorities facing one another: the family and the apparatus, but a series of concentric circles around the child: the family circle, the circle of technicians, and the circle of social guardians. A paradoxical result of the liberalization of the family, of the emergence of children's rights, of a rebalancing of the man-woman relationship: the more these rights are proclaimed, the more the strangle hold of a tutelary authority tightens around the poor family. In this system, family patriarchalism is destroyed only at the cost of a patriarchy of the state. The very frequent absence of the father testifies to this. Because he is busy working? Certainly, but that is not the whole of it, for when he is present, nine times out of ten it is only in order to keep quiet and let his wife do the talking. If he is present, one senses that this is at his wife's urging, or out of an acquired habit of yielding to summonses, but in any case not in the hope of participating. Because in actual fact there is no possible role for him to play. His symbolic function of authority has been usurped by the judge and he has been relieved of his practical function by the educator. Which leaves the mother, whose role is not suppressed, but on the contrary preserved, solicited. Provided it is placed somewhere between supplication and deferential dignity. It is that of a "natural advocate" addressing the tutelary authority embodied by the judges. In short, an arrangement that recalls the oldest patriarchal rules, the only difference being that the father has been replaced by the judge and the kinfolk by social mentors and technicians. Juvenile court: a visible form of the state-as-family, of the tutelary society.

A "familial" board of directors governs a domain of children that has been broadened by the obliteration of the separation between the familial and the judicial orders: it manages the child in his family and in special institutions as well. The founding of the juvenile court corresponded to a reorganization of the market of children. The state reformatories in which the law courts placed delinquent children, and the "parental houses" in which families had their rebellious minors confined, were slowly supplanted by a unified cluster of interventions starting with the noninstitutional milieu, the family (educative assistance), and proceeding toward the penal, itself revamped. The date for the official inauguration of the juvenile courts was 1912. In 1909, the scandal of the children's prisons broke, sparked by the suicide of a boy imprisoned in the Mettray Maison paternelle. A series of revolts ensued in the reformatories, occasioning the prosecution of the personnel and directors because of the resulting revelations. The left-wing newspapers and groups led a campaign against these "makeshift houses" that were only fit for manufacturing "rebel souls" with their cells, beatings, and exploitation of the work of adolescents. The year 1909 also saw the advent of remedial classes and boarding schools (the future I.M.P.[4]), these being annexes of compulsory elementary

---

4. *Instituts médico-pédagogiques.* Also the E.M.P.R.O.: *établissements médico-professionnels.*

schools, where one's unstable, feeble-minded, perverse, or assertive children could be dumped. This was also the period in which the modern forms of medical intervention in the delinquent milieu were sketched out. The old market of children was organized around monastic and military techniques, linked to familial and religious, police and judicial authority. The new looked to medicine, psychiatry, and pedagogy for its methods; it sought to supply itself more directly by its own means, such as educational screening and canvassing by social workers. But rather than a struggle between two systems, this was a metamorphosis—brought about with the help of acrobatic readjustments, it is true, but by and large rather painlessly. The Bonjean[5] family owned a number of houses that had been the scene of these famous revolts; to avoid seeing such a thing happen again, they converted them into boarding schools for the blind. The Congrégation de Nôtre-Dame de la charité du refuge, whose Saint-Michel convent had managed a reformatory for girls since 1825, bought an establishment at Chevilly-Larue that gradually became the main observation center for delinquent minors. It was presided over by prominent psychiatrists and psychologists, including Dr. Le Moal. The famous houses of the Good Shepherd, which were supported in the nineteenth century partly from donations and partly by the labor of girls brought there by their families who did not see any possibility of marriage for them, prudently placed themselves in the service of the new judicial and assistancial politics by having themselves financed by the state, at daily rates allocated for the care of morally endangered minors. Side by side with these institutions, there developed a new private sector of discreet houses, boarding schools, diploma mills, and private clinics, all of which were characterized by a strong "psy" infrastructure. Hence there was an expansion of the market of maladjusted children through the inrush of a contingent of "unmanageable" and "incapable" children drawn from the schools, cou-

5. Georges Bonjean was the author of an important book on the treatment of unruly children, *Enfants révoltés et parents coupables* (1882).

pled with the conversion of penal structures for use in the open milieu. Secondly, there was a modification of the modes of financing through a new relationship between the public and the private spheres: the state financed more and so controlled more, thus causing a rise in the cost of the forms of custody that could avoid that control. Finally, there was a unification of this market through its standard reference to psychiatric authority, which was delighted to discover its favorite clients in the confused population of the old system of confinement, a ready practical field for a brand-new psychiatric theory.

2. *A shift in the form of the trial*

Juvenile court puts one more in mind of a psychiatric synopsis, or of a presentation of patients in the good old days of Charcot's Salpêtrière, than of proceedings leading to a judicial decision.

In the unfolding of a conventional court session, the scene is built around two interlocking confrontations: that of the judge and the defendant, and that of the prosecutor and the defense attorney. The other actors called to the stand (witnesses, experts, or plaintiffs) are included in the quadrilateral traced by these four main protagonists, so that the accused at least has visual command of the field of forces in which his case is being debated. In a juvenile court, against a basic backdrop that is similar in appearance, the emergence of new actors, positioned differently in the scene, destroys this privilege and consequently alters the nature of the representation. Consider the order of the interventions and the respective positions of the actors. First, the judge on his platform; next, the accused, facing him and looking at him continuously, as it is forbidden to turn one's back to the court; then, behind the accused, his mother and—rarely—his father; and then, further to the rear, the educator. Last, to the defendant's right and to his left, the defense attorney and the deputy prosecutor. The scene has taken on a depth that escapes the defendant's gaze. Let us imagine: opposite him, he has the judge, a figure disembodied by the robe he wears, scrutinizing his expressions, his posture, and his dress. Behind him, people who see only his body and who speechify about his situation without his being able to look at them.

The main effect of this transformation is to nullify the notion of an equitable law that is ordinarily suggested by the formal opposition of the prosecutor and the defense attorney. Here, apart from the fact that they seldom intervene, it is not unusual to hear them saying the same thing. The prosecutor is noticeably handicapped by the "social" definition of the juvenile court. He is usually content to demand "that the law be applied," according to the time-honored expression. The defense counsel is nearly always appointed to the job owing to the family's poverty and the minor nature of the offense. But it is their very presence that is problematical for both attorneys, insofar as the classical formulas of defense counsel and prosecutor's charge appear out of place in juvenile court. Speaking after the educator, obviously with less knowledge of the situation of the minor and his family than he, the defense attorney selects out a few elements of the educator's report and arranges them to fit the rhetoric of the plea: "an unhappy childhood . . . I ask that the court give him the chance he has not had up to now"; or else: "an honorable family . . . nothing leads us to believe that the events that cause him to be here might occur again in the future." In these conditions, the contradiction between defense and accusation tends to zero. In order to get out of his uncomfortable position, the defense attorney identifies with the court, since in any case the court has appropriated the role of concern that would normally be his, and if the prosecutor happens to be dozing, he steals the latter's role—when all is said and done, an easier one to fill. This leaves the guilty child, surrounded by responsible adults.

The conventional confrontation between prosecutor and defense counsel, their rhetorical jousting, is thus relegated to the background by a new ordering of discourses, staggered according to a hierarchy of expertise [*hiérarchie technicienne*] that precludes any possibility of contradictory debate.

The discourse of the judge and that of the child are out of phase. For the judge, the evocation of the infraction is merely the occasion to test the character of the accused, or rather to furnish a corroborative demonstration of what is said about his character in the dossier: if he denies the charge, this only confirms the deceiving side of his character, as revealed by the psychological examination. One thinks sooner of the relationship between a teacher and his "bad" pupil, or of that between a psychiatrist and his "good" patient—the one producing the other, in any event—than of the confrontation of a defendant and his judges. The same principle of phase difference is repeated in the speeches of the parents and educators. In practice, they cannot hold a dialogue or question one another, since they only have the right to address the judge, and besides, unlike the prosecutor and the defense attorney, they do not speak the same language. In principle, the family is there to explain or defend the behavior of its progeny, but it is thwarted in this role by the implicit or explicit accusation that is brought against it: it is at least partly to blame for the child's being there. The results of the social inquiry concerning the family are read at the beginning of the session. Whence the little-varying repertory of its statements: self-justification—"I did what I could"; attempts at moving the judge—weeping scenes and promises of a new beginning; resignation—"I give up, Your Honor, he's too much for me to deal with."

To summarize, the juvenile court metes out punishments only selectively. In the main, it administers children over whom hangs the threat of application of a punishment. The official justification for the nonpublic nature of the court is this concern for prevention. It effects a discreet *dilution of punishment* instead of concentrating it. Preventive action aims at encircling the offending boy instead of stigmatizing him in an ostentatious way. In the range of sanctions at the juvenile court's command, in theory, incarceration constitutes the exception. When administered as a punishment, the sentence is usually suspended with a trial period or probation. It is in this cavity opened up by the suspensive character of the punishment that the educative measure takes hold. Whether it goes by the name of "educative assistance in the nonpenal milieu," "probation," "placement in a halfway house," or "conditional freedom," it is always by nature derived from prison. One must see the two facets of these educative measures, and not just one, as people generally do. In a sense, the system allows the guilty minor "his chance" by sentencing him only to measures of control. In another sense, by obliterating the separation between the assistancial and the penal, *it widens the orbit of the judicial to include all measures of correction.*

If we are to understand the interrelations of institutions dealing with irregular children, we have to represent them as being framed one within the other, according to a principle of superimposition which ultimately relies on the juvenile court to prop it all together. At the top, then, is this juvenile court, designed for minors who have committed offenses (ordinance of 1945). Directly beneath, the juvenile judge, that is, the same judge who presides over the court, but sitting alone in his chambers in order to rule in cases concerning endangered minors (ordinance of 1958). A minor qualifies for this designation when his health, his safety, his morality, and his education are in danger. In practice, this applies to children recruited, not by the police arrest procedure, but by that of informing. A teacher, a social worker, or a neighbor brings the existence of a "risky" family to the judge's attention. The possible modes of action for the judge are the same as in juvenile court, excluding punishment. One notch further down, one finds Social Aid to Children, formerly Public Assistance, an enormous administration that is independently directed in theory, but linked to the juvenile judge by a myriad of practical and juridical ties. It has the same sort of activities as the services of the juvenile judge: recruitment by the reports of informers or through the abandonment of the child, placement in institutions or educative assistance in the noninstitutional environment. The juvenile judge can send minors to it for placement, and when Social Aid to Children wants to make an important decision—for example, change a temporary placement into a permanent one (if it determines that it would be better never to return a particular child to his family)—it can and must rely on the judge's authority to have this done. At the base, finally, there is that immense nebula called child psychiatry: the I.M.P., the C.M.P.P.,* the clinics, the centers of infanto-juvenile guidance, and so on. Here the links with the judge become extremely tenuous on the juridical plane: a vague possibility of judicial control over the institutions, but a possibility with important practical consequences: the juvenile judge is responsible for the placements that are effected, and he "covers" their disciplinary problems. Hence *there is a feedback effect* [effet-retour] *of this dilution of punishment* on educative and assistancial measures. Through the continuity that it establishes between the different instances of corrective interventions affecting behaviors, *it places the latter in the gear train of the judicial apparatus and creates the possibility of a capitalization of surveillance which overexposes the minors to a penal identification.* Example: the placement of an overly truant child in a center is an educative measure that can be decided without the minor's having committed the least offense; but if he runs away, he thereby commits an offense and becomes subject to penal prosecution. Another example: the frequent accumulation by minors of suspended sentences that become enforceable with the first infraction they might commit on becoming adults, when tutelary clemency no longer applies.

Juvenile court does not really pronounce judgment on crimes; it examines individuals. There is *a dematerialization of the offense* which places the minor in a mechanism of interminable investigation, of perpetual judgment. The break between the investigation and the decision is obliterated. The spirit of the laws (those of 1945 and 1958) on delinquent and

* Centre médico-psycho-pédagogique. [Translator's note]

predelinquent children requires that more consideration be given to the symptomal value of the actions of which the minor is accused, to what they reveal concerning his temperament and the value of his native milieu, than to their materiality. The investigation is meant to serve more as a means of access to the minor's personality than as a means of establishing the facts. It is the occasion for instituting measures of observation of the child in his milieu, whether he is allowed freedom (O.M.O.—*observation en milieu ouvert*), is in a reformatory, or is in prison. It is the moment when he is examined by psychologists or psychiatrists, when an inquiry is ordered regarding his family via the police or social assistants. The actual investigation thus becomes an evaluation of the minor and his milieu, carried out by a host of specialists in social pathology. An evaluation that becomes a prosecution subsequent to sentencing, but by another name. It is the same educators, the same social assistants, the same psychologists who, after the trial, visit the family, intervene with regard to the child, and send regular reports to the judge recommending, on the basis of their impressions, that the measure be extended or transformed.

The effacement of the offense also has its feedback effect: *the judicial form of appeal is displaced from the justiciable to the justicier*, from the person subject to justice to the administrator of justice. The possibility of judicial appeal exists for the children and their families, but those who resort to it are ridiculously few in number. For how does one protect against decisions that hold in reserve the application of a punishment in the strict sense? And who would be capable of lodging the appeal, considering the fact that the disputable question (the offense, the *de jure* problem) is eclipsed by the question of behavior and the norm, by the problem of adjustment, thus becoming the business of specialists? Who? Why, the specialists, of course! They alone are able to argue the necessity of having the child pass from one status to another, of removing him from his family or placing him back in his family, of depositing him in an I.M.P. or sending him to a children's home, a reform school, a center for young workers, or a prison. The ranking, one above the other, of social services for maladjusted children, in order of seriousness, of increasing stigmatization, going from "petty psychiatry" to criminal justice, is the chief means they have of pressuring families. Sending your child into an I.M.P. is less serious, after all, than seeing him placed in a center of Public Assistance or a "house of correction." It gives the appearance of medical care: no disgrace or sneering from the neighbors—at least, not too much. It is well worth the trouble of submitting to a little area psychiatry [*psychiatrie de secteur*]. But if you balk at the prospect, if you prove to be "infrapsychiatrizable," then you are bound for one of the Social Aid to Children centers. This latter service has grown substantially over the last few years; it is the soft underbelly of a corrective system that never stops swelling. This being the situation, in order to unburden themselves of excessive demands, of indocile behaviors, the social services in turn can lean in the direction of juvenile law.

Juvenile court is not a minor jurisdiction for minors but the mainstay of a tutelary complex that also encompasses predelinquency (roughly 150,000 children), Social Aid to Children (650,000), and a large part of child psychiatry (figures not available, but certainly even higher than for Social Aid to Children). This central importance of juvenile law is due to the pivotal position it occupies between an agency that sanctions offenses (the retributive justice of ordinary law) and a composite group of agencies that distribute norms. Juvenile law relies on the former in order to guarantee and ratify the latter. On the one hand, it endows them with an authority, a coercive capacity necessary for them to function. On the other hand, it filters out the negative products of the work of normalization. In this sense, one can say it is the judicial apparatus that manufactures delinquents, since those who pass from the tutelary register to the penal register and who constitute a large proportion of delinquent adults have thus been previously tested and proved to be impervious to the normalizing process. This filtering orients those who have refused to play the game toward a career as delinquents. Starting with a child's occasional infraction, or with official attention being drawn by well-intentioned persons or certified specialists to the danger he risks in his family owing to the inadequate supervision he is under, a procedure of control and tutelage is set into motion, which eventually calls on him to choose between a subjection to norms and an orientation to delinquency that is difficult to reverse. The important thing for the apparatus is the individual's identification, his inflection toward an "uneventful" life or toward a career of catalogued delinquency. More than anything else, the system wants to eliminate surprises in favor of management in one category or another.

Let us illustrate this argument by giving an account of the trial of Ounadjela Boubaker, a fourteen-year-old Algerian adolescent who appeared in 1974 before the juvenile court of Lille. At the time his trial opens, Ounadjela is being held in the Loos prison. He is led into the room by the state police, his handcuffs are removed, and he takes his place on the defendant's bench in front of his parents dressed in their Sunday attire. The session commences with the examination of identity and the reading of extracts from his social and psychological dossier. From this, one learns that Ounadjela has already been the subject of educative and assistancial measures that have proved to be ineffectual and, above all, inapplicable. Singled out in the beginning for the inadequacy of his environment (his mother is divorced and his sister has been the subject of judicial measures), he has benefitted from educative assistance in the noninstitutional milieu.* But the social assistant assigned for the purpose was not able to do anything with him. She was relieved by an educator who was no more successful than she. As a result, he was placed in a school for rehabilitation where he remained only three days. Brought back, he ran away again. When the police arrested him, he appeared to be conciliatory, repentant; he was let loose and

---

* A.E.M.O.: *assistance éducative en milieu ouvert.* [Translator's note]

immediately disappeared. When psychologists tested him the first time—that is, at a time when he was under the risk of prison because of his repeated flights—he showed an intellectual coefficient verging on mental deficiency. Tested again inside an educative institution, he reveals an I.Q. that is clearly above average. The judge is furious: "Are you really an imbecile, or just pretending to be one?" It is the opinion of the magistrate that, given these conditions, nothing further can be expected on the educational plane. His precocious physical maturity and the cleverness of his replies make him out to be a little adult. The psychiatrists do diagnose an emotional immaturity in him, but the fact that he is artful enough to make fun of them leads them to conclude that nothing can be done in that regard, that one must change registers and assign him to prison, particularly in view of the fact that he is appearing this time for serious offenses: car theft, driving without a license, and stealing a substantial sum of money.

All would have gone according to plan, and in apparent good faith, if there had not been, on this one occasion, an attorney determined to defend Ounadjela. This attorney first more or less directly underscores the recording-machine aspect of decisions already made elsewhere in the surveillance practices that characterize juvenile court, its behavior in suspending or dispensing punishments. "For," he says to the court, "how does one explain that you waive the choice of an educative measure, in advance of any deliberation? What kind of court is it that comes to a decision before having debated? What is this juvenile court that calmly places a fourteen-year-old minor in a central house of correction where in theory only men sentenced to long prison terms are to be found? What is the educational value to this man (and to others like him) of the sticking on of labels and restuffing of chairs with which he will be occupied in prison?" Secondly, the attorney questions the strange relationship the juvenile court maintains with the offenses at issue, the way it has of treating them simply as the symptoms of a bad environment or of holding them up as proof of an irreducible penchant for delinquency. "What are these offenses, in fact? The theft of an automobile? But the owner of the vehicle has admitted to handing him the keys. It was at the urging of the police that he filed a complaint: he was informed that he would be reimbursed by the insurance company for the expenses of the accident caused by Ounadjela. Driving without a license? Certainly, but are all minors who have committed such an offense to be put in prison? One would have to empty the prisons of all their other residents to accomplish that. The theft of a sizable sum of money? But this money belonged to his mother and consequently no offense was committed." To give the act the character of a misdemeanor, the court tries to make something of the fact that it was concealed in a wallet belonging to Ounadjela's stepbrother, whom the mother entrusted with the safekeeping of her money. "So a theft was committed," says the judge, "since there was entry into the room occupied by the stepbrother." No such luck: there was no door separating his room from the common room, but simply a curtain. "Was this curtain drawn or not? It's too much to bear, from a judicial standpoint, these North African families with their extended sense of family relations, their custom of living in houses without doors!"

For this once, Ounadjela came off in good shape. But what a glaring light was thrown on the functioning of juvenile justice! A fictitious justice in that it has no judicial activity of its own but plays the role of a relay or exchanger between two jurisdictions possessing an autonomous logic: ordinary penal law and the invisible jurisdiction of the normalizing agencies grouped together in a single tutelary complex. Through its proximity to penal law, the juvenile court confers its legitimacy on surveillance practices; it extends the protective umbrella of the law to them, along with its potential for coercion. Through its links with correctional practices, it can relieve them of their rebellious elements, thanks to a mechanism that is unencumbered by the democratic character of the classical judicial forms: the public and contradictory nature of debates, and the genuine possibility of appeal.

Hence, to regard the evolution of social work as an expansion of the judicial apparatus is only half correct. Doubtless this apparatus has a function of mooring the various forms of intervention; doubtless it gives them a direct mandate, not to mention the indirect possibility of serving as a recourse for rebellious cases. But in this process, is it not just as important to note that it is the central apparatus that follows the movement rather than driving it forward? For while its authority does extend over an infinitely larger population than that of delinquents, it is an authority that is increasingly symbolic. It covers a broadened domain—in the feudal sense of the word—of practices of control, but it rarely instigates them, and it arrives at its decisions in reference to them. Further, it has a tendency to shed along the way the operational criteria that sustained its own credibility: public and contradictory debate, the possibility of appeal. From being the central mechanism for attributing penalties, it passes to the status of an accessory component of a control machinery whose logic depends on the judicial framework, but only to dissolve it in progressive stages. Between the judge, whose exercise is based on the law, and the educative social services, whose practice tends to indeterminate measures, there is always the threat of a conflict of powers, of a reduction of the one to the logic of the other. The educative vocation of the judicial apparatus arose when it became obvious that the penal system was inadequate to halt the substantial flood of "problem children," of all those adolescents who poured into the interstices between the old family order and the new educational order, taking advantage of the spaces that still remained in the junction of the two. Too numerous to be gotten rid of through prison, too shrewd and too "wild" to be dealt with by charitable methods, they made it imperative to find another solution. The solution hit upon was education under court order. But by thus filling this breach or "line of escape" created by vagrant minors, juvenile justice introduced another one at the core of the judicial apparatus: this very education, which could only be achieved at the risk of dissolving judicial logic, of reducing the power that prompted it to a mere role of support. Hence the need to devise a means of control over these educative activities, and the eventual emergence—in the vicinity of the juvenile courts—of psychiatry as an extrajudicial jurisdiction.

B. The Code

Open a few dossiers of delinquent or morally endangered children. In the multiplicity of documents, of decisions rendered with their reasons adduced, of reports of educative assistance, and medicopsychological opinions, you will have the impression of an endless reiteration of the same discourse. This is explainable in part by the typically bureaucratic effect: these documents are often copied from one another. But this homogeneity is due primarily to the gathering of the different observations made regarding the minor and his family into a single instance: the *consultation d'orientation éducative* (C.O.E.). Here the results of an inquisitorial, *investigatory* knowledge (the social inquiry) and those of a *classificatory* knowledge (medical-psychiatric examinations and psychological tests) are unified by an *interpretative* knowledge inspired by psychoanalysis. Heterogeneous knowledges are placed in a common perspective by the formation of an extrajudicial jurisdiction made up of educators, psychologists, social assistants, psychiatrists, and psychoanalysts. Their job is to draw up a synthesis and supply an expert opinion as to the most appropriate measure to administer to the minor.

At least this is the impression one has in the Paris region and the large cities, that is, in the areas where the *consultations d'orientation éducative* are firmly established, so that the juvenile courts refer the minors under their jurisdiction to them almost as a matter of course. In the "distant" provinces, however, and especially if one consults dossiers from a few decades back, one finds that they have an altogether different appearance. The social inquiry and the medicopsychological examination function in separate systems, along quite different lines and with a marked difference between them as to how often they are utilized. The social inquiry is more like the report of a police investigation than the subtle *mise-en-scène* of the history and problems of a family which a present-day social assistant is apt to formulate. Moreover, it was often police officers who were charged with conducting the inquiries subsequent to the reporting of an endangered child, just as the educators responsible for observations in the noninstitutional milieu (O.M.O.—*observations en milieu ouvert*) were often parole officers, that is, former police and military officers, and more rarely, former schoolteachers. The social inquiry, even in this summary form, almost always appears in the dossiers, whereas the medicopsychological examination becomes increasingly rare as one goes further back in time toward the advent of the juvenile courts. It then becomes quite similar in character to any psychiatric consultation in ordinary judicial matters. The medical expert is asked (1) to perform a medicopsychological examination of the minor; (2) to state whether this minor exhibits physical or mental disturbances or deficiencies capable of influencing his behavior; and (3) if such disturbances or deficiencies are found to be present, to state whether they necessitate a specific measure of protection, safeguarding, or re-education or a special program of treatment, or whether they imply professional or other contraindications. In short, the same questions as those for an adult (responsibility, concern for the division between the medical and the judicial), except that the question for adults concerning "accessibility to punishment" (read: the intimidating nature of prison) is here replaced by an inquiry as to the advisability of re-education measures.

Hence one sees the gradual emergence and extension of these three modes of knowledge—inquisitorial, classificatory, and interpretative—and their increasingly systematic combination and relative autonomization with respect to their commissioning authority, the juvenile court. In the beginning, social assistants, police officers, psychologists, and psychiatrists were the direct executive agents of the juvenile judge. The latter determined and specifically mandated his collaborators, and was himself responsible for effecting a synthesis and drawing conclusions from their reports. Social assistants were the systematic agents of his investigative mission, and psychiatrists occasionally assessed individuals suspected of belonging under the jurisdiction of medicine rather than law.

Why this transformation? What was it that caused these different modes of inquiry to diversify and evolve in a single direction? How were the psychological assessment of the child and the analysis of the educational value of his milieu able to pass from an *accessory function,* a mere supplement of the judicial investigation, to a *function of obligatory relay* between the judicial setting and surveillance practices that could be traced back to it, however far removed from it in appearance? How were these practices thus able to constitute a semi-autonomous jurisdiction that transformed the judicial setting into a chamber for recording or soliciting their opinions?

1. The first material to be placed in the dossiers of dangerous children, and still the most important, was furnished by the *social inquiry,* which came into general application at the same time as juvenile law itself (1912). It was made necessary, in fact, by the two operations that established the juvenile court. On the one hand, the fitting of assistancial practices into the judicial framework called for a search for better ways to counter the unpredictable or self-interested behavior of parents, resulting in a codification of the conditions under which Public Assistance and the philanthropic groups could intervene. On the other hand, the removal of the right of correction formerly belonging to parental authority, its transfer to the judicial apparatus and to social notables, necessi-

tated the perfection of a procedure for verifying parents' complaints, with the more or less explicit objective of turning the procedure into an indictment of their educative abilities, of the value of the child's environment. The social inquiry was thus situated at the meeting point of assistance and repression. It was the technical means by which an attempt was made to efface the weaknesses of both.

The limitation of repression was a weakness, in that repression could not intervene except on the grounds of an offense having been committed—too late, therefore—or on the parents' demand, which was suspected of arbitrariness. There was weakness too in the quandary of public or private assistance, whose maneuverability was restricted to the space between the parents' shame, which appealed for assistance only when it was too late, and their effrontery, which set money in motion for unworthy ends. As a preliminary to coercive measures and aid measures alike, the social inquiry ideally would represent the means of eliminating the drawbacks of both the repressive character of the former and the charitable character of the latter by converting them into a single process, by linking them in an effective reciprocity. The social inquiry thus brought about a conjunction of two lines of control of the family. Starting with assistancial practices, this procedure spread with the expansion of the "social" sphere in general. It began with the measures for protecting endangered children; then it was employed for the assistance of poor women giving birth, for families demanding special subsidies from social-aid offices, and for poor families with one parent placed for a long period in an institution of health care (sanatorium, psychiatric hospital) or repression (prison). It was next put to use in the surveillance of delinquent children, becoming a preliminary to parole measures, the first form of educative assistance in the noninstitutional milieu (A.E.M.O.). Finally, the social inquiry became necessary for the settling of contested cases involving the allocation of social benefits—family allowances (devised in 1930 and systematized in the postwar period), national insurance, special allocations. To which should be added the recourse to the social inquiry for divorce proceedings and, quasi-officially, for the allocation of social housing units. *The social inquiry is thus the chief technical instrument for regulating the new logistics of social work:* the possibility of deprivation or restitution of children, intervention in the family for purposes of re-education (A.E.M.O.), the monitoring of social benefits, inaugurated in 1946 and restricted at first to family allowances, but later extended to cover all social benefits. It is brought into play by the order of a juvenile judge in cases where the family is accumulating debts, or wants the benefits of social housing although its income and budgetary behavior appear inadequate, or again, when the husband is suspected of chronic and more or less deliberate unemployment.

The nineteenth century had produced many procedures of investigation into family morality, among them that of Gérando, explained in his *Visiteur du pauvre*. But their utilization had been limited to works of charity. The social inquiry that was devised at the beginning of the twentieth century was conceived in the same spirit, with the same obssessive concern for preventing the investigator from being tricked by the popular methods of staging poverty. But it completely changed the position of the investigator, the points of support at his disposal. Gérando dreamed of introducing a new technique in the service of the old form of tutelage. He made innovations in the method of observation of the poor, which penetrated the interior of the domestic economy instead of keeping to the "external signs of poverty," and in the technique of economic blackmail ("control your needs if you do not wish to be controlled on their behalf"). But Gérando did not imagine any other "visitors of the poor" than the well-intentioned rich and in particular their spouses, for whom the practice of charity was a way of regaining their vigor, of avoiding conjugal confinement. In his plan, the initiative for charitable activity would remain with private individuals, with people of standing, with philanthropic societies who might get support from the public-aid structures, though this would be of a secondary kind only, such as for the centralization of information (an inventory of the genuine and false poor), the stocking of means of material aid (layettes, suits of clothing, food supplies, heating apparatuses), and partial financing. In any event, this is the way things actually worked during the greater part of the nineteenth century. At the end of the century, organizational superiority passed from the private to the public sphere. Protected financially by the organizing of public assistance, sheltered politically by a screen of administrative procedures, relieved in the field by paid technicians, philanthropy began a new phase of its career—less spectacular, perhaps, but more serene, as it was now housed in the body of the state. The technology that Gérando had engineered for investigating poor families could thus become an extensive type of social control, with agents mandated by public authorities and supported by the administrative and disciplinary system of the state.

This new structuring of assistance, in conjunction with society's disciplinary infrastructure and the laws for the protection of children (1889 and 1898), made possible the generalization of the investigatory technique by sweeping away everything that had restricted its effectiveness, enabling the investigator to disengage his work completely from the logic of *reputation,* which was replaced by methodical, police-like *investigation.* Without this technique, an article written in 1920 explains, "the inquiry will not be conducted by the investigator, but by the investigatee."[6]

First rule: *the circular approach to the family.* Before entering into contact with the family to be monitored-assisted-protected, it is necessary to gather all the information possessed by the administrative agencies responsible for assistance and observation. This accomplished, the investigator can set out to locate the schoolteacher, preferably before anyone else. He is usually well informed and always impartial, so his testi-

6. "L'Enquête sociale," *Revue philanthropique,* 1920, pp. 363 ff. Cf. also *Services auxiliaires des tribunaux pour enfants* (1931), and René Luaire, *Le Rôle de l'initiative privée dans l'Assistance publique* (1934).

mony is of primary importance, whether in the cities or in the country. In point of fact, as he sees the child every day, the schoolteacher knows all about him, his state of health, his appearance, the education he is receiving, the care and super- vision he is given. With the teacher's help, the investigator can get a clear notion of the life of the family itself, for it is not unusual for mothers to come to him for advice. Through him, one can also be informed about the occupation of the family head; one can learn the name of his employer in par- ticular. The employer's statement comes next. One should be a little wary of it, however, because he will tend to present his employee in a favorable light when it is a question of obtain- ing benefits for him other than wages, for "obvious reasons." On the other hand, "the employer is in a good position to appraise the ability, conscientiousness, and industriousness of his personnel." Next come the landlord, the concierge, the neighbors, and the shopkeepers. The statements of the land- lord and the concierge are worthy of consideration, but they must be handled "with a pair of tongs." If they are favorable, they can be trusted; it means that the tenant pays his rent and leads a quiet life. In the contrary case, "one must try to ascer- tain the true causes of the hostility expressed." The neighbors are less reliable, and among the merchants, one must beware of the wine dealer, "who is too willing to talk, and should always be treated with suspicion."

Second rule: *separate and contradictory questioning*. "It is always preferable that the visitor not arrange a meeting in his own home, but appear rather at the client's house, and that this visit occur without advance notice." This is still one of the ABC's of the job of social assistant. She will always choose the middle of the afternoon for her first visit, when she can be almost certain of finding the mother at home alone. "The investigator must not let it be guessed right away that he is already informed in part, this being a good way to test the mother's sincerity, to inspire confidence and obtain a maximum of confidential disclosures. A second visit, still without prior notice, but in the evening this time, when the husband and children are there, will allow the investigator to match what the mother says against the evidence of the father. The latter is often hesitant to speak. The best way to get him to talk is to use the elements supplied by his wife. He will then put aside his reserve and, resuming his hegemonic role in the home, will try to become the investigator's chief interlocutor."

Third rule: *practical verification of the family's way of life.* In addition to what can be learned from it, conversation with the family should always be enjoyable to the investigator (and to the investigatee: "this is the most engaging aspect of his duties"). It should "give rise to as much talk, back and forth, as possible. These conversations always give pleasure to the persons one is questioning." A show of interest, a giving out of advice. This is the price one pays, so to speak, in order to carry out a relatively painless and systematic collection of information. "While conversing, and taking a few notes, the visitor will look about him, examining the dwelling, its layout, its appearance, the promiscuities it imposes, the sanitary conditions in which the inhabitants live. He will take stock of the furniture, utensils, articles of clothing, and so forth which attract his attention." It is not considered inappropriate, either, to raise the lids of a few cooking pots, to examine food stocks and bedding, and if need be, to take a few telling photographs.

All things considered, a technique that mobilizes a minimum of coercion to obtain a maximum of verified information. On paper, it is the ideal formula for doing away with the dangerous stigmatization of an overtly policelike intervention and the no less dangerous charitable practice, which creates social hypocrisy, replacing these two approaches with a discreet and enlightened administration. But only on paper. In practice, the formula has not worked as well as might have been hoped, and this fact became apparent as early as the 1930s. The social inquiry did establish a bridge between the administration of assistance and the judicial apparatus, but more for the purpose of discriminating those who would come under the authority of one or the other than of establishing a continuous and functional circuit between the two. By means of the social inquiry, the social assistant tested the family's receptivity to a mild intervention. If all went well, if the family still wanted and asked for aid, they were referred to Public Assistance, later called Social Aid to Children. If they appeared uncooperative, they were sent into the judicial sphere as a quasi-punishment. Each of these circuits came to insist on keeping its "clientele," on preventing their transfer to another service. Poor families know what they are doing when they put on a good face as a tactic for dealing with services that dispense the most subsidies while bringing the least coercion to bear and being the furthest removed from the judicial apparatus. Whence the enormous swelling of services provided by Social Aid to Children (650,000 children aided), which are clearly out of proportion to those of the juvenile justice system, even though the latter is also mandated for the protection of children. This fact testifies to a problem of adjustment of administrations whose equivalent will be encountered in our discussion of child psychiatry.

2. From the time of its founding, juvenile law provided that "the social inquiry will be completed, when appropriate, by a medical examination" (1912). That is to say, the recourse to psychiatry was envisaged for the first time in juvenile law in the form of a complement to the investigation. Since the Napoleonic Code, the question of the responsibility of minors was regarded from the viewpoint of the *discernment* manifested by the child in the accomplishment of his misdemeanor. A discernment whose value would be determined by the judicial examination, at the end of which the judge would decide in one case to assign a punishment, and in the other to have the child benefit from an educative measure (in actual fact, placement in a correctional institution was always involved, but in the latter case without entry in the police record). The new juvenile law thus removed this power to

determine the responsibility of minors from the judge's list of prerogatives and conferred it on the doctor. But not entirely, since the judge still decided as to the advisability of perform- ing a medical examination. The judge no longer had the means of testing the discernment evidenced by a young delin- quent, but he had the function of distinguishing those who were subject to a psychiatric examination from those who were not. An acrobatic position that was to dominate a rela- tionship of intense proximity, causing as much quarreling over the definition of the respective powers of the judge and the doctor as collaboration between them. The situation that resulted for juvenile law was not, properly speaking, excep- tional. It was simply the site where the effects of a decisive redistribution of relations between law and psychiatry were to have the greatest impact, for reasons that had to do precisely with the nature of this transformation.

In the last third of the nineteenth century, psychiatrists be- gan to refuse the terms according to which they were asked to offer their opinions regarding a particular defendant, even when adults were involved. To declare whether a criminal had acted in a state of insanity appeared pointless and meta- physical to them. To be called upon only in cases involving major crimes, "monstrous" affairs that baffled the judicial ap- paratus, seemed to them a vexatious limitation of their prac- tice, as did the restriction of their field of action to adults. They no longer wanted to be "that law of the extraordinary" which the law born of the Revolution had invited them to be, but to which it had also confined them. But for them it was not so much a question of giving up an old function as of extending the existing one. They wanted to be able to concern themselves more with minors than with adults, more with petty offenses than with major crimes, more with the detec- tion of anomalies, with orienting those sentenced to a particu- lar mechanism of correction, than with grading the responsibility of those accused. They proposed to go beyond their minor function in the judiciary and achieve an autono- mous position as prime movers in the prevention and treatment of delinquency, which in their eyes had become a mere symptom of mental aberration, on a par with all the other "antisocial reactions" such as running away, lying, sexual perversion, suicide, and so on. For them, delinquency was not the always possible and hence "excusable" product of a (momentary or lasting) loss of reason; it was the manifestation of a deficiency that was present at the start, a constitutive— hence detectable, foreseeable—anomaly. The madman, that disinherited son of reason, was succeeded by the abnormal individual, society's bastard offspring. After the person who had accidentally lost something came the one who had never possessed "the morally and socially necessary equipment." A shift of interest that made possible *the transition from restricted psychiatric expertise to generalized psychiatric expertise.*

This transformation of the psychiatrist's position, the broadening of his social vocation, resulted first from an internal critique of psychiatry and secondly from the external concern of which it became the subject, owing to the rise of disciplinary mechanisms that required its services in a way that the judicial apparatus had not.

An internal critique. In the decade of the 1860s, a part of the psychiatric profession concluded that the asylum was beginning to show a marked resemblance to the thing it had the mission of replacing, the old general hospital, that repository of an undifferentiated gamut of sick, criminal, and indigent individuals. The suspicion was aroused "that the asylum might not be that medicalized space which Pinel and his successors conceived it to be. In reality, a deep upheaval in the very conception of mental illness was undermining this notion of an order that was indissociably spatial (the disposition of patients over the space of the hospital) and theoretical (nosographic classifications.)"[7] The theories of the first alienists operated on the basis of a symptomology. The diagnosis of madness was determined by the description of its manifesta-

7. Robert Castel, *L'Ordre psychiatrique* (Paris: Éditions de Minuit, 1977).

tions, which produced the different varieties of monomania. Intelligibility resided, therefore, in exterior signs. Starting with Falret, Baillarger (1854: *De la folie à double forme*), and above all with Morel (1857: *Traité des dégénérescences*), this intelligibility was no longer to be found in the explicit sign but had to be perceived in what lay underneath this sign, the latter being nothing more than an apparent stage in an ongoing process of development which was predictable by anyone capable of interpreting it. Similarly, mental illness was no longer a spectacular exception that must be isolated and eventually treated, but a phenomenon that was always latent, necessitating early detection and a prophylactic intervention embracing all the causes in the social body which favored the mechanisms of degenerescence: to wit, miserable living conditions and the intoxications, such as alcohol, to which the poor population were exposed. Thus, well in advance of present-day segmentation, the psychiatrist yearned to leave the asylum in order to become the agent of a project of social regeneration.

In any event, the emergence of the psychiatrist from his institutional preserve was ordered by an imperious summons issuing from two social apparatuses in full expansion: the army and the schools. Making education free and compulsory caused the schools to be filled with a mass of individuals who were either unwilling to submit to scholastic discipline or ill prepared for it. Their outbreaks of undisciplined behavior and their avowed incapacities for scholastic achievement presented teachers with insurmountable problems. Which of these individuals needed to be weeded out? What were the signs by which one could recognize an idiot, a mental defective, a child who would never be able to adapt to school, or on the contrary, one who only needed a little time and special attention? In 1890, the Elementary Education Administration appealed to Bourneville—the Salpétrière alienist who specialized in the treatment of abnormal children—for assistance, requesting that he furnish a schema of observations for the detection and orientation of scholastic misfits. The army experienced the same problems, owing to the generalization of conscription and especially to a change in military tactics that made special kinds of training and, consequently, continuous selection necessary. "Nowadays it is no longer the intoxication of battle that must ensure victory, but the steadfast and personal courage that is demanded of the least soldier. Instead of neglecting his wits in the heat of battle, he must stoically await death in the silence of the ranks and master his giddiness of nerves through a relentless effort of will." A premonitory text, seeing that it was written in 1913.[8] It punctuated the first phase of an evolution in which, from the 1880s onward, psychiatry assumed an increasingly important position in military medicine. After having been merely a technique for managing confinees, the disciplinary perspective was expanded to take in the great domains of social life, developing into the main surface of emergence of madness and abnormality. Régis, one of the noted psychiatrists of the end of the nineteenth century, expressed this well when he proclaimed that "the disciplinary requirement is becoming the touchstone of general psychical deficiency."[9]

The whole theoretical effort of psychiatrists in this period was to consist in trying to align their own reasons for wanting to extend their work beyond the asylum to the social body as a whole with the reasons for which they were being called upon to intervene in the social apparatuses. In other words, to bring about a fusion between a pathology of race and a pathology of the will. The three cardinal figures of modern psychiatry, the hysteric, the mental defective, and the pervert, can only be understood on the basis of this project. Where the pathology of the will was dominant, one had the hysteric, with his fugues, his senseless lies, his partial amnesias. Where the pathology of race held sway, there was the mental defective, that product of a biological involution. Lastly, at the point of maximum convergence between the two discourses, there appeared the pervert, the individual in whom the will,

---

8. Gaston Haury, *Les Anormaux et les malades mentaux au régiment* (1913).
9. Albert Pitres and Emmanuel Régis, *Obsessions et impulsions* (1895).

which was completely inverted with respect to the moral faculty, coincided with the instinct, with its most "animalistic" features. The main focus of this theoretical effort was the vagabond as a social figure, one which brought together, in wondrous fashion, psychiatry's two major concerns, race and discipline. The vagabond, that "impulsive degenerate," that embodiment of atavism combined with indiscipline, was much too interesting in the eyes of psychiatry for it to make him into a special category, as the legal system had done. For roughly ten years (1890–1900), the vagabond was to become the universal of mental pathology, the prism through which all the categories of madness and abnormality could be distributed.[10]

Beyond the vagabond, however, the ultimate objective of this psychiatric strategy was children in general. The universality of the symptomal value of vagabondage, its ability to blend all the varieties of nosography, derived from the fact that virtually all the components of the vagabond attitude had their roots in the nature of the child, the child's suggestibility, his emotiveness, his excessive imagination.[11] The vagabond was interesting only in that he displayed to the maximum all the pathological effects of the weaknesses of childhood when these were not corrected or checked in time. "Why is the will of even the most gifted children generally so vacillating and fickle? This is primarily because their brains, still poorly organized, are scarcely capable of maintaining a balance between two opposing tendencies and do not allow

10. Regarding this psychiatrization of vagabondage at the end of the nineteenth century, see Auguste Marie and Raymond Meunier, *Les Vagabonds* (1908); Armand Pagnier, *Du vagabondage et des vagabonds* (1906); and the countless articles in the penal reviews, the archives of criminal anthropology, and the medicopsychological annals. The article that seems to have set the tone for the rest is Achille Foville, "Les Aliénés migrateurs," *Annales médico-psychologiques* (1895). There is a parallel literature of the vagabond, with Maupaussant (*Le Vagabond*) and Richepin (*Le Chemineau*). The Vacher case, from which the film *Le Juge et l'assassin* was made, should also be mentioned, because it lies at the meeting point of these two discourses. One might read "Les Vagabonds criminels" by Fourquet, *Revue des deux mondes* (1899), concerning the philosophy of the judge in charge of the case.

11. Regarding this continuity, see Jean Hélie, *Le Vagabondage des mineurs* (1899).

them to exercise a great power of abstraction. It is this weakness of abstraction that is the cause of their inability to escape fascinations. Consequently, when the desire to wander, born of a curiosity, an attraction, or an example, takes control of the child, if he is not under supervision, if the circumstances are favorable to him—in a word, if nothing stands in the way of the realization of his desire—he will plunge headlong down the path of adventure, an adventure capable of degenerating into a complete flight [*fugue*]."[12]

This is how the advent of child psychiatry should be understood. In the beginning, it was not tied to the discovery of a specific object, of a mental pathology peculiar to children. Its appearance derived from the new ambitions of general psychiatry, from the need to find a base, a ground in which to root all the anomalies and pathologies of the adult, in the form of a presynthesis; to designate a possible object of intervention for a practice that no longer wanted to limit itself to the management of confined individuals, but sought to preside over the whole social enclosure. *The place of child psychiatry emerged in the space hollowed out by the search for a convergence between the prophylactic cravings of psychiatrists and the disciplinary requirements of the social apparatuses.*

Consider the book that officially established child psychiatry in France, *Enfants anormaux et délinquents juveniles* (1914), by Georges Heuyer. Not that this work contained a lot of new statements. It is easy to see in it the resumption of work and of remarks that were scattered through the field of psychiatry thirty years before its publication. But it gathered them for the first time into a tactical design that became a basic element in the subsequent expansion of child psychiatry. The objective is explicitly stated: how to preselect and pretreat those unfit for military service, the mentally ill, and the professionally unstable; how to identify these elements before they have done any damage; how to direct them into

12. Marie and Meunier, *Les Vagabonds*.

channels that will separate them from the normal population; and how to administer a treatment that will only affect them after the event.

On a practical level, this tactic was made possible by a double operation:

1. *The designation of a standard institution: the school.* What link was there, what common denominator could be found between the children of Bourneville's abnormal ward at Bicêtre and those imprisoned at the Petite Roquette for theft, vagabondage, or insubordination to parental authority? The answer: scholastic behavior. As proof, a series of record cards made on the basis of observations of delinquent children, abnormal children, and others placed in remedial schools. Although the mixture was different in the three categories, it was made up of the same ingredients of instability, feeble-mindedness, and perversion. The school could thus be regarded as "a laboratory for the observation of antisocial tendencies" (Heuyer).

2. *Ascribing the origin of the troubles to the family.* If one examines the records used by Heuyer, one notes two types of questions. The first is concerned with discipline: Who supervises the child at home? What kind of supervision, weak or brutal? Was the child attending classes? His behavior during recess? And then, another set of questions dealing, in a very detailed way, with the morphological aberrations and pathological past history of the parents: What was the moral condition of the parents or guardians? What was the father's state of health (alcoholism, tuberculosis, syphilis, criminality)? The child's deficiencies could be related in turn to two types of family deficiency: educational insufficiency and the existence of degenerative anomalies. Thus, more than the patient, more than the problem child, the family became the true locus of illness, and the psychiatric doctor was the only one capable of distinguishing in this pathology between that which belonged to the sphere of discipline and that which belonged to organic treatment.

The decisive effort of this child psychiatry consisted, therefore, in displacing the juridical category of discernment on behalf of the category of *educability*. It thereby gave itself the theoretical means of exercising a decision-making function in the juvenile justice apparatus, where it promoted a system of behavioral justice that was parallel and competitive with the system based on offenses. At a time when juvenile law was being constructed on the basis of the desire to replace punishment with prevention, repression with education, the psychiatrist appeared at the judge's side, motivated by the same project as he, but endowed with a theoretical capacity for assessing the suitability of a particular educative approach, a capacity that was matched only by the juvenile judge's capacity for ordering the measure to be carried out. It is true that no time was wasted in searching for an idyllic complementarity between these two capacities—for example, the collaboration of Georges Heuyer, André Collin, and Henri Rollet—but there was also mistrust and competition. The least one can say is that in the discussion concerning the Law of 1912 it was mistrust that prevailed.[13] A majority of the magistrates insisted that a medical examination of children should not be obligatory; otherwise, they argued, their specific power to judge would be at an end.

In the years between the two wars, the collaboration of the doctor and the juvenile judge remained very limited. Doctors Collin, Alexandre, Orly, Boffas, Paul Boncour, and Rabinovitch began a first phase by publishing one article after another demanding that the psychiatric examination be made mandatory for all delinquent children (Heuyer was already aiming his sights higher in 1914, subtitling his work "The Necessity of a Psychiatric Examination for All School Children"). In 1917, Paul Boncour and Rabinovitch organized a medicopsychological examination service for young inmates at the Petite Roquette (a boys' prison). This formula was in

13. See André Collin and Henri Rollet, *Médecine légale infantile* (1920).

the nature of a compromise, in that only minors subject to a parental-correction measure were held there. Criminal law still was not being tampered with. In 1919, the girls imprisoned at Fresnes were given the benefit of the same examinations. In 1925, Henri Rollet launched his initiative (Rollet was on the faculty of the Paris School of Medicine and was in charge of the child neuropsychiatry clinic—later to be directed by Georges Heuyer—run by the Association for the Protection of Children and Adolescents). First intended for the children of the association and hence outside the direct judicial sphere, this initiative gradually extended its activity to children brought to the clinic by their parents, or on the instructions of schoolmasters; then to those sent to it by the juvenile court. It was not until 1927 that these initiatives received official approval, in the form of an authorization for the medicopsychological examination of young detainees out on bond who consented to be examined.[14]

Reading the extensive publications of this clinic of child neuropsychiatry, however, one has the impression that they were marking time. A whole school of child psychiatrists gathered around Heuyer and set about refining classifications to an extreme degree, inventing endless varieties of perverts and publishing alarming statistics on the rate of mental pathology in young delinquents (80 percent). This was a formidable affirmation of knowledge that did not correspond to a real power. They were given a few guinea pigs to keep them occupied and to keep them at a distance.

3. At first, it seems hard to understand why psychoanalysis did not really enter the field of juvenile law until the years immediately after the war. Its birth was contemporaneous with that of the juvenile court; it had an aptitude for dealing with pedagogy; it could not have been more concerned with family organization; in short, on paper it was the ideal dis-

14. Regarding all these efforts, see the book by Henri Gaillac, *Les Maisons de correction, 1830–1945* (Paris: Cujas, 1971).

course for the protagonists of a *prevention* of child maladjustment. The psychiatry that originated with Magnan, Heuyer,
Dupré, and company seemed to have its natural place in the
general movement of hygienization. This campaign was
aimed at the organic defects of the poorer classes: tuberculosis, syphilis, alcoholism. "Psychical pauperism," as Heuyer so
neatly put it, was part of this cluster of curses; more often
than not, in fact, it was the result of them. Why, then, did this
psychiatry experience so many difficulties in harmonizing its
activities with juvenile law, even though the latter was motivated by the same intentions? Why did juvenile law, after first
ignoring psychoanalysis, proceed to integrate it? What was
there in psychoanalysis that psychiatry did not have; what
was it that opened wide the gates which had been under siege
by it for more than thirty years?

To answer these questions, people generally point to the
traditional resistance to new ideas, the shrinking back of Car-
tesian minds from the discovery of the unconscious, minds
more interested in classifying than in getting down to the
difficult task of listening to something that was apt to disturb
their mental comfort. This argument hardly stands up, since
psychoanalysis is just as old as their psychiatry, and the psychiatrists firmly believed they had discovered the unconscious
in race, that hidden instance in relation to which they observed the variations of moral will. People also call up a more
materialistic argument: defense of the corporatist interest.
But this is no more convincing. To cite only one example to
the contrary, the ubiquitous Georges Heuyer lost none of his
social status by his late recognition of the merits of psychoanalysis. In 1946, he was appointed to the first chair of child
neuropsychiatry, and he went on to preside over the destiny
of the new pedo-psychiatry (revised and corrected by psychoanalysis), easily steering this flourishing association by sometimes bringing the helm over toward psychoanalysis and
other times toward psychiatry. To understand the social fortune of a knowledge [*un savoir*], one has to locate the reasons
favoring its acceptance, find the existing link between its dis-

cursive properties and the problems posed by the functioning of institutions. What was there, then, that was inadequate in the link between the discourse of classical psychiatry and the development of juvenile law?

We have seen how the juvenile justice system implied a redistribution of the market in maladjustment. Gone were the prisons full of convict children, the notorious penal or correctional colonies, those hotbeds of revolt and objects of scandal. At any rate, the administration retained only a small part of them, as a "harsh" solution for its most disobedient clients. Most of the minors were placed with private protective associations approved by the courts.[15] These organisms assigned children to various institutions that specialized in vocational training, in physical and moral treatment (the development of physical education and the ideology of scouting), or in the medicopsychological approach (very few of these). The years between the two wars were *a period of pioneering exhilaration in the pedagogical mission.* Not a year went by without a scandal breaking out in the children's institutions that still had a strictly penal discipline. These were ideal conditions for the expansion of the private protective societies. A few figures will indicate the extent of this disaffection from the old system of correction. Before the creation of the juvenile courts, the number of young people sent into the penal and correctional colonies was around 10,000. In 1930, there were scarcely more than 1,000. By contrast, the average yearly number of minors placed in the charge of charitable institutions increased from 479 in 1919 to 1,860 in 1925, and reached 2,536 in 1930. Strengthened by the growing discredit of the penitentiaries in the eyes of public opinion as a result of press campaigns, and by the juvenile judges' inclination to affirm the special preventive character of their mission, the protective societies collected a maximum number of children—all who had not committed very serious offenses. They then redistributed them in their various institutions according to the chil-

15. Regarding these *sociétiés de patronage,* see especially Albert Constant, *Les Sociétés de patronage, leurs conditions d'existence, leurs moyens d'action* (1898).

dren's professional, correctional, or medical peculiarities; according also to the space available, since it was a question of maintaining the profitability of each establishment by bringing in a necessary minimum of subsidies at daily rates. *The private organizations worked out among themselves an informal system of subcontracting for both technical and financial reasons.* The practice of parole [*liberté surveillée*] was to undergo an evolution that paralleled these modifications in placement techniques. Understood at the start as a kind of reprieve from being sent to a correctional colony or to a charitable institution, as a first degree on the scale of punishments, this function of surveillance was to be transformed by the voluntary parole officers into a more gratifying activity—for them, at any rate—of *moral regeneration of the family.* Although they were chosen and mandated by the courts, the parole officers came to be *representatives of the interests of the protective societies, more engaged in recruiting for the latter than in applying the decisions of the judges, while acting in accordance with their "desire to educate."*

This rapid sketch of the evolution of juvenile justice between the two wars was essential in order to understand the lines along which supervised education [*éducation surveillée*] was reorganized beginning with the Pétain government and continuing through the Liberation, especially the central place that psychiatry—amended by psychoanalysis—was to occupy in this new organization. Simplifying things somewhat, one might say that the extensive and intensive form of educative practices set up by the protective associations and voluntary representatives rendered inadequate the classical psychiatry defended by the clinic of child neuropsychiatry, while the judicial apparatus, on the other hand, discovered the usefulness, indeed the necessity, of having recourse to a specialist ally in order to re-establish undisputed control over the practices of surveillance.

As for the practices themselves, what purpose could be served by psychiatry? For the volunteers assigned to observe children in the family milieu, and to "moralize" the latter, psychiatry was as much a handicap as a useful instrument. What did it have to say, in fact, about the family with a problem child? Either that the family was not performing its educative task satisfactorily, gradually "conditioning" the child to become perverse, so that it was urgent to take the child away from the family; or that the family was genetically (degenerescence), medically (tuberculosis), or socially (indigence) tainted, and consequently it was again necessary to take the child away from the family and place him in the appropriate institution. The bluntness of these diagnoses was bothersome. But *prestige de science oblige,* of course, and the volunteers scrupulously noted down family defects. That sort of thing could always turn out to be a useful means of pressure. But the detection system that the doctors called for would have practically nullified their action—their reverie of a gentle moralization of the child in the family surroundings. Moreover, the principle of the alternative diagnosis—ill/not ill—could turn back against them to the benefit of families who, in the absence of confirmed medical problems, would have the means of challenging the intervention. Hence, starting in 1930, Heuyer's clinic applied itself to the difficult task of *making its grid of analysis more flexible; it set out in search of parameters that could be manipulated by educative action.* And what it came up with, first of all, was the concept of *opposition reaction in the child* (Heuyer and Dublineau, *Revue médico-sociale de l'enfance,* 1934). This was a splendid synthesis of the Pavlovian conditioning to perversity and the Freudian Oedipus complex. Prior to this discovery, the practice was to criticize the bad example set by the parent for the child, or to ascribe the example to pathology, or perhaps to a congenital defect. To get out of this dilemma, Heuyer and Dublineau announced that the emotional state of the child at the time of receiving the example counted for more than the example itself. Good parents could have opposing children if the latter were jealous of one of their siblings or troubled by unspoken hostility in the family climate. A good father could "freeze" his son into an opponent status if he did not put up with the child's necessary but passing opposition at the age when the child needed to assert himself. The reception of the example would be good or bad, the child would be normal or would give evidence of indiscipline, dreaminess, and laziness, would steal or attempt suicide, according to whether or not there existed a climate of jealousy, for example, in the family atmosphere, or an excessive severity on the part of the father, and so on. Some small resistance by the child was normal (Oedipus complex), but if it increased, this meant that "the child's personal affectivity does not resonate in harmony with that of the surroundings." The analysis of disturbances in the child which resulted from *conjugal dissociations* marked a second stage. Beginning in 1936, there was a flowering of articles and theses by Heuyer's cohorts, proving, with the help of statistics, the negative effects of separation, divorce, widowhood, and even of large poor families, as the last implied a guidance of children that was almost unilaterally maternal. In this way, the Freudian theory of deficiencies in parental images was linked up with the classical analysis of the environment. It was only when they were provided with this resource that the psychiatrists were able, on the eve of World War II, to begin instructing social workers and ladies of charity.

Psychiatry was scarcely any better suited to the needs of the protective associations and their establishments. Of course, these organizations had a problem in assigning minors according to the particular nature of each of their institutions. To improve the situation, they set up a few regional observation centers (at Lyons, in particular) in order to organize the distribution of children. These places took on high-sounding names, but their purpose was more to test children's behavior, docility, and aptitudes in a collective and disciplinary milieu than to produce a precise medical diagnosis or prognosis. In any case, for these people animated by a feverish educative zeal, psychiatry's aptitude for distinguishing, a priori, the educables from the ineducables had the effect of an authority that inhibited their devotion and restricted their powers. It questioned the validity of their results, introducing the worm of scientific doubt into the fruit of these fine projects. At the heart of this misunderstanding was the *notion of perversity*.

A distant derivative of the concept of moral degene-rescence put forward by Morel, it was carried to the firma-ment of psychiatric nosography by the eminent Dr. Dupré at the congress of French-speaking alienists held in Tunis in 1910. Dupré was a military psychiatrist assigned to the colo-nial disciplinary battalions. Through the observation of the army rejects in his African *biribis,** he was to formulate a "scientific" definition of the pervert. What was a pervert? He was an "unemotive, unaffective, unintegrable" individual. These were the traits which characterized a "mental substra-tum" that expressed itself through "an inclination to exclusive hedonism, with a basic need of 'festive' living, a prevalent taste for easy solutions, an immediate refusal of effort," "an ideological and moral subversism, with rationalized adher-ence to a prescribed conduct; the whole personality is polar-ized into malfeasance; one is confronted with a coherent, perfectly organized system, satisfying the 'subject' in every respect"; "capping it all, a kind of prideful rigidity, with an extreme susceptibility to, and a systematically malevolent in-terpretation of, the intentions of others. One cannot tell them a thing, and they have the right to say anything."

In his thesis on abnormal children (1914), and again in his child neuropsychiatry clinic, Heuyer sought to "apply" this definition of perversity, a definition he could count on to arouse the interest of a psychiatry seeking its place within the disciplinary apparatuses. If the harshest discipline, that of the African battalions, had been unable to break down the resist-ance of certain individuals, there must exist a mental substra-tum that was structurally oriented toward antisocial activities; there must be a perverse constitution, similar to the paranoiac constitutions brought to light by Kraepelin at about the same time. Thus, the role of the preventive psychi-atrist was to be that of detecting the early signs indicating

* Disciplinary companies. [Translator's note]

such a constitution: an irrepressible tendency to petty theft, an incurable disposition to lie, a propensity for playing hooky, a taste for cruel teasing. The first question posed by the child neuropsychiatry clinic about every child referred to it was "Is he a pervert?" Was it an instinctive (and hence congenital) perversity? An acquired perversity (resulting from illness—encephalitis, for example: in the twenties, an encephalitis epidemic supplied Heuyer with a considerable number of guinea pigs); a perversity engendered by bad treatment (conditioning)? An educative treatment was indicated or not, depending on this scale of severity of the sickness. But the thing to note is that psychiatrists buttressed their will to intervene with the hegemonic figure of the pervert, and therefore concentrated on the detection of ineducable individuals, whereas the juvenile judges, the protective societies, and the unpaid agents postulated the educability of all minors as an a priori, even if they were prepared to acknowledge their ultimate failures by resorting to psychiatric labeling. Let us say that psychiatrists and educators took strictly opposite approaches to the educational process, and consequently were incapable of reaching an understanding.

The development of educational methods, the opening up of a range of mechanisms of reception and treatment, and the organization of educative action in the noninstitutional milieu slowly signaled the discrediting of this notion of perversion. In 1950, the review *Rééducation* tried to evaluate the use of this classification in the practice of magistrates, educators, and psychologists. It addressed a detailed questionnaire to the leading representatives of these professions: Should doctors make use of the term "pervert" in their diagnoses? Should the juvenile judge faced with a "pervert" forgo an educative measure and pronounce a penal or social-defense measure instead? Should the educator regard him as an ineducable subject, and confine himself to a systematic mistrust of such an individual? In the replies, one finds a still large coefficient of irreducible supporters of the "perverse" label. But the general tone was set by the educators: "The notion of perversity cannot be employed in practice except with extreme caution. It crushes the child, and it has been shown that one is often mistaken in this matter. It discourages the educator and disturbs his mind. It is hard to imagine that these young educators, fresh from their training, will have the courage to confront an instinctive pervert if he is placed in their hands with the hopeless prognosis that this notion, in its conventional form, implies." And by the psychoanalysts, the educator's new allies. Juliette Favez-Boutonier declared: "As a psychoanalyst, I am inclined not to agree with the notion of constitutional perversity. Every time I have had to do with young children labeled in this way, I have had the impression that I was dealing more with children who were especially disturbed and difficult than with perverts in the strict sense of the term. The subjects who correspond to the standard clinical table of the forms of perversion strike me as being less the representatives of a sort of peculiar and monstrous human species than of the serious forms of character disorders." There was a gentle shift, therefore, from perversion to character. The table is the same, but the etiology changes: relational deficiencies in families, resulting in immaturity and aggressiveness. The hysteric suffered the same fate, and even the mental defective, who was so labeled only with an etiological corrective attached: "defective through environmental insufficiency."

There was a slow dissolution of the unholy trinity on which child psychiatry had been founded: at the center, the little pervert, that gray eminence of evil, on the one hand seducing the suggestible little hysteric and inducing her to run off, and on the other hand pushing the young mental defective into committing antisocial acts by taking advantage of his docility and the primal character of his instincts. They would no longer be designated by their meeting on the steep trails of adventure against the Good, but by their lost wandering in the obscure maze of relational disturbances.

Was this the inauguration of a new golden age of pedagogy, guided this time by the lights of a science of the invisi-

ble and not by the edicts of a knowledge that only wanted to
inscribe bodies with the stigmas of its diagnoses? In this same
issue of *Rééducation,* there appeared two texts which, by
being brought together after the event, will allow us to measure the scope and the limits of the introduction of psychoanalysis into the field of re-education. Two texts which were
marginal in relation to the group as a whole—not surpris-
ingly, since one was written by Fernand Déligny and the other was made up of selections from the little-known work by
Jean Genet entitled *L'Enfant criminel.*

Déligny replied only in order to challenge the question: "I
no longer read the reviews or books which debate these problems. . . . I was acquainted with a doctor, an experienced
psychiatrist, who detected perverts everywhere in the children's ward he had charge of; he saw as many traces of their
perversions as there were broken windowpanes, stolen pas-
tries, and clogged toilets. . . . By contrast, the doctor who
succeeded him was intransigent about several points of doctrine, among which was the following: no perverts. He was
not willing to see a one. What he wanted for himself was a
clean white shirt every morning and no perverts in his ward.
. . . By and large, in this establishment it was as if the pervert
were a psychiatric myth whose skin, or envelope rather, was
made of that especially impermeable and stretchable fabric
which is exuded by every discussion having to do with defini-
tions, and whose internal pressure (hence the increase in size,
the imposing presence) is fed by all the by-products that are
so generously secreted by totalitarian atmospheres."

Jean Genet had just got out of prison on the strength of
Sartre's intervention. He was asked to participate in a radio
broadcast in order to present his ideas concerning criminal
children. He accepted on condition that he be allowed to
question an official psychiatrist on the air. This requirement
refused, he had to make do with publishing the text of his
address in a little brochure, parts of which were later ex-
cerpted by a representative of the Protection de l'enfance,
Henri Joubrel, under the title "Jean Genet, a pervert and

proud of it . . .": "The young criminal demands that his punishment be devoid of leniency. It is with a kind of shame that
a child will admit that he has been acquitted or given a light
sentence. He hopes for severity. In his heart, he dreams that
the form his punishment takes will be a terrible hell. . . . The
criminal child is one who has forced open a door giving access to a forbidden place. He wants this door to open onto the
most beautiful landscape in the world; he demands that the
penal servitude to which he has won the right be ferocious; in
short, that it be worth the trouble he has taken to win it. . . .
Over the past few years, men of good will have been trying to
soften all that somewhat. . . . Such an attempt at corruption
leaves me cold, for . . . what leads to crime is the feeling for
romance, the projection of oneself into the most perilous of
lives. . . . They do not know where they venture, but they
know it is outside that place where *you* live. And I wonder if
you do not also prosecute them out of spite, because they
despise and abandon you. . . ."

These two texts are akin to one another, certainly, by virtue
of the humor and irony they manifest with regard to the self-
righteous men of the field of correction; but everyone will find
in them, to his pleasure or dismay, an indication of a basic
misunderstanding inscribed within the educative intention.
The educator and the delinquent are at cross purposes, in
effect, for the educator wants to give up any reference to
punishment in order to be more agreeable in the eyes of the
delinquent, whereas the latter proves the firmness of his personality through the seriousness of the punishment imposed
on him. In any case, these texts reveal the fear that perma-
nently haunts the judicial apparatus in its will to reform, to
replace coercion with education. For how could one help
fearing that once this apparatus has shed its walls, no longer
opposing its violence to those who defy it, no longer recognizing them, the effect will be to exacerbate *their* violence? How
could one not be afraid that without this constraint, the educative relationship would find no other ground rule than the
mutual and endless seduction between those who only dream

of venturing against the rules of the Good and those who only want what is good for them—the educator becoming less and less an educator in order to approach a being whose existence in his own eyes is asserted in proportion to the show of daring he is able to muster. This is where psychoanalysis enters in as a vehicle for the softening of punishment, for the controlled "freedom" of surveillance. Psychoanalysis is certainly not the only discourse required by this process, but it is without doubt the most effective. It lays bare the emptiness, the lack that is seen as lying behind the excesses of the delinquent, by shifting his performance of the act to the act of speaking. The delinquent becomes interesting when he lets himself be heard, and no longer when he turns a deaf ear to the injunctions of order. Furthermore, the psychoanalyst ensures that the educator is always on the good side of this game of seduction that he will enter into with the delinquent by supervising the latter's investments and identifications. The new landscape of supervised education is here given in its entirety: a gradual dilution of the spatial structures of correction, impelled by an educative desire which endeavors to be free of any hindrance, but which can accomplish this only by replacing the coercion of bodies with control over relations. Moreover, at the outer limits of this process, where the "milieu" becomes so open that nothing is controllable any more, where the educator comes in contact with the delinquent without the benefit of markers or railings, the cordon of police reappears, seizing upon both partners of these dealings without distinguishing between the two. Look at the violence of the quarrels between the police apparatus and the street educators who appeal to the right of professional secrecy in order not to come through with the denunciation that is expected of them.

Psychoanalysis proved to be just as timely in the formidable question of the link between juvenile justice and the enormous administration of Social Aid to Children. In 1973, Dupont-Fauville, of the Chamber of Deputies, published a report entitled *For a Reform of Social Aid to Children*, which was mainly the work of a commission headed by the psycho-

analyst Dr. Soulé. What could be done to stem the alarming
increase in workers of the A.S.E.?* How was one to impose a
technical rationality on the functioning of an apparatus inflated because of the tacit complicity between social assistants
and families who traded on the myth of prevention to the
satisfaction of both parties? There was protection of families
by the A.S.E., which kept them in its domain so as to save
them from judicial marking, and protection of children from
their families through placement with wet nurses or in institutions. With such methods as these, exclaimed Dr. Soulé, little
wonder that Social Aid was becoming so swollen. These social assistants who took themselves for Saint Vincent de Paul
whenever they saw a child of poor parents and for benevolent
ladies of charity whenever they were dealing with a needy
family! This charitable vice was a throwback to former times,
creating an individual pleasure but prolonging, even aggra-
vating, social ills. In it one saw traces of those clientelist customs which the eighteenth and nineteenth centuries had
already fought hard against. (Of course, the psychoanalyst
did not speak in precisely these terms, but I am being faithful
to the spirit of his discourse.) What was to be done, then?
How was this double game of families and social services to
be opposed? First, it was necessary to put an end to the latitude which families had to abandon their infant children
when they were costly to rear, an abandonment that took
wrongful advantage of the availability of the A.S.E., of the
excessive adoptive capacity of the social services. The solution, therefore, was to replace ill-considered placements with
the forms of treatment that were applied in the noninstitutional milieu—that is, within families, instead of allowing the
latter to shed all responsibility. To leave children in their families, but oversee the education they received in the home.
Later, when they were adolescents, placement in centers for
young workers, for example, might become more advisable, a
matter of socializing them quickly and of preventing the fam-

* *Aide sociale à l'enfance.* [Translator's note]

ily from reconstituting itself as an organic and autarchic ag-
gregate. Secondly, in order to combat the ambivalence of
social workers, to extricate them from the network of emotional and contradictory entanglements they became involved
in with the population of social cases, it was necessary to
place their work under psychiatric and psychoanalytic supervision. In this way, capricious choices in placements and the
practice of maintaining families in the sphere of assistance
would disappear. Finally, and consequent to all the foregoing,
the juvenile judge had to be brought back into the social
workers' favor; they needed to be shown that he could have
"much more of a restructuring effect on families than a traumatizing one."

This left one last point of contention, occasioned by the
array of preventive practices: for example, the practice of
apportioning minors in different centers. It was necessary to
take up this problem of orientation through protective societies and their mechanisms of subcontracting which escaped
the judge's supervision. This system of selection had to be
brought under control without offending the protective societies, those indispensable allies of the techniques of prevention, without whom juvenile law would not even have been
conceivable. Constitutionalist psychiatry was useless for this
purpose, since it too sought to slice off a part of the domain of
the juvenile judge, to claim its share, in competition with the
protective associations, leaving the judge his meager portion
of certified delinquents. This tripartition caused conflicts, suspicion, reciprocal encroachments, and institutional aberrations. Given a lack of coordination between neighboring
services, history had sufficiently proved that the one which
was the moving spirit was paradoxically the subject to be
modified, and not the modifying institution. Because of its
psychoanalytic improvement, psychiatry was able to furnish
the judge with the means of joining together in a single bun-
dle, under his juridical control, the disparate categories of
delinquent, assisted, and abnormal children. The genesis of
the concept of maladjustment bears witness to this develop-

ment. Prior to World War II, works on the observation of problem children always employed the label "abnormal" (the last of them was that of Nobécourt and Babonneix in 1939: *Les Enfants et les jeunes gens anormaux*). In 1943, the psychoanalysts Lagache, Le Guillant, the cofounder of area psychiatry [*psychiatrie de secteur*], and of course Georges Heuyer established the classification "irregular children." The word "irregular" was agreeable because it did not sound too medical, though it did preserve the idea of anomalies transposed to a moral plane. This suited the Pétainist context rather well. The essential elements of the classification would remain as follows: (1) those suffering from serious mental and organic illnesses, who came under the authority of the psychiatric hospital; (2) the mentally retarded, who were shared among the psychiatric hospital, the medico-pedagogical institutes, and the medico-professional institutes, depending on the seriousness of the case; (3) those with character disorders, who were distributed among the rehabilitation schools and the protective societies; (4) the scholastically maladjusted, who were assigned to the medico-psycho-pedagogical centers; (5) children suffering from deficiencies in their environment. But in 1956, the term "irregular" was officially supplanted by that of "infantile maladjustment." This was an evolution corresponding to the deployment of psychoanalysis in the tutelary machinery. Why? Because psychoanalysis brought in a grid of analysis that made it possible to overcode, to meld into a single mold, categories of children derived either from the judicial sphere (delinquent children) or from the sphere of assistance (unfortunate and abandoned children). The use of a single codification, a homogeneous etiology, provided the judge with a crucial instrument for apprehending children right and left.

In the observation centers, in the educational orientation consultations that flourished after the war on the basis of this unifying concept of maladjustment, one could observe an important transformation of the two primary modes of knowledge concerning children: the social inquiry and the medicopsychological inquiry. A greater editorial initiative was demanded of the social investigator so that she might account for the "dynamic" of the family, its "developmental possibilities." She was expected, therefore, to stop limiting herself to a determination of the family's budgetary, conjugal, and educative morality. Conversation was no longer that gratification by which the investigator bought a certain quantity of information; it became the most important part of the job: listening, getting people to talk, illuminating the dark areas of conflict where the malaise that had an impact on the child originated. Thus there was an effacement of the juridical categories to which the assessment of family morality had been restricted. Indications such as "false household" (concubinage) or "normal (legitimate) couple" gave place to the "risky" family. In the medicopsychological inquiry, the importance of medical examinations, tests, and descriptions of features diminished in favor of corrective interpretations of these "appearances" through a familial explanation of their manifestations. A junction was established between the two types of knowledge; there emerged a homogeneous grid that set up different levels of communication between parents' behavior, the educative value of a family, the moral characteristics of children, and their pedagogical problems. There were no longer a moral judgment and a juridical appraisal, or rather, these continued to be used, but more as a reminder; they were linked together by an interpretative continuum that blamed nothing in particular and everything in general. A dense grid that wove a considerable number of ties between apparently minor elements, placed them at the entry to a pathogenic circuit, and—at the end of this circuit—deduced the indication of an immaturity or aggressivity that was subject to a particular type of intervention. And poor families knew nothing about this grid, since it went against their customary experience of assistance, repression, and medicine and placed them, without defenses, in the field of a tutelary complex whose internal boundaries melted away and whose external limit became imperceptible.

In this way, the psychiatrist, who had been the judge's rival, now became, with the help of psychoanalysis, his indispensable ally, the relay that was needed in order to control the endless array of preventive practices by means of a homogeneous code. He furnished educative action with a technique of intervention which limited the unpredictability of the voluntary organizations [*le benevolat*] and the hazards of the "desire to educate." He placed at the judge's disposition a flexible selecting mechanism for the apportionment of minors, giving him a choice of measures to apply. He throttled the autonomy of the protective societies and surmounted the abrupt barriers that were raised between the assistancial, medical, and penal domains. This was the completion of a migration that had brought the psychiatrist from the minor and infrequent role of last resort for difficult cases to that of declared instigator of the lowliest judicial decisions. The juvenile judge saw his symbolic role increase in value at the very moment when the mechanisms of effective decision eluded him. He became the visible simulacrum of a jurisdiction that depended at least as much on specialists of the invisible as on him.

C. The Practices

As the last stage of this long voyage through the tutelary complex, we will now examine its actual work, its everyday practices, its ordinary maneuvers. This is the culmination of our study, since it seemed logical to prepare for the description that follows by first directing our gaze to the brightly lit, official stage where decisions are made before proceeding gradually to the semidarkness of the places where these decisions are carried out. First we needed to understand how juridical power and psychiatric knowledge were connected to one another, while trying to avoid facile notions regarding the development of the state apparatuses, expressed in terms of an indefinite excrescence or a greater and greater humanization, notions that permit one to denounce or praise but not to understand. We have located the element, contained in the rise of educative practices, around which the psychiatric and judicial agencies pivoted. We have seen that when correctional activities moved outside the confined space of the penal institution and the psychiatric hospital, psychiatry and judicial authority were repositioned in relation to one another, changing their respective "dimensions" in such a way that the decision-making power slowly changed from a penal jurisdiction to an extrajudicial jurisdiction, the former now serving only as a guarantor and executor. But precisely what necessity was met by the shift that occurred? It is easy to understand how this new strategic arrangement of the judicial and the psychiatric agencies was commanded by the growing incapacity of the courts to control these new technicians, but we still fail to see why these practices became uncontrollable by judicial power alone. The first educators and the first social assistants were sent on their missions by a judicial authority that said to them: "There are a considerable number of children who are poorly cared for and who escape all authority. We cannot and do not want to put them in prison. Go see what you can do in the field. Do what is necessary in order for the parents to fulfill their obligations. They will not be able to challenge you, since we have just had a series of laws for the protection of children voted in, authorizing you to go beyond parental authority and, consequently, constrain the family." We must now try to understand why this explicitly judicial *politics of the family* became in fact the business of the psychiatric agencies.

This seems an appropriate point for a quick review of the results of a lengthy survey that was carried out in the social services of the juvenile courts in the North of France (Lille and Valenciennes) and the Paris region (Bobigny). These two areas were chosen intentionally in order to assess variations that are due to the primacy of juridical or psychiatric authority. An analysis of the way the code is constituted in the two areas showed an uneven promotion of the "psy" infrastructure in the business of the juvenile courts. In the northern region, "psy"-related services and facilities are much less significant (especially in Valenciennes) than in Bobigny, where recourse to the medicopsychological examination is all but systematic. This fact also corresponds to a pronounced unevenness between industrial regimes (old and established industries in the North, textiles and coal mining; and more recent industry, with a mobile work force, in the Paris region) and between the forms of social management (the North is the primordial land of paternalism). We undertook a systematic examination of dossiers pertaining to endangered children (under the Law of 1958, which made it the duty of the juvenile judge to intervene whenever the health, safety, morality, or education of a minor is in jeopardy). The objective was to reconstruct the politics of the family that was brought to bear in each locale by the social services. In order to achieve this, the targets of these services had to be reconstituted; it was necessary to reach the sociocultural singularities that were aimed at through the juridical, medical, and moral specification of cases; we had to reconstruct the effects obtained by a range of measures; in short, it was necessary to decipher everything that had been coded.

Here then are the results—for the northern region first.

In the literature of the dossiers, under a thin psychological layer, a more substantive vocabulary soon emerges, one richer in economico-moral notations, which makes it possible to identify the main poles of social life on which the action of the services is focused. We will describe them by using the vocabulary that is peculiar to the social services: unstructured families, normally constituted but rejecting or overly protective families, and deficient families. Not that the social services actually employ this type of classification; their ethics obliges them to speak only of particular cases. But if we list the characteristics of the families for whom this kind of terminology functions, it is easy to reconstitute their social targets in terms of these three major constellations and to assess the differential tactics the social services bring into operation for each one.

1. *Unstructured families: conversion or destruction*

These are families whose dominant traits (in the eyes of the court services, of course) are professional instability, immorality, and slovenliness. Consider the example of the D. family. The father, thirty years old, is a truck driver. He changes employers often, is often away from home because of his work, and is always being fined or prosecuted for one thing or another (indecent acts committed with young female hitchhikers, for example). The mother, who has no occupation, lives in an old farmhouse with her alcoholic and deaf father and her four children, who are always dirty because there is no running water in the house. They frequently play host to young people passing through, with whom they "dance in the courtyard and engage in unmentionable acts." The oldest daughter is pregnant, and this is the doing of a "frequently idle young man." To complete the picture of the unstructured family, one must imagine it surrounded by a retinue that is at times less amusing. For instance, the father T., who spends his nights shooting at streetlights with a rifle and his days in bed with both his alcoholic wife and her retarded sister, while the children, on reaching the age of twelve, are initiated into plundering and the pleasures of red wine. Or else, V., who persists in frequenting the riverbanks with a fishing rod instead of going to the factory, thus endangering the health, safety, morality, and education of his children; and then, higgledy-piggledy, all those who do not, or no longer, see the advantages of a life of work, those who have no jobs, and those who are in no hurry to find one; women who hang out with North Africans; people who drink because it is something that is done in the North, and people who drink in order to forget that they drink. In sum, that fringe of the working class where misconduct is joined to fatalism, described over and over again by moralists and hygienists, particularly in the last century and especially in this region where it is taking longer than elsewhere to disappear.

Taking charge of a minor always begins with the procedure of *notification;* that is, the juvenile judge is advised by agencies, which may be public or private, that a critical situation exists in a particular family. In the case of this category of family, fully half of these denunciations come from other social services: social assistants of the family-allowance office or area social workers.

The husband's loss of work or his unexcused absences may entail the discontinuance of family allowances. In this event, after a visit to the family, the social assistant sends a report to the juvenile judge. Next come the police and the mayor's office: the first when they are called upon to put an end to drinking bouts or overly noisy domestic scenes; the second in order to subdue families of marginals (scrap merchants, vagabond families who have set up house in vacant lots) who disturb the peace. Last on the list are the school and the neighbors: truancy reports, and anonymous letters in the style of "I take the liberty of writing to tell you that someone should be sent to X's home because some funny things have been going on there of late."

Second step: in order to establish the credibility of this information, the juvenile judge orders an *inquiry* to be conducted by the police and the social services to determine whether an intervention for the protection of children is warranted. The reply is in the affirmative almost every time, and it is supported by a profile of the families whose major constants are the laziness of the man, the moral laxity of the mother, and the dirtiness and malnutrition of the children despite their "apparent good health." In the reports, one finds passages underlined by the redactor or the judge which one can assume to be those on which the decision hangs. The following is a sample of these underlined statements drawn from five dossiers taken at random:

—"Negligent mother who runs from bar to bar, leaving her children in the care of her cohabitant . . . apathetic, indolent, nonchalant father. . . . On one occasion, the minor was found to be in possession of a special type of brochure entitled *The Tariff of Love.* It was reported to me that at one time in her room the girl had assumed a position that left little of her anatomy concealed."

—"Lymphatic, shameless mother, who occasionally gets drunk with her lover. This cohabitant is said to have a tendency to sponge off her. . . . The two daughters (aged seven and fourteen) were once present for the amorous play of the couple, and they related what they had seen to other children."

—"The mother regularly frequents the workers of the construction sites. . . . The father is reputed to be a heavy drinker . . . the older daughters run loose."

—"The mother drinks while her mate works. . . . She sometimes abandons her children and goes off with lovers."

—"The household is poorly maintained. The mother appears to be lacking in good sense. . . . He is an irregular worker. . . . The family allowances have been stopped; given this degree of apathy, it is essential to think in terms of placing their children with the A.S.E."

Third step: *taking charge.* The average time for the wardship of children is quite long: eight years, with a maximum of fourteen years. It is on these years that a whole battery of measures at the juvenile court's command is concentrated, including educative assistance in the noninstitutional milieu, supervision of social benefits, and placements. It is difficult to assign an end to this sort of tutelage with any certainty. The interventions often do not end until the children are grown, get married, or begin working, and they may recommence when the children have children in turn. At any rate, after several years have passed, a rather perceptible alteration in the families' circumstances is noted, which orients them either toward a supervised advancement of their living standard or toward pure and simple destruction. This supervised advancement may be in the form of an opportunity for obtaining housing, with the chance of coming into ownership conditional on the avoidance of bad company and the regularization of the husband's work habits. Changes for the better may be merely fictitious, however; thus the social services can always keep an eye on the family via tutelage. At the other pole, destruction derives from the systematic placement of children once the results of the inquiry are known. But the destruction can also come after years of tutelage. The C. family was first the subject of educative assistance in the noninstitutional milieu because the mother took very poor care of her home; then it was noticed that the father was accumulating unexcused absences from work, which jeopardized the obtaining of family allowances and so constituted a threat to the children. This resulted in a first measure of supervision of social benefits. All at once, the father stopped working altogether, started drinking, and closed the door in the social assistant's face. The allowances were discontinued; the children were taken away, and conflicts between the parents ensued, leading to a separation. In due course a tendency emerges in these families: the banishment of the father. Immature couples, who let their children run about more than is proper, separate. The wife returns to her parents with the children, who have been given back to her, and she begins working. Typically, she pretends to reject the husband, which gives her the right to Social Aid to Children, in addition to the certainty of obtaining allowances. The husband comes back and tries to conceal his presence from the social assistant, but one day the latter makes a point of showing that she has not been fooled, and suddenly everything recommences.

Hence the form of these interventions in unstructured families is characterized by a decisive tussle between the services and the recipients. In order to retrieve their children, the latter set about producing all the exterior signs of morality that are expected of them: detoxification cures, scrubbing the house on days when a visit by the social assistant is rumored, moving into a new apartment (even if they are unable to pay the rent—the important thing is to show a spirit of cooperation), and especially a flood of letters testifying to the most sincere repentance, the grim determination to live as one ought to. But as for the social worker or educator, how are they to be sure, and what is there to rely on? Faced with these professions of faith, which are often nothing more than one day's ruse, they practice the restitution of children in driblets; they make the periods of guardianship last as long as possible. Even if these unstructured families represent only a third of the dossiers, it is they who absorb the largest part of the social services' energy. They are the preferred target of these services, as the high percentage of complaints lodged against them by the social services themselves indicates. Why is this? Doubtless because of the nature of the supposed sex and filth representing for them the ideal terrain for fulfilling their dual vocation, moral and medical. Whence comes that ceaseless interventionism that sometimes promotes and more often destroys, but always replaces autarchy, insouciance, and truculence with dependence.

2. *Normally constituted but rejecting or overly protective families: assignment of culpability and selection of scapegoats*

This bizarre designation corresponds in fact to a "clinicization" of the most widespread living conditions in the working class. In every case where this incrimination functions, the picture is actually the following. A large working-class family lives in a modern but cramped apartment. The mother sends the older children outside so as to be able to attend to the younger ones. She is what is called an "overburdened" mother. The father, when he comes home from work, demands quiet and turns on the television or reads his newspaper instead of devoting himself to educative talks with his children. He is what is called an "inaccessible" father. Consequently, life in the street forms a large part of the children's framework of existence, with all that this implies in the way of "bad company" and exposure to police authority. So, depending on whether the parents prepare for the possibility of the police arresting their children by alerting a social worker, or cover for them, reckoning that if the children hang out in the street it is nothing serious, nor are they to blame, the parents will be classified as either "overly protective" or "rejecting."

The denunciations issue in fairly equal proportions from the family or from the police and the social services. Letters from parents generally try to reconcile a demand for the strengthening of their authority with a discourse that does not have the look of a denunciation: "I have the honor of requesting your intercession on behalf of one of my sons who is seventeen years old and whom I cannot get to obey me. Despite his courage and goodness, he goes out late at night with God knows who. Although I punish him during the week and even Sundays, either by locking him in his room or by taking his clothes away, he somehow manages to get out anyway." Such a request is almost never denied by the juvenile court, but a significant stylistic twist is given to the response. The parents ask the judge to create a beneficial fear in their child, to show that he is on their side, that the child has to obey them. Instead of the desired admonition, however, the juvenile judge, after reviewing the results of the social inquiry, decides in favor of an educative assistance that has another purpose altogether, since it brings the adolescent into the sphere of the tutelary complex, leading to his detachment from family authority and transferral to a social authority, steering him smoothly toward a center for young workers or something similar, all in order to prevent him from contaminating his brothers and sisters and to enable his parents to devote themselves to the younger children.

With "normal" children, the tactic is very different, therefore, from that observed with regard to unstructured families. In the former instance, we saw that the object was to convert or destroy. Now, however, it is a question of guaranteeing the child-rearing function and of bringing a disciplinary function into play rather than of reinforcing a position of authority. It is as if the tutelary apparatus addressed working-class families in the following terms: "Send your children to school, to the C.E.T.,* into apprenticeship, the factory, or the army; watch over the company they keep, the way they use their time, their movements. Vacuity is the danger. If you do not see to these things, we will make them *our* responsibility; it is we who will reinsert your children into the disciplinary mechanisms, the difference being that we add our centers for young workers, our centers for educative action, and our reform schools and prisons to the list of such mechanisms."

3. *Deficient families: social aid*

We shall give this designation to families in which either the father, the mother, or both have died or are the victims of a critical disability. Example, the B. family: the father, sixty-six years old, suffers from an advanced stage of silicosis; the mother has been missing from the family for ten years, having been chased away by her husband. He lives with his three children (nineteen, sixteen, and fourteen years old) in a little house belonging to National Coal Mines, a house that is his to enjoy until his approaching death, after which nothing obliges the company to leave it to the children. This is the category of the crippled, of those mutilated by work or prison. In the North, with the mines and the severity of the Assize Court of Douai, this amounts to a large number of people. At the head of this category come the fathers' disabilities due to work-related illness, whether or not they are recognized as such. These are typically cases of silicosis, asthma, or chronic bronchitis: three out of five at Valenciennes; one out of three

* *Collège d'enseignement technique.* [Translator's note]

at Lille, where National Coal Mines employs fewer people; and in both places, a high percentage of Arabs. The picture is nearly always the same: at the age of fifty or thereabouts, the man's health starts to decline seriously and his activities are curtailed. If he does not die, his incapacity and the paltry pension he receives soon provoke a conflict with the wife, who is often much younger, especially in the case of Arab families (as much as twenty or thirty years separating the two). So, either he has retained enough strength to send her away, or it is he who gets himself thrown out of the house, leaving him no better prospect than a small room in an Arab café-hotel. If the age difference is less, the disability is not a special cause of separation. There is simply an inversion of relationships: the husband remains at home and looks after the children, while the wife does housekeeping on the outside. This small contribution does not prevent the family from living according to the rhythm of the successive evaluations of the husband's percentage of disability, nor from joining the sad procession of "welfare cases." In a decreasing order of importance, the second cause of deficiency is the death of one of the parents at an early age, resulting of course in a dramatic situation, more or less so depending on whether it is the father or the mother. Finally, the last heading: parents who are absent by reason of penal detention or psychiatric confinement. This category is concerned for the most part with penal cases, the consequences of absence for psychiatric reasons being more likely to fall under the independent authority of the Office of Social Action.

In child-protection cases, the origin of the distress notice is distributed equally between the families themselves and the social services. The paltriness of disability pensions, the death of one of the parents, or their separation causes the survivors to appeal to Social Aid to Children, either to obtain money, which is most often the object, or to place a burdensome family member with that agency when there are "too many mouths to feed." As to the notifications brought by the social services, these result from a previous observation of the family by area assistants or the Family Allowance offices.

As regards the measures taken, the general tendency is partial or total placement of the children, with a few instances of A.E.M.O. (*assistance éducative en milieu ouvert*) and of guardianship. A list can be drawn up following an order of increasing chances of placement according to the different possible sets of particulars in this category of families:

1. The mother is alone, with several young children. Exhausted by successive pregnancies, her time taken up by the little ones, it is practically unthinkable for her to engage in a life of debauchery or to take a lover, the latter being always suspected of diverting the allowance money to his own profit. And besides, placing eight or ten children is no small matter. For this sort of woman, the social services put forth a maximum amount of energy in order to get them new housing, or to make the administrative, scholastic, or other procedures easier for them. A little overseeing of benefits is in order, however, when one is dealing with Arab women.

2. When the mother lives with one or two children, the situation is much more difficult. The family allowances are not enough for her to live on; she has to work, and if the child is very young, she must place it with a wet nurse— which leaves her all the latitude she needs to lead an irregular life. If the nurse is not certified by the D.A.S.S., or if the mother draws attention to herself, placement quickly ensues. Things are even worse if the child or children are older: mother-daughter complicities are very much frowned upon, since the relationship does not include the necessary pedagogical distance. They lead each other astray, entertaining the daughter's "fiancés," who are sometimes parole violators, under the family roof. In fact, the mother encourages the daughter to marry. Her dream is for the couple to work and let her lodge with them so that she may attend to the children, which can lead to a series of shady maneuvers that provoke the constant irritation of the social services.

3.   When it is the father who remains, especially if he is disabled, the chances of placement are increased by two-
thirds, owing to poor resources, illness, his advanced age,
and his diminished authority. The older boys tend to leave
this kind of home to seek their fortune elsewhere; the
younger children suffer from "lack of supervision." They
are all placed, although one of the daughters might be
allowed to return if she is "abnormally attached to her
father" and runs back to him so many times that the judge
relents. When none of the children is the talk of the town,
the father's inevitable financial request is taken advantage
of in order to prescribe an A.E.M.O., intended as a preliminary to placement after the impending death of the
father.

4.   Last stage: the father and mother both are practically or
morally out of the picture: the father in prison, the mother
retarded; the father deceased, the mother confined, etc. In
these cases placement is certain, and with little possibility
of the child's return. From the depths of prison, the father
sends one missive after the other to the judge, so that the
woman he says he wants to marry may have the right to
visit his children, whose mother has disappeared. Or else,
in order to complain that the Social Aid nurse-guardian is
not respecting visiting rights. As a rule, the judge lets matters stand, after inquiring about the state of the children.
It is worth noting that this category includes a significant
proportion of mothers who are former pupils of Social
Aid to Children or former pensioners of the Good Shepherd. Marginality is capitalized on at this level, through
contraction of a social horizon that combines the various
types of down-and-out individuals and redoubles surveillance. It provides the social services with constant and
renewable raw material.

In this northern region, the tutelary complex appears se-
curely fastened to the rails of nineteenth-century philanthropy. It has the same strategic aims of destruction of
popular organic aggregates, of those islands of economic autarchy, of cabaret complicities and "free thinking." There is
the same concern with the fabrication of a wholesome work-

ing-class family by fostering mistrust among its members and involving them in a system of mutual surveillance; the preoccupation with establishing a blanket wardship over the population, deriving from the relentless economic administration of individuals whose familial system can no longer enclose them in its structure. The tripartition of the social targets of the juvenile court corresponds rather neatly to this process of fabrication of the working-class family, achieved by uprooting it from the old forms of life (unstructured families), by "disciplinizing" it (normal families), and by restricting its objectives to reproduction and child rearing (deficient families). The climate of paternalistic philanthropy is noticeable at the level of the attitudes of the population *vis-à-vis* the social services. In a region where not so long ago all the housing and even the churches and schools belonged to the employers (National Coal Mines still owns 200,000 dwellings), where the doctors who made the house calls were also paid by the employers (the doctor was called "the spy"), it is rather logical that the inhabitants should become accustomed to a sort of total wardship. Traces of this paternalism are still to be seen in the make-up of the administrative boards of the private or public organizations attached to the juvenile court. It is not rare to find direct descendants of the nineteenth-century employers' association—a great builder of orphanages and technical training schools, those reservoirs of docile manpower—represented on these boards.

The way these social services operate still preserves the two basic principles of this philanthropy: (1) insertion into the economic sphere in the name of morality: this is the struggle against family autarchy, under the guise of a campaign against moral laxity, the creation of the "tireless little worker" in opposition to the unstructured family; (2) the economic administration of individuals in the name of morals: this is the technique of removing individuals, especially children, from a family when the cost of its social maintenance becomes too high. Juridical authority has a decisive part in this forced assimilation of morality to economics. It is the instrument necessary in order to counteract family authority where the latter is neither economic nor within the economic domain. It is also the means of holding out possibilities of obtaining housing, work, and social advancement through the legalization of marriages and compliance with educational requirements. In this sense, the juridical is a pure category of nineteenth-century political economy.

The first feature that stands out in the comparison between the northern region and the Paris region is the lessening, in the latter, of the crude folklore that goes with the regional policing of families I have just described.

When we draw up the list of problems raised with respect to the source of interventions, we discover that scarcely a third of the cases conform to the tripartition that we were able to establish for the northern region. Out of fifty dossiers, only eighteen originated with a notification by neighbors denouncing the state of abandonment in which the children were left during the day. The area social assistants notify the judge of children whose parents are deceased, or request a tutelary measure for families who are in debt and threatened with eviction because the father can no longer work because of illness; they also refer to him children of immigrant families roaming about in the streets. The scholastic social assistants signal instances of absenteeism and suspected malnutrition. It is only in this first batch of cases that we reencounter the aspect of direct moralization and authoritarian management of families that we saw in operation in the North, and here it is undoubtedly less successful. The resistance of families to this type of authority is very clear-cut. On his release from prison, the father will go and reclaim his daughter from the Social Aid nurse and then place her with another one whom he knows. Another father will encourage his children to run away from the establishments in which they have been placed, in order to rejoin him in a locale on the border between two parishes where he can play the social services of one against those of the other. Algerian families appeal to the consul of their country in order to obtain formal protection against placements; and so on.

The great majority of dossiers are concerned solely with problems of family dislocation: parents placing their children with the A.S.E. following a separation; minors fleeing the family milieu, arrested by the police who address themselves, on their own initiative, to the juvenile judge so as to obtain a placement in a center, or authorization for the children to reside with friends; parents requesting placement of their children because they can no longer put up with them. Thus all the possible forms of weakening of family life are associated with an unabashed utilization of the social services. Going more into detail, the picture is the following:

1. First, ten cases of placement by one of the parents following a separation. More often than not, it is the father who takes his children to the A.S.E. on parting, or to some center that wastes no time in unloading them onto the A.S.E. There are also couples whose separations alternate with reunions and who place their children periodically with the social services, or again and more rarely, cases similar to that of the woman, more or less classified mentally ill, living for years in a hotel with her mate, who dumps her children at the A.S.E. as they are born (money is not the problem, seeing that the lover earns 3,000 francs per month as the chief of a security crew). To which should be added the couples who place their children under the temporary hospitality of the A.S.E. so as to be able to go away on vacation.

   By and large, parents who undertake a placement after separation hope it will be for only a short period of time. But things get complicated owing to the policies of the A.S.E. To understand the attitude of this agency, one must bear in mind that it has to administer three kinds of lists: (1) that of parents who abandon their children temporarily—there is a large number of such cases—or, in fewer cases, for a lasting period of time; (2) that of certified nurses paid by the A.S.E. to care for children in need of "temporary homes"; (3) the longest list, that of fully deserving families seeking to adopt a child. One can readily guess that the temptation of the A.S.E. is to have as many children as possible transferred from the first list to the third by making effective use of its position of power over the second. For example, a child is considered to be abandoned by his parents when they have not seen him or written to him for the space of one year. An abandonment to which the A.S.E. can contribute by sending the child for placement in a distant locale, or by suggesting to the juvenile judge a limitation that discourages visiting rights. In addition, before being obliged to return the child, the A.S.E. has the option of requesting a social inquiry concerning the father or mother, to be carried out by the social services of the juvenile court.

2. Next, we find ten cases of children who run away from their parents' home and are arrested, or address themselves directly to the juvenile judge in order to obtain a modification of their situation: to be placed in the home of an uncle or an older sister, or in some establishment of the social services. Six of the minors are asking for the judge's help on their own initiative: three boys who have told the judge that they can no longer bear their father's or mother's excesses of authority; all are placed but one, whose rebellion is found by the judge to be too "intellectual"; three girls who have more specific grievances: the first tells of being raped by her mother's lover, the second accuses her father of giving her intramuscular injections and then masturbating in front of her, and the third states that her mother's mate has been pursuing her alternately with physical blows and kindnesses ever since he found her diary containing a scrupulous account of her sexual emotions. The other four minors arrested by the police at the end of their flight say they left home because of a disagreement with the father or stepfather.

3. In the last eight cases, it is the parents who notify the police or the judge of their children's running away or, in fewer instances, their bad conduct at school. For example, the father who requests that his son be placed in an

I.P.E.S.* because he got expelled from the C.E.S. for insubordination. Or the older sister who is disturbed about her sister's wandering in and out of night clubs. Moreover, when one of the children (generally the oldest) of a family has been placed, the others want to follow suit, and the best means is to run away.

Whether it is a matter of families' greater resistance to the decisions that are imposed, or the large-scale misuse these families make of the services of assistance and repression, everything points to the failure of the old juridical, economic, and moral formula of intervention in working-class families. That system functioned so long as access to a profession and the obtaining of housing and social benefits were tied to a strict family life. Normalization could rest on juridical authority to the extent that the latter made it possible to distinguish a settled population from a marginal one. But the juridical apparatus no longer exercises such a secure hold on families moved by the centrifugal and destructive forces (the very high rates of depression and suicide) that are created by the new conditions of work and habitation, and by the requirement of mobility (the often considerable distance between the workplace and the dwelling). No longer being linked to specific living conditions, it no longer possesses the same force of imposition. Hence the rise in resistance. Determined as they are to absorb all the products of this dislocation, the social services have had to de-dramatize their utilization. Hence the fraudulent schemes of which they are the object.

That this field was ripe for psychologism, with its aptitude for relaying juridical authority in the coordination of normalizing activities, is easy to understand. In point of fact, it allows the system (1) to dissolve the resistance of families to the placements that are imposed, on behalf of the necessary socialization of adolescents; (2) to interdict the lines of escape that are constituted by the irresponsibility of parents with

* I.P.E.S.: *institut de préparation aux enseignements du second degré;* C.E.S.: *collège d'enseignement secondaire.* [Translator's note]

regard to infant children, on behalf of the necessity of a familial education; (3) to perfect a new system in the utilization of the family for normalization practices. As the old juridical diversion between legitimate families and illegitimate families is no longer good for much, it is being replaced by the double register of contract and tutelage. All families who issue demands for placements, financial grants, and so forth will be likely candidates for tutelage. Under this system, the family ceases to exist as an autonomous agency. The tutelary administration of families consists in reducing their horizon to supervised reproduction and in the automatic selecting-out of "socializable" minors. To this end, the psychiatrist-psychoanalyst oversees the performance of social work; he does not intervene directly, since the demand of families is monopolized by material concerns, and also because the imposition of guardianship implies a measure of direct coercion. But at the same time, it is he who designates the threshold from which the family can start to function as a contracting party, the moment, that is, when it is capable of both a financial autonomy and a purely psychological demand. Through the use of intermediary social workers, and thus without getting his hands dirty, the psychoanalyst marks out the threshold from which his reign becomes possible.

5.

The Regulation of Images

It was already no small matter to get a man to stretch out full length on a couch and recount his life story, his childhood, his dreams, and to keep him there through the promise of a distant cure for his anxieties, his phobias, his obsessions. Nor is it easy to explain that singular event. But how does one account for the enormous diffusion of psychoanalysis, for the historical good fortune of that method which has invested all areas of social life? Why did the analytic technique break out of the limited framework of its exercise; why did this ritual explode into a multitude of fragments, clinging to the contours of nearly every institution? A first piece of it can be found just outside the doors of the school, in a building that resembles the latter, but with classrooms that have been subdivided into little cubicles for listening to our first mental aberrations. It is what is known as a medico-psycho-pedagogical center (C.M.P.P.). Other fragments are found in a discrete room of the divorce courts, in the services for the protection of mothers and children, in the birth-planning centers, and in the sex-education organizations. Perhaps the best known of these are marriage counselors, although they may have other names. You may find them by tuning in to their radio programs, where they open their arms to suffering and dissect personal problems at fixed hours for the edification of all listeners.

You find them because you look for them, but they do not come looking for you; they do not come to your home as a social worker or educator would do. There is no risk of confusing them with social workers, for the distinction is very dear to them, and they explain why. In the first place, they do not want any other mandate than the subject's demand. For them, there is no question of notifying authorities, of denunciation, or of direct intrusion into people's lives; no question of inquiries, of investigation of people's behavior, of surveillance and correction. They work only on the basis of what is furnished by their clients, of their client's account of things without any verification process. They reject beforehand any possibility of intervention, even when it is requested by the subject himself. In the second place, they operate in scattered fashion. No coordinating body centralizes their information or harmonizes their activities. To hear them tell it, competition reigns between counseling centers, which jealously guard their autonomy, entering into private contracts with their clients and guaranteeing professional secrecy. There is even a strong dose of hostility between the different groupings, in accordance with the more or less technical or political emphasis they give their action and the splits within each of these registers, and according to the degree of radicality they exhibit. In the third place, they never resort to any sort of blackmail based on constraint or the obtaining of "solid" services. On the contrary, they hold out the possibility of achieving, through their help, a freedom from constraints, from the heaviness of customs, from the arbitrariness of rules; promises of a removal of sexual inhibitions; the hope of an existential autonomy. Placing themselves between the rigor of institutions and the enclosure of families, they will help you rediscover the true path your life should follow, for a few bills and a dash of those images that prowl about in our psyches. But how did they acquire this position? What makes them just as able to supply the needs of institutions as those of families and individuals? Why them, and why now? What gives them such a privilege in this society and others like it?

A. The Priest and the Doctor

Sexuality, the couple, pedagogy, and social adaptation are brought together in a single mold by the recent appearance of the constellation of counselors and technicians of human relations. But who attended to this kind of problem in the past? The priest and the doctor, the priest *or* the doctor—in any case, they occupied two clearly separate registers.

The priest managed sexuality from the angle of family morality. An ancient complicity, consisting of mutual benefits, operated between the system of matrimonial exchanges—the key to the old familial order—and the religious apparatus. The family received the guarantee of its unions through the distribution of blessings by the Church. For its part, the clergy received money, for the expenses of celebration and for the exemptions it granted for the contraction of a marriage when the partners had a certain degree of kinship; under the *ancien régime,* this favor was a necessity, for village organization implied a high rate of consanguinity. The convent served the family by preserving those of its offspring whom it destined for marriage and by relieving it of those who were a burden to it. It was just as useful to the Church in recruiting a population that the Church could employ for its own missionary purposes. The mechanism of confession furnished the family with the means to deal with the inevitable variance between the strategic nature of alliances and sexual attractions. In return, it obtained for the Church a direct hold on individuals, the possibility of a direction of consciences. The Church increased its benefits in money, power, and expansion precisely insofar as it reinforced the family's hegemony over its members: it constituted a veritable Mafia grafted onto the system of alliance.

For a long time, medicine maintained a prudent distance from this social regime of sexual exchanges. In the eighteenth century, it began to take an interest in sexuality, from the viewpoint of a specifically corporal as opposed to a spiritual flux. It attached a great importance in the explanation of illnesses to all frauds in the performance of the reproductive functions. The withholding of the mother's milk, the refusal to breast-feed—a tendency commonly found in women who were drawn into the artificial concerns of society life—was designated as the cause of a litany of ills. The dissipation of sperm through onanism could be equally calamitous for the man. We have seen how this type of discourse provided an increasingly important place for doctors during the eighteenth and nineteenth centuries in the activity of family counseling. The family doctor intervened in the domestic organization of the home; through his suggestions concerning hygiene, through his educative advice, he substantially altered its internal arrangement. But he did not dare meddle with the system of alliances, that sacred preserve of the family and the Church. This can be ascertained from the behavior of the medical profession in regard to the question of venereal disease, a symbol of moral depravity and the object of a fear that bolstered the power of the family and the Church. In 1777, a certain Guilbert de Préval, who had discovered an "antivenereal specific," was expelled from the faculty of the Paris School of Medicine by solemn decree.[1] A century later, the hygienist Tardieu was to heap sarcasms on one of his colleagues who had wanted to develop an antivenereal vaccine. This, he declared, would mean that the door would be opened to all sorts of abuses, that medicine would be used against morality, that passions would be unleashed and would begin to proliferate at the expense of the interests of families.[2]

This restriction of medical intervention in sexuality solely to private hygiene slowly came undone during the nineteenth century. An examination of the popular medical books intended for the use of families reveals an increase in the size and importance of articles devoted to sexual behavior. At the beginning of the nineteenth century, the medical encyclope-

1. Cf. F.-F. Potton, *De la prostitution et de la syphylis dans les grandes villes* (1842).
2. Regarding this question of venereal diseases in general, see the works of Louis Fiaux, *La Police des moeurs,* 3 vols. (1907), and *Les Maisons de tolérance* (1892); and Ambroise Tardieu, *Dictionnaire d'hygiène publique,* 3 vols.

dias supplemented the standard diatribes concerning onanism and the refusal to breast-feed with rather vague remarks on the greater longevity of married individuals, the doubtful advisability of marriage between persons of widely different ages, and the best compatibility of temperaments. In the middle of the century, the dictionaries of hygiene inserted a few positive considerations regarding nonartificial means of contraception. Starting in 1857, that is, after the publication of Morel's *Traité des dégénérescences,* they grew rich in imperious advice regarding indications and contraindications for matrimony.[3] Eugenism was not far in the future. The end of the century saw the proliferation of a new genre, the medical library, with titles like *Bibliothèque médicale variée, Petite bibliothèque médicale,* and so on. In the catalogues of small low-priced books, sexual questions, often dealt with by highly acclaimed physicians, occupied a prominent place. The mandarins of the end of the nineteenth and the beginning of the twentieth century used their pages to wage a campaign of hygienization of sexuality, based on a general mechanism of prevention of the social diseases (venereal disease, alcoholism, tuberculosis).[4] For the doctors, it was a matter of treating sexuality as the business of the state, thus transcending the arbitrariness of families, morality, and the Church. After setting out to rule over bodies, medicine decided the objective could better be reached by legislating on marriages as well.

What was at issue in this campaign? What was judged by the hygienists to be dysfunctional in the system of alliances? In the main, what they called the two-faced morality of families, the way they had of professing a highly moral behavior and of practicing another composed of egoism, ambition, and a secretly unbridled sexuality. Why did families have this attitude? Because they organized their existence so as to maintain a tight grip on the contraction of alliances. Hence the

3. See Alex Mayer, *Des rapports conjugaux considérés sous le triple point de vue de la population, de la société et de la morale publique* (1857).
4. The list of catalogues would be too long to draw up. The *Librairie du gymnase* will do as an indication of the rest.

separate education of girls and boys, the protection of the former and tolerance, indeed encouragement, of premarital experience for the latter. Hence too the high social cost of this practice: a substantial percentage of illegitimate births doomed to a high sickness ratio, the maintenance of a significant number of prostitutes who spread venereal disease, and the contraction of marriages that were contraindicated medically but carried through in the interests of the families concerned. An expense, an entire social pathology that appeared to be coextensive with the freedom of families to act as they saw fit. The notorious double morality, the hypocrisy of adults which was so roundly denounced, were not due to an undefined prudishness or a repression born of guilt. If parents taught their girls to preserve themselves while encouraging the amorous exploits of their boys, this was because their interests were at stake in the game of matrimonial alliances where the contractual ability of a family, and consequently its power, was the greater as its daughters were better preserved and as those of other families were less so. The system of alliances brought about and ratified the results of a permanent civil war, a series of mini-battles that were called debauchery, seduction, misappropriation . . .

The beginning of the twentieth century presented itself as the moment of ultimate competition between two ways of managing sexuality: the priest's way, on which the power of the family still rested, and the doctor's way, which was promoted in the name of public hygiene and the best interests of society. However, the impact of this *technological moment of reckoning* is not reducible to a two-dimensional clash between an old figure and a new one, nor can it be adequately described as a war between the secular sphere and the denominational sphere. It *crystallized a set of issues*—in the politico-military domain, the institutional domain, the medical and social domain—which, because they overlapped one another (some more clearly than others), caused a *general confrontation between two great strategies* to emerge. One was nationalist and familialist, linking the technical option of populationism to the political themes of Vichy paternalism. The other was socialist and individualist, finding in neo-Malthusianism the means to create a collectivist organization.

From the 1840s to the 1880s, Malthusianism had underlain the behavior of the philanthropic bourgeoisie. In the eyes of the philanthropists, the excessive fecundity of the lower classes constituted the chief cause of their misery. Moreover, the lack of foresight of the laboring masses placed a strain on public finances in the form of the rising cost of welfare procedures. It created a political danger through the growth—in the heart of the nation—of the less "civilized" social classes. Philanthropy completely reversed its position as the result of two events. First, the crushing of the Commune liquidated the problem of the internal threat. Second, colonial imperialism went into high gear. It became the sector on which profits depended, the locus in which they were redistributed as a function of internal competition. The bourgeoisie had nothing further to fear internally, and it needed men for its external schemes. Hence the replacement of the old Malthusian moralization of the lower classes by a new discourse that now inveighed against the growing sterility of families, the unpardonable lack of concern of those who refused to procreate, thus placing the nation under the menace of its rivals. In 1902, the statistician Bertillon and the philanthropist Émile Cheysson (a graduate of the École Polytechnique and a promoter of social housing and workers' garden plots) established a "National Alliance" against depopulation.[5] They called on all those with an interest in reinforcing the military and industrial might of the nation, its numerical capacity for enterprise and intimidation, to come together as a group.

A fine example of the permutability of political themes: those who did not want to be the objects and eventual victims of this politics seized on the old Malthusian discourse, updated it with medical knowledge in the areas of contraception and prophylaxis, and then set it against the nationalist dis-

5. "Alliance nationale pour l'accroissment de la population française," with a quarterly bulletin carrying that title.

courses. A decisive connection was formed between rebellion against employers and generals (the "wombs strike") and medical progressism. The militants of the group Ligue pour la régénération humaine (founded by Paul Robin), then of its successor, Génération consciente (founded by Eugène Humbert, who took over from Paul Robin), were leftists of the Belle Époque.[6] Doctors like Klotz-Forest, Jean Marestan, and the woman doctor Pelleresse Pelletier, together with feminists like Nelly Roussel and Jeanne Dubois and anarchist militants like Sébastien Faure, traveled across working-class France in order to broadcast their subversive ideas. They took advantage of every hotbed of struggle, every strike that broke out, in order to establish a link between worker revolt and unsubmissiveness to biological fatality, leaving behind clandestine posts for distributing contraceptive devices in every place they visited. It seems they created havoc in the areas containing the great paternalistic complexes. The populationist statisticians produced rueful comparisons regarding the reproduction rate before and after the great strikes of the beginning of the century.[7] These groups were to have a resonance in our own day: they had no successors before the "Maoists" installed themselves in the factories and the Drs. Carpentier began to distribute their leaflets at the doors of the *lycées*. In 1906, Paul Robin urged prostitutes to unionize in order to fight against the vice police, and he dreamed of a cohabitation agency that prefigured the classified columns of *Actuel* and *Libération*. They were leftists in the sense that they came up against both the judicial repression of the self-righteous bourgeoisie and the political and union armature of the institutional left. Obviously they presented a threat to the privileges of the former, but they also threatened the bases of combat of the latter. "We do not want a proletariat that is

6. The review *Régénération* was published from 1900 to 1908, and *Génération consciente* carried on the struggle until 1914.

7. See Paul Bureau, *L'Indiscipline des moeurs* (1920); Pierre-Paul Leroy-Beaulieu, *La Question de la population* (1913); Fernand Boverat, *Patriotisme et paternité* (1913).

happier, workers' families that are better cared for, whose children are protected from dangerous promiscuities, women of the people who are no longer exposed to the danger of repeated abortions; we want the abolition of the proletariat as such" (Dr. Vargas, of the Guesdist tendency).[8] In Germany, the neo-Malthusians fared better with syndicalism and the left. The revisionism of a Kautsky and the liberal positions on women of an August Bebel allowed neo-Malthusian themes a place within state socialism. The only allies they were able to find in France were anarchists. In the Belle Époque, one could only be an anarchist or a patriot.

At the center of the debate between neo-Malthusians and populationists there emerged the question of law. The bourgeoisie insisted on strong juridical structures that guaranteed its privileges, property, inheritance, and the labor agreement. The political and union left contested this law, but was reluctant to see it amended by medico-social legislation that would blur the clear dividing line it traced between oppressors and oppressed. It was around the juridical status of the family that the issues carrying the greatest passion were to take form.

The populationists went to war against a course of events that tended to reduce the importance of the family. Divorce legislation had already been passed (1884), and women had entered the labor market. If birth control were established as well, the juridical character of the family would become a useless formality. Why this fear? Their argument has the virtue of simplicity. The stronger the family structure, the greater the chances that the family would be prolific. Restoring the authority of the man over the woman would make it possible for him to confine her to the home, to "liberate" her from all but reproductive and domestic activities. The ensuing loss of profit would be offset by an increase in revenues due to the offspring, the family allowance that would have to be advanced, and the wages of the children once past the age of twelve. Thus the family would be given the character of a

8. Quoted by R.-H. Guerrand, *La Libre Maternité* (Paris: Casterman, 1971), p. 58.

small business interested in multiplying its members. This was a rather cynical reversal of the philanthropists' program. To those who reminded them of how much they had once deplored the impoverishment of large families due to the enormity of their burdens, they replied that in a working-class family, having a lot of children might be a sacrifice at first but would turn into an enrichment when they were of working age.

All those with social privileges to defend were also interested in the maintenance of juridical power because it was through the continuity of filiations and the interplay of alliances that vested interests could be preserved or expanded, and the organic family was the best support for the vertical relations of dependence and prestige. This amounted to a large number of people. A network of family-oriented organizations was woven around the National Alliance: the leagues of fathers of families, the league of mothers of large families, the Association of Parents of Elementary and Secondary School Students, the Parents' School, the directors of family-allowance bureaus, the union of social assistants, the scout organizations, the leagues for moral hygiene, the groups for sanitizing newspaper kiosks and the areas surrounding *lycées,* and so on.

An enormous assembly that was to constitute a lasting pressure group, fighting against everything that might weaken the family: divorce, contraceptive practices, abortion. We have it to thank for the notorious Law of 1920 prohibiting any propaganda relating to contraception, and for the no less famous family code, which sought in every way possible to strengthen the status of the family. First of all, by means of the family vote—an old idea, since it had already been put forward by Lamartine as early as 1848. How was one to optimize the civic importance of the family by assigning it an electoral capacity that took the number of children into account? The procedure was difficult to establish and full of hazards. Must this power be granted solely to fathers? But this would be to slight mothers, whose reproductive instinct one wanted to flatter. On the other hand, giving this power to mothers as well would be to introduce a seed of division into an entity whose organicity one wanted, on the contrary, to reinforce. Moreover, didn't this entity contain a political danger? Weren't the lower classes, the dangerous classes, the most prolific? By giving them an increased right to vote, the privileged classes would be distributing the rods with which they would have themselves beaten. It was true—some said— that these classes were the most prolific, but they were also the ones with the greatest numbers living outside the legitimate bonds of marriage and hence would not be able to avail themselves of the vote. So what good was a policy like this, which aimed to strengthen the juridical importance of the family, but could do so only by damaging the over-all strategy? Troubled by these difficulties, the family-vote plan was gradually to be abandoned.[9] On the other hand, the development of the family-allowance fund and the proliferation of the social-work antennae were given a major and successful push forward by these regroupings.

The initiatives of the neo-Malthusian movement took two forms opposite this familialist movement. First, as we have already noted, the militants grouped around Paul Robin and Eugène Humbert set their little war machines into position against the family, celebrating cohabitation, distributing contraceptive devices, and propagandizing for the "wombs strike." Secondly, gathered in the vicinity of this hard core was a constellation of famous doctors such as Auguste Forel (a professor of psychiatry from Zurich), Sicard de Plauzoles, Tarbouriech, and the illustrious Pinard; writers like Octave Mirbeau; political men like Alfred Naquet (the father of divorce) and Léon Blum. These were men who accepted the neo-Malthusian label with some hesitation, especially because of its association with anarchism in France. Being notable technicians, they were particularly concerned to incorporate hygiene, and consequently birth control, into the functioning

9. The ups and downs of this business of the family vote were amply reported in the *Bulletin de l'Alliance nationale.*

of institutions. They made their views known through books and reviews for the most part, given the unwillingness of the political classes to allow hygienist themes to be introduced, for the two reasons we have already seen. There was a belated attempt at a *rapprochement* between them and the political left in 1933, with the creation of the review *Le Problème sexuel,* whose editorial board was composed of Bertie Albrecht (a Communist), Victor Basch, Paul Langevin, Jean Dalsace, and Sicard de Plauzoles. The Communist Party and the Socialist Party published in the review separate programs for reforming the Law of 1920, both of which advocated sex information, birth control, and therapeutic abortion. But as early as 1934 the Communist Party reversed itself as a part of its plan for a people's coalition with the Catholics, and the review ceased publication after six issues. In order to defend their positions, the innovating doctors fell back on the Ligue des droits de l'homme, chaired by Sicard de Plauzoles, and the Société de la prophylaxie sanitaire et morale, under the leadership of the same Sicard de Plauzoles, two organizations that were to fight persistently against the Law of 1920, but without significant political support.

Everything was confined, therefore, to publications. At the beginning there were books: Auguste Forel's *La Question sexuelle* (1906), Sicard de Plauzoles's *La Fonction sexuelle* (1908), and Léon Blum's *Du mariage* (1907), which was to have a long series of reissues during the period between the wars. Then a series of little brochures and short-lived reviews, the last of which was *Le Problème sexuel,* not counting the *Revue de prophylaxie sanitaire et morale,* which lasted into the 1950s. The discourse they contained went something like this: Since the family is being destroyed by the economic necessities of the social order, the community must replace the father in order to ensure the survival of the mother and the children. The mother will thus take the father's place as the head of the family, since she is its fixed center. The children will be under her guidance, a tutelage that will be centralized by public authority. They will all bear their mother's name, so that chil-

dren born of the same mother but of different fathers will
have the same name. There will no longer exist any difference
between legitimate and bastard children. The man's influence
over the woman will depend on the love and esteem he in-
spires in her; he will have no other authority than that deriving from his moral value; the only place he will have in the
home will be the one he has earned. . . . In short, a medical
administration of sexuality would free women and children
from patriarchal tutelage and would break up the interplay of
alliances and filiations on behalf of a greater public control
over reproduction and a pre-eminence of the mother. A state-
directed feminism, in other words.

To understand the degree to which the question of law was
vexatious to the hygienists and eugenists, it should be helpful
to cite the example of Tarbouriech, a doctor and the author
of a scientific utopia, *La Cité future* (1902). He specialized in
work accidents and was instrumental in the passage of the
modern legislation dealing with this subject. In this he was
motivated by one special concern: reducing the number of
appeals to the courts in this kind of case, so as to facilitate
settlements and thereby eliminate the uncertainty that was
experienced by the company and the worker alike. He explained to the company that the new legislation would oblige
it to pay compensation in every case but would also save it
from any surprises, the amount of this compensation being
limited by a prior agreement between it and the worker. To
the latter, he conceded that he would not always be fully
compensated for the injury that was done, but that he could
be sure of always receiving some indemnity in exchange. This
was a way to avert risk, surprise, conflict, and the always
debatable arbitration of the judge. Then why not extend this
kind of solution, this administrative form of dealing with
problems, to the whole social sphere, since these problems
were cropping up at the end of the century in other areas as
well—such as public assistance? *La Cité future* was a portrait
of the family-state that would be brought into being under the
auspices of medical science. Jurisdiction was to be entirely

administrative, modeled after the civil courts and divided into three authorities: accountable justice, which managed the public fortune, determining investments and wages; civil and disciplinary justice, which dealt with violations of the public order; and medical justice, which handled offenses implying a deficient mental state in their perpetrators and decided who was permitted to propagate life and who was not. To prevent the evil consequences of the division between civil and criminal law, "which (criminal law) fails to protect children adequately and allows them to satisfy their lust even though they are not yet able to contemplate marriage (civil law is too slow in authorizing marriage), this medical jurisdiction will require all children having reached the biological age of reproduction (fifteen to seventeen years old) to appear before the court and undergo an individual examination. The doctor may then decide to issue a 'voucher for social service,' which will give them permission to effect temporary or permanent sexual unions, or he may defer the individual to the following year, or order his sterilization." Hence, by eliminating the variations between civil law and criminal law, all family power would be obliterated. The father and mother would have no right of any kind with regard to their offspring, only obligations. The legislation concerning loss of parental authority that was contained in the Law of 1889 had to be done away with, since it still presupposed the idea of a familial power. It was the state which would declare a man or woman fit to collaborate in the mission of rearing a future citizen, and if they did not fulfill their mission in a suitable manner, the state could replace them at any time with a child rearer or educator who offered more guarantees. What was wanted, therefore, was to extend the tutelage system to all of society, the allocating of educative assistance and medical supervision to all mothers, so that they might be "paid as nurses of their own children, rearing them not for themselves but for the state."

The neo-Malthusian discourse was more on the offensive in this regard, by its elaboration of a theory of prevention of degenerescences, of physical and moral anomalies, that was both sexual and social. What was behind the proliferation of those innumerable disturbed individuals with their mental deficiencies, their character disorders and behavior probelms, of all those people who were locked away in asylums and prisons but also of the countless numbers who were at large, spreading their mischief and imposing a burden on the functioning of society? There were two main causes: alcoholism and syphilis. Alcoholism was the logical result of the maintenance of social misery by the irrationality of production. By socializing the latter, one would be able to ensure everyone a healthy job and decent resources, putting an end to the moral despair that created alcoholics and lineages of damaged individuals. Syphilis was linked to an organization of family life governed by a dual morality that supported prostitution, and by the predominance of family self-interests over the concern for healthy procreation in the forming of marriage ties. It was also the whole system of family assistance that was under challenge, denounced by Sicard de Plauzoles in no uncertain terms as early as 1908: "We cannot help but observe that if the goal is to hinder the reproduction of undesirables, to prevent or if possible to stop degenerescence, to prevent the multiplication of misfits and encourage the reproduction of capable persons, we are doing just the opposite through the organization of our assistance and our protection of the family and children, for the greater part of our effort is spent protecting, preserving, and cultivating degenerates and misfits."[10]

Medical discourse thus linked up with the utopias of the first half of the twentieth century while furnishing them with a powerful technological support. In 1903, Paul Robin launched a violent polemic against the health and assistance administration. His slogan: "Empty the asylums and fill the phalansteries." The familialists countered by accusing the doctors of being too ready to pull children out of their natural

10. *La Fonction sexuelle* (1908).

surroundings, to hospitalize them on the slightest pretext, a procedure that was socially costly and morally destructive. Even the traditional medical establishment rebelled. Pointing the finger at Toulouse, an eminent "social" psychiatrist and a leading advocate of sectorization in the interwar years, Dr. Gouriau emphasized the danger of medicine's becoming a totalitarian omnipresence: "He dreams of a federation of psychiatric republics where ordinary citizens would be examined, assembly-line fashion, from the beginning of their main activities, by an army of prophylactors, orientators great and small, sexologists of every stripe, specialists in suicide, head colds, automobile driving, and statistics; in sum, by all the secondary products of 'noology,' those born or soon to be born of its creative inspiration."[11]

It would seem that all of recent history has been implicated in the advances and retreats of these two strategies, in the clash between the defenders of progress, of the liberalization of sex, and the traditionalists, the men of the Church, the barracks, and the courts. A first phase marked by brutal repression, persecution of the forerunners; then a slow evolution of mores which loosened the strangle hold of customs; finally, the obsolescence of repressive laws becoming obvious, they were abolished after a last fight, for honor's sake, by the upholders of the past. The work of time served to tone down the candors, excesses, and utopian qualities of the new ideas. It made it possible to reduce oppositions, to take the edge off fears of the will to destruction which many people impute to what is out of the ordinary. Progress cannot be resisted for long, nor can it be brutally imposed on people. It is in terms of this languid evolutionism, through this platitudinous manicheism, that we all tend somewhat to decipher this chapter of

11. Dr. Gouriau's reply to an "inquiry concerning the open services," an investigation Toulouse was commissioned to conduct by the minister of public health, *Aliéniste français*, November 1932, p. 563, quoted by Robert Castel in *L'Ordre psychiatrique*.

our present, so vital is our notion of power as repression, our representation of freedom as an affirmation of sexuality. One has only to consider texts rather than hagiographies, however, in order to discard this representation. The opposition between populationists and neo-Malthusians does not boil down quite so simply to a stereotypic antagonism between a fierce traditionalism and a naïve and generous utopianism, any more than it can be reduced to a preoccupation with repression versus a hope of liberation. The boundary line between the two was of another order. The populationist current comprised a significant number of doctors who favored normative intervention in family life in order to ensure, not just an increased productive yield, but a better standard of reproductive quality. The best example of this was Dr. Cazalis,[12] the author of a famous phrase that was to figure for a long time in manuals of special hygiene for use in the teacher's colleges: "A day will come when two families, before deciding on a marriage, will meet with their two physicians in the same way as they now meet with their notaries." We are indebted to him, as a matter of fact, for the law requiring the prenuptial medical visit. Moreover, everyone knows how this sort of legislation was able to be broadened to include a prohibition of marriages with various categories of individuals declared unsuitable for social or racial reasons (recidivist delinquents in the United States, Jews in Germany under the Law of 1934). Cazalis, with his violent anti-Semitism, his literary quest for a new mystique for the West (he wrote Parnassian-inspired poems under the pseudonym Jean Lahor), was one who shared this way of thinking. Céline also comes to mind, as another doctor-writer whose thought comprised the same ingredients: the medical mission, anti-Semitism, the obsession with a decline of the West through the proliferation of "inferior" peoples.

As regards the neo-Malthusians, medicalization was not always synonymous with liberalization in their case either,

12. Henry Cazalis, *La Science et le mariage* (1900).

judging from the notion of sexual education they tried to introduce between the wars, from their base in the Société de prophylaxie sanitaire et morale. Education, or rather "the civilizing of the sexual instinct, to go back to Pinard's expression, should consist in a sort of vaccine capable of creating a certain psychical automatism, of getting the brain into the habit of associating erotic ideas with the representation of their possible consequences."[13] Said consequences being, of course, the various forms of venereal disease, with charts and edifying illustrations in support. By instituting such an education before the awakening of the sexual instinct—meaning, for them, before puberty—in a collective and anonymous setting, one would defuse its disturbing charge and thus contain it until the age of normal reproduction; in this way, one could expect to obtain a healthy, vigorous, and disciplined sex. The ideal was to eliminate nonreproductive sexuality as if it were an illness. This was all in the nature of routine tactics. The grand design sometimes showed evidence of a totalitarian planning. In 1934, Sicard de Plauzoles gave a lecture at the Sorbonne, in the presence of the minister of health, on "human zootechny" (thus fulfilling a wish of Cazalis). This is his definition of the term: "Human zootechny is the end-stage of hygiene: after private hygiene, which is addressed only to individuals, and public hygiene, which is concerned only with collective spaces, it is the true social hygiene, that which considers the individual only in terms of his social value and utility. Social hygiene is an economic science that has human capital or material as its object, the latter's production or reproduction (eugenics and puericulture), its conservation (hygiene, medicine, and preventive assistance), its utilization (physical and vocational education), and its output (scientific organization of labor). Social hygiene is a normative sociology: let us think of man as an industrial material, or more precisely, as an animal machine. The hygienist, then, is the engineer of the human machine."[14]

13. Sicard de Plauzoles, *Revue de prophylaxie sanitaire et morale,* 1920
14. *Revue de prophylaxie sanitaire et morale,* 1934.

Another proof of the theoretical proximity of these two strategies could be furnished by pointing out all the quotations from Hitler's *Mein Kampf* in the respective publications of the two groups. Up to 1933 or so, both of them treated that work more as a model of transformation than as a subject of criticism. The populationists lauded its phrases on family politics, where the child should count for more than the adult. The Malthusians took pleasure in its vigorous pronouncements concerning the prevention of venereal disease and its heralding of new marriage legislation. I do not bring this up for the pleasure of showing that things are always more complicated than one thinks. It is simply a matter of bringing to light the fact that these two strategies opposed one another only on a part of their surface, whereas on another level they communicated. The image of the horseshoe suits them better than that of two opposing blades. When the debate is framed in these terms, the traditionalist, legalist, and familialist tendency and the innovating, medicalizing, and socialist tendency both implied an interventionist, coercive pole that welded them to one another.[15] The maintenance of a strong family structure and the preservation of social privileges went by way of *social fascism,* while the dissolution of organic moorings and the social and medical annulment of inequalities were manifested in a *social-sector fascism.*

Hence there was a historical solidarity between these two strategies which, in the first third of the century, formulated the problem of the medicalization of sexuality and the family in terms that are no longer ours. The opposition between the reverie of a sort of family-state (nullifying the family process in favor of a more or less "statized" reproduction) and the aim of a juridical and organic restoration of the family no longer speaks to us, any more than does the conflict between priest and doctor, denominational and secular. For how can we fail to notice the eclipse of issues that were dimly per-

15. See the praise given to the forms of youth training practiced by Mussolinian Fascism, Soviet Stalinism, and Hitlerite fascism in the articles of Mme Caillax in the *Revue médico-sociale de l'enfance* (1932 and after).

ceived in that period as being the important ones surrounding the medicalization of sexuality? Only someone like Michel Debré can still see the promotion of sexuality as a war machine directed against the potency of the nation. Who would still make sexualization out to be a pure and simple tactic of destruction of the family, when the latter takes from this sexualization, at least in equal part, the means of its reinforcement? How can we see this process as a means of suppressing "abnormals," when on the contrary it serves them as a support for boldly asserting their differences? Let us also take note of the virtual disappearance, from this terrain of the administration of sexes and souls, of the two protagonists who laid conflicting claims to it, the priest and the doctor, these having been replaced by the recent categories of counselors and psychologists, our new directors of conscience. An effacement or displacement of the issues and at least a relative withdrawal of the leading combatants. The history of sexuality has taken another path, one more discreet, less glorious, less epic. Indeed one can continue to call up the phantoms of past struggles around it, the marvels of repression, the obsessions with destruction, but this is only a way of breathing new life into something that has none left. That sort of thing is meaningless except when the right accuses the left of wanting to create a collectivist society or when the left denounces the traditionalism of the right. The solution of the family question has deserted the thorny field of medicine for the more comfortable one of psychoanalysis. Staying within the metaphorical, let us say that we shall try to show how Freud is to medicine and psychiatry what Keynes is to Marx.

B. Psychoanalysis and Familialism

If somehow we had to declare a victor between these two tendencies, this would be—probably contrary to the idea that most people have of the matter—the familialist current. Between the early neo-Malthusian pioneers of birth control and free abortion and the Family Planning movement created by Dr. Lagroua-Weill-Hallé in 1956, the only evident continuity is that of a sentimental reference. The *Bulletin du planning familial* pays homage to the martyrs of the cause and bows to Sicard de Plauzoles; in it, the survivors can recount their epic tale and count their departed ones. But that is all. There is no theoretical or practical thread linking the first movement to the second. Eugenist psychiatric theory relinquished its place to psychoanalysis, designated by Mme Lagroua-Weill-Hallé as the only discourse that made it possible to frame the problem of sexuality scientifically. The militant inspiration of Family Planning plainly dissociated itself from the utopian, anarchist, or collectivist reveries of neo-Malthusianism. *Planning familial* began with an apprenticeship in the Anglo-Saxon forms for the spread of birth control. Its authority is backed by the international standing of the Family Planning Association. That is, a very apolitical form of propagation of contraception, combining philanthropic techniques of aid to the poor with the distribution of contraceptives and marital advice. Above all, it is a militantism that devotes itself to the aim of developing family life, based on the celebrated theme of the "happy family." Gone, then, is the direct political dimension of neo-Malthusianism, and its antifamilialist dimension as well. The weapons may be the same, but it is another fight between other combatants, who bear a passing resemblance to their former enemies. And just as there is a great practical and theoretical break between the school of Paul Robin and Family Planning, it is easy to observe an unbroken nervure leading from the populationists of the beginning of the century to the current specialists in the promotion of family life and sexual liberation: a strange continuity of the familialist movement, which has converted the theme of sexual liberation to its own ends.

First let me underline the common origin of a good part of the men and women who in the 1950s were to develop the discourse on the modern family that is summed up by the term "the happy family." They emerged in the thirties and formed an original cluster: the Parents' School. The latter took shape as early as 1929 within the boundaries of the populationist current: its first offices were those of the Alliance nationale (A.N.), graciously lent by General Borie, the director of the Alliance and a member of the administrative board of the Parents' School. In addition to him, this board was made up of Bonvoisin, director of the Family Allowance offices; Hunziker, president of the Association of Parents of Elementary and Secondary School Students: and last, Mme Vérine, founder of the Parents' School. Thus, assembled around a project of pedagogical activation of family life, there was this pressure group obsessed with the Bolshevik threat, the fear of collectivization and medical positivism. All these tendencies were unambiguously set forth in the Parents' School's profession of faith. Its four objectives were in fact: "(a) to teach parents to educate and instruct one another in order to make their children into future social and moral assets; (b) to work toward a reawakening of the familial spirit in France; (c) to safeguard the rights of the family over the child: (d) to achieve a sacred union through the family."[16]

To illustrate the continuity of this first grouping and the postwar movement, let me begin by giving a few career profiles of the leading participants. First, that of Georges Mauco. In 1930, he defended a geography thesis on the role of immigration in French society, showing it was a necessary palliative to the reproductive shortcomings of the French, but balancing this argument by supplying a set of recommendations for coping with the risks of demoralization that came with an influx of immigrants. By virtue of his twofold concern with population quantity and family morality, he won over the directors of the A.N., who praised him in their review. He then devoted himself to psychoanalytic training and to the founding of the first Centre médico-psycho-pédagogique (C.M.P.P.) in France at the Lycée Claude-Bernard in 1945.

16. This presentation figured in all the reports published by the Parents' School.

Soon after, he became chairman of the Select Committee on the Family and Population. In the course of the fifties and sixties, he published numerous books on education and sexuality, based on experience with scholastic maladjustment gained in his work at the C.M.P.P. Next, the career of André Berge. He started out, in the 1920s, as a novelist, taking his material from misunderstandings between parents and children. It was a subject that was guaranteed to please. Typically, the author established that young people got out of hand when their fathers were away at the front, this being accompanied by a parallel criticism of the inadequate behavior of parents, of their shallow, purely formal morals. The best example of the genre is the novel by Kleber Haedans entitled (ironically?) *L'École des parents,* published in 1932. In a word, André Berge was a precursor. Mme Vérine took notice of him and wrote long articles praising his novels in her literary column in the Alliance review. She invited him to give lectures at the Parents' School, and he soon became one of its mainstays. He went on to study medicine, becoming a psychoanalyst and the cofounder, with Mauco, of the Claude-Bernard C.M.P.P. In the fifties and sixties, he was one of the chief propagandists of Family Planning. Beginning in the interwar years, he published books on sex education that gained authority in France and abroad, serving as a model for all those that have proliferated since then.

It is possible to see the symbolic fulfillment of Mme Vérine's desire in the meeting of these two men. The one came out of an interest in quantitative problems, population figures, the management of the lower classes; the other emerged from dealing with qualitative problems, the educative relationship, problems of middle-class children. They converged on the question of scholastic maladjustment, where psychoanalysis would realize, on the basis of its modernization techniques, that dream of a "sacred union through the family."

Let us also examine the way in which the modern groups, organizations, and institutions dealing with sex and the family were linked together logically and practically, the Parents' School being the first link in the chain.

A first phase was begun when that organization established contacts with centers for the production of specialized knowledge concerning children. There was the Child Neuropsychiatry Clinic (N.P.I.) directed by Heuyer since the beginning of the century, with an entire archipelago of disciples around him. His field was maladjusted children, focusing on the lower classes and delinquency, with a solid attachment to constitutionalist psychiatry, its labels, its scholarly racism. There was the psycho-pedagogy of the Claude-Bernard C.M.P.P. from 1945 on. Its inspiration was resolutely psychoanalytic, with a clientele of middle-class children (the Lycée Claude-Bernard is located squarely within the sixteenth *arrondissement*). It concerned itself, therefore, not with delinquent children, but with "difficult" children. A systematic circulation was organized between these three agencies: the Parents' School, the N.P.I. clinic, and the C.M.P.P. Specialists came to give lectures at the Parents' School, which in return referred parents who came to the meetings for consultations with the specialists. One can imagine that a certain principle of social discrimination was applied between the two types of specialists. They returned the favor by drawing up a series of educative and relational recommendations whose dissemination was ensured by the Parents' School via radio broadcasts and the publishing of a considerable quantity of inexpensive brochures written in a simplified, didactic language. The establishment of this circuit created a set of secondary internal benefits for each of these agencies. Heuyer's neuropsychiatry continued its a priori labeling of minors, but moderated it through psychoanalysis in order to justify flexible interventions in the social milieu. Inversely, psycho-pedagogy grounded in psychoanalysis took support from references to delinquency in order to reinforce the dissemination of its advice in the middle and upper-middle classes. The Parents' School in turn depended on the familial etiology of delinquency and character disorders to raise its level of intervention from the simple educative relation to a treatment of the general problem of family life and the marital understanding.

Hence the transition to a second phase, involving groups of intervention in sexual and family life. Starting out with child maladjustment, one arrived at the problems of the couple without leaving the "scientific" register of prevention and educative qualification. In what children presented to them, the staff of the Parents' School, the psychoanalysts, and the psychologists thought they could perceive a different demand begging to be heard: that of the parents themselves. It was more or less disguised, in their judgment, because there was no interlocutor qualified to receive it. Thus the parents were using their child as an indirect way of talking about themselves. Through the child, they were pointing to a wound, an accident that had happened to them, or else they were using him to manifest a symptom of their own difficulties. The *child-as-accident* and the *child-as-symptom:* two themes that must not be confused with one another, since they refer to two different realities—which are strategically unified, however, in the "psy" language.

In actual fact, who were the children who most often landed in Heuyer's consultations, in the centers of observation of delinquent minors? Where did these little delinquents, these future social misfits, come from? They were unloved children, and unloved because they were unwanted. Either because they belonged to a family too large and too poor to provide them with a constant share of affection, or because their mother had conceived them without any love for her partner, and he had deserted her, leaving her with that burdensome gift. She now supported the child grudgingly; indeed, consciously or not, she *rejected the child* because for her he was the product of an accident and not of her desire. What category of children headed the list of medicopsychological consultations (C.M.P.P.) in the fifties? Only children, the exclusive objects of their parents' attention, particularly those who suffered from evident *overprotection* on the part of their mothers. Now, what exactly was this overprotection of the child, if not the symptom of her own anxieties and frustrations? If she invested so much in him, this was in order to compensate for her dissatisfaction in an adult relationship, in the conjugal relation, where she was not finding fulfillment—sexual fulfillment, to begin with. There was a double surface where the theme of the desired child emerged: through the critique of the poor, overly prolific family, and through the critique of the middle-income family, of its reproductive egoism and its pathological effects on the mother and the child. The child who was desired too little and the child who was desired too much. The common denominator, therefore, was desire, *desire appearing as a legitimate area of intervention at least as much as it was a domain of liberation.*

These two lines of intervention remained separate in a first phase. On the one hand, they gave rise to Family Planning, an instrument of struggle against the "child-as-accident," and on the other hand, to groups of marital counselors who plugged into the theme of the "child-as-symptom," analyzing marital problems in terms of their somatic repercussions (psychosomatic illnesses), social repercussions (vocational overinvestment or underinvestment), and pedagogical repercussions (a child evidencing disorders that refer back to the family climate). Family Planning was formed in 1956. The aim, as stated in its first bulletin, *Happy Motherhood,* was to avoid unwanted children: "The practice of deviations of the sex act being subject to varying degrees of success, they might be tolerable, to some extent, for couples who share an understanding . . . but the problem becomes a conflict when husband and wife do not act in agreement with one another . . . when the wife, for health reasons, is in dread of a new pregnancy, or when the husband is irresponsible due to an illness or defect (alcoholism, derangement, character disorder). . . . The problem is to avoid having these tainted children, brought up without strength of purpose and without joy, frequently abandoned by the husband, who is put off by the familial atmosphere."[17] In 1958, André Berge, the Parents'

17. *Bulletin du Planning familial,* 1956.

School and Family Planning rolled into one, wrote an article entitled "Individual and Familial Psychological Problems Posed by Family Density." What was at the root of scholastic maladjustment? he asked. It came from overcrowded conditions in the schools, and as the schools were becoming all the more selective, the parents experienced an anxiety that reflected onto the children. "Starting from a viewpoint that had nothing normative about it, the search for the etiology of character disturbances, neuroses, and delinquency, *psychopedagogy links up with, and confirms, the conclusions of family planning.* Voluntary procreation has become an integral part of the budgetary responsibility of couples."[18] On the one hand, Family Planning brought forward the statistics of Heuyer: "Out of four hundred cases of petty delinquents, one finds that 80 percent are children whose parents did not want them, had difficulty supporting them, and grudgingly tolerated them."[19] On the other hand, it displayed the results of an American survey conducted in Indianapolis in 1950, demonstrating that the category of couples who had planned the number of births and the intervals between them contained the largest proportion of parents who took a great interest in their children, and further, that these couples were the ones who appeared to be the happiest.

Marital counseling groups sprang into existence at about the same time as Family Planning. The most important of them joined together in 1962 to form the Association française des centres de conseillers conjugaux (A.F.C.C.C.). But they made less of a stir than Family Planning. Their name is a handicap, because it cannot help but evoke the parochial tutelage of the past. This is not without good reason: the A.F.C.C.C. has its roots in the Catholic "circles for preparation for marriage." It is led by the Catholic psychoanalyst Jean Lemaire.[20] Few people expect anything new to come out of a context in which the Church has long embodied the sex-

18. Ibid., 1958.
19. Ibid.
20. See his book *Les Conflits conjugaux* (Paris: Éditions Sociales Françaises, 1966).

ual taboo. One can measure the effort they put into shedding their origins by reading their review, *Dialogue,*[21] and the publications of Lemaire. It would be hard to find books in France as heavily laden with Anglo-Saxon references as those of the marital counselors. An exorcism of the past, but also the longing for a future: in England and the United States, marital counselors abound, and they enjoy as good a reputation as all the other forms of psychotherapy. In those countries, the Protestant ethic has produced birth control and counseling in conjunction with one another, while in France the Catholic ethic fell back on the celebration of the couple: it is no accident that the founders of Family Planning include a large number of Protestants. Their emergence was discreet, a bit bashful even, but their expansion was rapid, accelerated by the propaganda produced for them by radio programs like that of Ménie Grégoire.

The meeting of these two currents in the late sixties came about on the question of education, a common denominator of marital difficulties and scholastic maladjustment, and at the same time, an instrument for their prevention. This was the third phase of the process.

In 1967, the Neuwirth Law authorized for the first time a special course of instruction on sexuality in the schools. The only stipulation was that the administration of a *lycée* or a parents' association had to request it. Who was to be in charge of administering it? Practically all the organizations that were established in the train of the Parents' School, and including the latter. In no special order, let us mention: the Groupe d'étude et de recherche sur l'éducation a la sexualité (G.E.R.E.S.), an offshoot of the Parents' School; Family Planning and a splinter group that formed the Institut de formation, de recherche et d'études sur la sexualité (I.F.R.E.S.); Couple et famille, originating in the parish circles for the preparation of engaged couples for married life; the A.F.C.C., which made this its second activity; and a myr-

21. A quarterly beginning in 1961.

iad of micro-organizations created for the occasion by every category of family and women's associations, plus the hygiene leagues. The differences of origin among these groups—some were denominational, others secular, familial, or medical—were virtually obliterated. Families and *lycée* students saw scarcely any difference and called upon them on the basis of their available means. The message was always the same: harmonious psychosexual development of the child; preparation for adult life in its individual, conjugal, and parental aspects; prevention of the mental disturbances of scholastic maladjustment, and so forth. Sex, the field of mission, still created local rivalries, but it provoked no further doctrinal disputes. Moreover, this was the conclusion of the process set in motion by the Parents' School, the closing of a circle that started with the schools, with the problems of maladjustment, then proceeded to the problems of procreation, family life, and the marital understanding, only to return, finally, to the schools, with the introduction of sex education. In this school-family circuit, the instigator of each new stage was psychoanalysis. It was psychoanalysis that authorized the shift away from the problems of scholastic performance to those of the family compact. It was again psychoanalysis that taught a sex education no longer centered on the venereal diseases but on the question of mental and emotional balance. In view of the array of psychologists, counselors, and educators who orbit around the school-family relation, it is not enough to say that psychoanalysis went that route. It would be more exact to say—indulging in a play on words—that this familio-scholastic activism was the way by which psychoanalysis was able to make a go of it. When one consults the brochures of the Parents' School, one discovers that nearly all the well-known psychoanalysts of today made their debuts in that milieu. In addition to Berge, Mauco, and Juliette Favez-Boutonier, one finds the names of Amado, Lébovici, Maud Mannoni (in those days a specialist in disobedient children), and Françoise Dolto, who now compete with Ménie Grégoire in the field of radio consultation.

For a lover of paradoxes, there is pleasure in affirming that between the materialist, medicalizing, socializing current and the populationist, familialist, Pétainist current, it is the latter that has won. If indeed it is around this current that we can locate the advances of the movement of transformation of family life, we must not overlook the internal conflicts that each of these stages has provoked. Consider the polemic between the defenders of the old familial authority and the supporters of an educational liberalization; or that concerning psychoanalysis and sexual liberalization: for example, the violent hostility of the Christian psychoanalyst Hesnard to contraception and abortion. The important thing was to stress that whatever the turbulence in this area, it was less than elsewhere, that familialism was the locomotive to which all the elements of today's policy in matters of sexuality, reproduction, and education were progressively attached.

But the populationist current no doubt lost as much as the neo-Malthusian current in this affair. It rediscovered some of the reasons for its battle, a certain priority of the family in the organization of sociality, but this was at the cost of liberal techniques that undermined its strategy aimed at a social order based organically on the family and directed militarily toward the fabrication of a combat capacity. Was there a mutual neutralization of two politics, then, which favored the gradual liberation of sexuality? In appearance, yes, in the sense that the terms of the old political debate were displaced, the two former strategies were disbanded, and the official political authorities ratified the transformations without giving the impression of deciding between two radically different and antagonistic plans for society. But certainly not, if one takes this to mean a victory of the evolution of mentalities over the register of short-lived political designs. The familialist current was the focus of a continual working-out of a discursive politics governed by psychoanalysis and serving as a support for all the current techniques for the management of relational life.

C. Familial Strategy and Social Normalization

How do we explain the fact that psychoanalysis succeeded where medicine and psychiatry failed? We can bring in the history of judicial repression in order to account for the dissolution of the neo-Malthusian groups. We can understand the link that psychoanalysis established with the familialist current as being the result of the left's compromises with eugenist doctrines. But this fails to explain how psychoanalysis managed to suit the purposes of familialism while making it possible to solve the problems of social normalization. Whereas these two objectives appeared contradictory in the first formulation of a medicalization of sexuality, psychoanalysis was somehow able to resolve this antagonism and efface the political points of contention, the clash of opinions which, as we have seen, dominated the first third of the century. How, in fact, was this accomplished? The slow assumption of psychoanalytic sex was fitted into the problem of the ties between school and family. This was a discreet laboratory for the perfection of a new mode of social regulation, one that was far from the areas that were saturated with absolute antagonisms, areas like the army or the domain ruled over by employers. Not that the education system was devoid of sociopolitical issues, but the issues that were raised had to do with its rate of expansion (to what extent could the schools infringe on familial prerogatives with respect to the qualification and orientation of individuals?) and its techniques for the diffusion of social norms (how were norms of hygiene to be implanted in families?). Two objectives that can be lumped into a single question: *How could the family be divested of a part of its ancient powers—over the social destiny of its children, in particular—yet without disabling it to a point where it could not be furnished with new educative and health-promoting tasks?* It was on this question that psychoanalysis entered into competition with the psychiatry of the thirties in France. Then, *what was there in psychoanalysis that allowed it to meet both the standard of familial ambitions and that of the propagation of social norms?*

A first aspect of this question: How and why did psychoanalysis became *operational* in the familialist current? *What was the junction point of the Parents' School (that focus of resistance to medical, positivist, Bolshevik collectivization) and psychoanalysis?*

On the face of it, the creation of the Parents' School was an event of little importance. In 1929, some ladies of the best society decided, on the initiative of one of them, Mme Vérine, to meet in order to organize a program of mutual improvement for parents, with a view to adapting the timeworn and rigid family morality to the requirements of modern life. The Great War had loosened the bonds of authority, with sons taking advantage of their father's absence to break away sooner, and the wives back at home finding it necessary to take on responsibilities which they were not about to relinquish. Moreover, new and more liberal concepts were flourishing all across Europe, concepts that placed greater trust in children's spontaneity, and new forms for training young people, such as scouting. It was the declared objective of the Parents' School to take note of these innovations and reconcile them with the essential features of the old familial morality. Hence the convening of a series of congresses to which these ladies invited psychiatrists, educators, and the leaders of youth movements and family organizations to expatiate on children, the problems of adolescence, the future of young people, the dangers of motion pictures, of the street, of morally corrupting literature—of that entire "countereducation," as they put it.[22] There was a steady output of brochures, lecture series, and speaking tours in the provinces, a plan for training family educators, and so on. In short, a program that

22. The Parents' School published the results of these congresses in separate volumes: 1930, *Adolescence;* 1931, *Youth;* 1932, *On Personality;* 1934, *The Education of Effort;* 1935, *Education and Countereducation;* in addition to a volume of lectures on *Marriage Apprenticeship* in 1934.

would seem rather unoriginal if we did not situate it in the precise historical context of the school-family relationship of the 1930s.

What was this context? It was characterized, first of all, by a declared supremacy of schooling over all the other forms of socialization. The secular mission was at its peak. "Republican" cultural values were being inculcated in children of the lower classes, and families were being colonized through the diffusion of the norms of public and private hygiene by means of lectures given to parents by schoolteachers, or instilled into families through the children. Enrollments swelled in the *lycées* and *collèges*, and they gradually lost their elitist isolation. Before, they had their own elementary grades (tenth, ninth, eighth, seventh*), with special teachers, progressing to the sixth in four years instead of the five it took for ordinary primary schools. Little by little, this privilege was to disappear. In 1924, the lower grades of the *lycées* and the *collèges* were placed under the same system of inspection as the primary schools. In 1927, sixth-grade classes were made tuition-free, with entrance based on obtaining the certificate of primary studies, a requirement that prefigured today's entrance exam for advancing to the sixth. From 1928 to 1929, this fee exemption created a "wave of scholastic hordes," as the parents' associations of the time expressed it. Enrollments doubled from one school term to the next. This was an obvious sign that the directors of the scholastic apparatus aimed to establish a *unified school system.*[23]

The question of sex education was linked to this context of unification. The question had been raised since the beginning of the century in the framework of a hygiene campaign that saw compulsory elementary education as the privileged instrument in a struggle against alcoholism, tuberculosis, and venereal disease. A first attempt at concretization occurred in

* French school grades start at the high end of the scale and finish at number one. [Translator's note]

23. See Antoine Prost, *Histoire de l'enseignement en France: 1800-1967* (Paris: Armand Colin, 1968).

1906, with the authorization of a special course in hygiene in the elementary schools, adapted from a manual of Debove and Plicque (lessons on child rearing for young female teachers and on venereal disease for young male teachers). Similar endeavors in secondary education made little headway. In 1923, the national education minister organized a referendum on the subject among teachers and parents' associations. The former were in favor, although not without a certain discomfort, and a large majority of the latter were against. A second poll was taken a few years later, covering the Paris region alone and submitting a more subtle proposal which only suggested an optional sex-education course. It met with the same opposition: the optional plan, said the parents, would create a differentiation between children who knew and children who did not, and would reinforce the importance of their games of mutual initiation at the expense of family prerogatives.

Children "of good family" were not only being threatened with a common school system, but, through a collective teaching of sexuality, they would also be exposed—incited, even—to temptations that clarified, in the sphere of sex, the danger of the social promiscuities that the schools imposed. At the end of the twenties, a violent polemic erupted over this twofold question of a unified school system and sex education, involving political issues that appeared in sharp focus. The tone of the dispute can be measured from the following excerpt of a letter sent by the president of the Association of Parents of Elementary and Secondary School Students to Sicard de Plauzoles, who, as you will recall, was a prime mover of the Société de prophylaxie sanitaire et morale and a well-known propagandist for compulsory sex education. The letter was published in *Le Temps*, a newspaper whose readership corresponded to that of today's *Figaro*. "Your statism, sir, is but a precursor to socialism. This is the same road that has led to the destruction of the humanities, the amalgam (of the ancient and modern disciplines), tuition-free secondary studies in the *collèges*, and, even more serious than all this, it is

now leading to a unified school system and to sex education."[24]

I emphasize the description of these polemics surrounding
the schools in the interwar years in order to suggest that a
shift be made in the way we are currently asked to consider
the social role of education. The recent bringing to light, by
Baudelot and Establet,[25] of two systems existing within the
scholastic apparatus—the primary-vocational system and the
secondary-higher system—seemed to reveal a kind of anti-
egalitarian conspiracy at the core of the capitalist school system in France. In actual fact, these two systems are the trace
of two forms of education that originally were strictly separate and explicitly intended for two distinct groups: the primary system for the masses of the country and cities, and the
secondary system for the urban bourgeoisie and rural rich.
Baudelot and Establet are right in showing the limits of the
unification process, in pointing out the perpetuation of two
older systems underlying the new, in saying that this unity of
the scholastic apparatus is more formal than organic. But if
we change our line of sight and look at levels of transformation instead of constants, we will have a guiding thread for
understanding the modifications of the familial regime for
which the schools were the catalyst. Perhaps this will also
enable us to explain—in terms of local tactics and not of a
comprehensive system—the pre-eminence of the socio-familial legacies that are reflected in the scholastic mechanisms of
selection.

I would point to *the formation of parents' associations* as a
first relay of these modifications of the family by the schools.
As regards the elementary schools, the first associations were
religious in inspiration. The "leagues of family fathers"
fought against "the godless schools," aiming their criticism at
the history and civics textbooks. These associations represent-

---

24. From a letter also reprinted in the *Revue de prophylaxie sanitaire et morale*.
25. Christian Baudelot and Roger Establet, *L'École capitaliste en France* (Paris: Mas-
pero, 1973).

ed a minority, but it was an active and vocal one. Set off against them were the teachers who, after the Liberation, were to establish the Cornec Federation. Under their direction, and limited at first to the elementary schools but eventually climbing up the scholastic grades with the creation of the C.E.S., it basically consisted in utilizing families as a means of applying pressure to the public powers in order to obtain increases in equipment and supplies, teaching positions, and the like. It traded on the quantitative expansion of the scholastic apparatus. As to the secondary schools, this time it was not teachers but former students who served as a platform for launching the first parents' association in 1902. It is important to note that the alumni associations had a longstanding elitist function, shared by all "old-boy" networks: to maintain the privileges of a body by means of discreet allegiances. A second difference from the elementary schools was that these A.P.E.'s (*associations de parents d'élèves*) of the *lycèes* and *colleges* utilized the medical discourse as a means of control over the schools: criticism of the overworking of students and of unsuitable classrooms, keeping watch over the moral relationships of teachers with students, surveillance of areas around the *lycées,* and so on.[26] An additional means of pressuring the public secondary school apparatus was available to them in the form of the threat of withdrawing their children from it and placing them in the private sector instead. This A.P.E. of the *lycées* entered into the major question, the unified school system, by trying to bring its movement to a halt, or failing that, to control its direction. After insisting on participating in the departmental committee charged with the question, it used the occasion to bring out various arguments drawn from the medico-pedagogical repertory: the danger that overcrowding would harm the quality of teaching, the difficulty of carrying out a selection at too early an age (an admirable interchangeability of themes: in a first stage, tests served as a means for the administration to resist the pressure of groups

26. See their review, *Lycée et famille,* published from 1908 to 1938.

of privileged parents, before they were denounced as the alibi for an unjust social selection). At last, the ultimate argument: the need to differentiate *instruction* from *education*. In 1928, the director of the A.P.E. made the following statement to the departmental committee: "Grant the sixth grade to everyone, if you must, but do it while avoiding unity of place, for next to instruction, there is education to consider. Parents think it important for their children to have the speech of good breeding and to preserve good manners."[27]

It was at this very time (1928-1929), on this precise point of the distinction between education and instruction, that the Parents' School intervened as a second relay. At a moment when the requirement of scholastic segregation of children of "good family" and children of the lower strata depended on nothing more than the all too visible, fragile, thin partition that separated two classes where the same subject matter would be taught, the Parents' School was to bring relief by suggesting a more acceptable solution: shifting the task of producing an educational quality, a distinction, to the interior of the family. The A.P.E. used medicine to control the quality of the *lycées* and *collèges*. The Parents' School was to use it in order to supply the family with the means of fabricating individuals who would escape scholastic leveling by virtue of their quality. It aimed to preserve a power of the family over its children which the schools were threatening to obliterate.

Sex: was it a subject of instruction or a subject of education? This was the first question raised by Mme Vérine when the Parents' School was formed. In 1929, she put out a call to the parents' associations, asking them to construct a barrier against collectivist initiatives in the teaching of sexuality: "Sex is not a sport to be learned in the stadium." In this, she was not manifesting a puritanical refusal of sex but rather urging the family to recover possession of it and form it into an inalienable asset. In her books on the "initiatory mother" (*La Mère initiatrice,* 1929) and women and love *(La Femme et*

27. *Lycée et famille,* 1928.

l'amour, 1930),[28] she proposed a total change in the behavior of families with regard to sexuality. If one compares what she wrote with a book that was still authoritative among the bourgeoisie, *Conseils aux parents sur l'éducation morale de leurs enfants* (1881), by Elizabeth Blackwell, one does not find a substantial difference as to moral options, granted, but one does notice a decisive break in method. Following in the tradition of everything that had been written about sex education since the Counter-Reformation, Blackwell recommended a meticulous surveillance of the child against all sources of corruption and initiation. But in Mme Vérine's view, this would only make the child hypocritical; a considerable amount of energy would have to be put into developing such an attitude, and the success of the family project would be jeopardized, the child tending to become secretive, introverted, or hypocritical. Consequently, she said, you must answer all the young child's questions, even and especially if they have to do with sexuality. Not only will you thus prevent him from being initiated by his little playmates, and deprive the advocates of compulsory sex education of an argument; you will later reap the benefits of your candor, for as an adolescent this child will not hesitate to confide to you the things that happen to him in this domain to which you have introduced him. In this way, you will avoid surprises.

More important still: by establishing with the child such a relationship of confidence, of trust, of attentive observation, you will give him the benefits of modern techniques of education which allow full play to the child's spontaneity so as to encourage the rhythm of his attainments. The change in the attitude of parents toward their children can serve as a support for the spread of methods like those of Maria Montessori or Decroly in family life. In short, you will be able to display the qualities that parents have to acquire if they are to become true educators, capable of influencing—through the intensity of their action—the scholastic career of their children,

28. She had previously written *Maman nous dira: Le Sens de l'amour* (1927) and *L'Éducation des sens* (1928).

of improving the children's chances at a time when they are being threatened with scholastic leveling.

Hence it was not a matter of opposing the schools in a reactive way; on the contrary, one should go along with them, but in a way that would augment the family's role instead of diminishing it. Thus one would be able to re-create, parallel with the schools, with their horizontality, a vertical dimension of familial behavior where moral values, higher cultural proficiencies, and emotional assests might reclaim their rightful place. This meant making the family into a missionary field that exploited educational requirements in order to make the most of the familial register. And this was where psychoanalysis came in.

What use could constitutionalized psychiatry be to these people who were anxious to find, in the activation of family life, a means of strengthening their children's chances against the "wave of scholastic hordes," of furnishing them with a separate education that was no longer guaranteed once the doors of the secondary schools were opened to all comers? The reply came in a best-selling book entitled *L'Enfant sans défauts* (1930),[29] by Gilbert Robin, a disciple of Heuyer: it would be useful in diagnosing the state of their children. "There are no lazy children," Robin declared, "there are only ill or badly educated children." He had much to say on the subject of illness. His book is a long enumeration of psychiatric labels applied to the unsatisfactory behavior of children: the nervous child, the depressed child, and especially the endless varieties of perversities—acquired, constitutional, conditioned, and so on. On the subject of remedies he became more discreet, and he was conspicuously silent as to what might distinguish a good education from a bad education, except for his reference to a "healthy authority." This was not exactly what parents wanted to hear, and one can easily understand

29. See also Gilbert Robin, *Enfants d'aujourd'hui* (1932) and *Guide du dépistage* (1936).

the infatuation with the psychoanalytic discourse that was to take hold of them, the delicate educative advice that was to be provided by Freud's disciples in order to save children from traumatisms that might harm their development.[30] How to avoid traumatisms, but also how to detect the traces, in their lies, in their silences, of a relational problem they would eventually be able to resolve, rather than the sign of a future lot as a pervert or mental defective. Respect for medicine demanded that doctors like Robin be invited to the congresses of the Parents' School. They would reel off the awful list of degenerescences, which did not upset the assembly too badly, since it was well aware that the descriptions were based on delinquent children, the children of the lower classes. Then André Berge or Father Viollet would appear, fresh from psychoanalysis, and explain the means whereby a particular opposition or difficulty of a child could be worked through. Families anxious to join up with the schools only received an either/or response from psychiatry: either illness, or fault of the family. Apart from the difficulty of establishing such a division, this formula affronted the family through direct as well as indirect attribution of blame (your child is badly brought up; your child is defective). It also offended the school by calling on it to model its classifications after medical categories, thus disallowing its role in the distribution of capacities. In contrast, psychoanalysis avoided the fatalism of diagnosis as a matter of principle; it recognized the possibility of the family's improving the child's behavior and made a royal truce with the scholastic apparatus. Better still, it flattered the schools by appealing to their intrinsic desire for pedagogical improvement.

The question of scholastic maladjustment was the lever by which psychoanalysis was introduced into the social domain, well in advance of its utilization in health institutions in the strict sense, and with more important consequences. It brought in the principle of a *relaxation of psychiatric nosogra-*

---

30. For an inventory of psychoanalytic works intended for families in this period, see Horst Richter, *Psychanalyse de la famille* (Paris: Payot, 1971).

phies by promoting an increased flexibility of relational structures, a *loosening of the familial vise.* By playing on the educative strategy of the family, psychoanalysis introduced a concern with the observance of social norms in the family without colliding head on with it, but rather—now is the time to say it—taking support from its desire. Psychoanalysis made the family *amenable to social requirements, a good conductor of relational norms.*

In what, then, did the psychoanalytic solution to the heteromorphism of the family and the social machinery consist? What was the technique that made it possible to harmonize the differences of regime between, on the one hand, an agency like the traditional family, which operated on the basis of the exchange of its members according to rules that combined genealogical determination and the strategies of alliance, thus requiring them to be accessible to its own designs—and on the other hand, an agency like the school, which formed individuals according to its norms, deciding on their qualification so as to orient them socio-professionally? What made it possible to reduce the rift between the register of the religious, and hence familial, management of sexuality and that of its medical and social management? What made it possible to combine confession with expertise?

A cursory look at the functioning of the educational, sexual, and conjugal conselors who have thrived on the problem gives us the impression of a hasty compromise between the two registers, *a mixture of the scholastic and the familial, of the medical and the religious, of expertise and confession, with variable proportions of each.* The Parents' School was the scene of a kind of permanent consultation between parents and educators. Doctors came to its meetings in order to learn to listen to family problems, and priests set about absorbing the familial vocabulary, detecting the pathological in the telling of faults. One might mention the birth of the review *L'Éducation,* in 1936, as a symbol of this preoccupation with synthesis. *L'Éducation* was a regrouping, around the Parents' School, of the former *Revue familiale d'éducation,* the organ of the Fédération générale des familles, directed by Father Viollet, a specialist in confession and preparation for marriage, and the review *Éducation,* a pedagogical bulletin directed by Bertier, a former patron of the École des Roches and a great enthusiast of pedagogical innovations. Did not Mme Vérine, presiding with the likes of André Berge, Father Viollet, and the pedagogue Bertier, presage the customary threesome of the current broadcasts of Ménie Grégoire, flanked variously by a sexologist reverend father, a psychiatrist, or both at once? Generally speaking, the co-presence of the expertise form and the confession form is easy to observe in all the technicians of relational life, whether they practice in ultra-private offices or in public edifices, or spread themselves over the air waves. With the psychologists in the strict sense, there is the double game of tests and anamnesis, the expert inventory of individual possibilities and the confessional account of family life. With the sex educators, there is a game that alternates between questions concerning the norm and questions leading to "implication," the evaluation of the subject's relationship with sexuality.

However, there must be something else to these relational techniques besides the simple juxtaposition of the old prestige of the priest and the new prestige of the doctor. Otherwise it would be difficult to understand why they have become the object of so inflational a demand. Above all, it would be hard to understand why the priests have been divested of their confessional function (except for those who have reconstituted themselves in the guise of the analyst-priest, parallel with that of the worker-priest), or why doctors have given up their claim to the function of family guidance which they coveted so much (except for those who have made themselves into psychosomaticians). Then what is there in the relational technique that has called for the formation of new technicians? What is new and specifically effective is the *establishing of a process of circularity between the two practices of expertise and confession.* When you go to a psychotherapist or marital counselor, the principle of diagnosis is maintained as a preliminary (it can be used to eliminate cases that are too "heavy"), but it is also formally nullifed at the outset, treated as a provisory and, above all, nonpreferred, nonrecorded appearance. This is a crucial suspension, in that it removes the handicap of an a priori judgment, creating an opening where the confessional account will be lodged, the discourse of avowal out of which, precisely, there can issue an a posteriori revaluation based on the "work" of the subject in his discourse, which is no longer expected to serve exclusively to verify an a priori. This circular displacement eliminates worries about manipulation, since every formulation of a social judgment is associated with its possible calling back into question through the subject's participation. The individual's resistance to norms, like that of the family, is thus no longer anything but an *internal* resistance to a process whose outcome can be a greater well-being for him and for it. *The resistance to norms becomes a resistance to analysis,* a purely negative and blind blockage in the way of one's own welfare. The strength of relational technology lies precisely in the fact that *it does not impose anything—neither new social norms nor old moral rules.* On the contrary, *it allows them to float in relation to one another until they find their equilibrium.* This is an economic technique in the strict sense, and the most economical one to use in terms of both administrative and conflictual costs. One can understand why doctors renounced a type of function in which they would have lost the security of their terrain, the reassuring clarity of the diagnosis. And one can understand the pains priests have taken to adhere to these methods, which have much to thank them for, even if only for this floating of values and norms. It is all the more understandable inasmuch as they have nothing to fall back on.

The first job of the relational technician consists, therefore, in *discouraging the demand for expertise.* Don't expect an opinion from me, an immediate and imperative piece of advice, a discourse of truth concerning your case. Or if, as in the C.M.P.P., there is indeed an inventory of the child's intellectual possibilities, do not think that it is a conclusion; on the contrary, it is more in the nature of a beginning. You come in order to find out if the mediocre scholastic results of your child are due to a hereditary defect or if he does it on purpose. It is not, in any case, the one or the other; and if the tests show a discrepancy between his abilities and his scholastic performance, it is for this very reason that you must tell us how he behaves in school and at home, how he gets along with his brothers and sisters and with you, what your educative attitudes are, your own problems, your marital understanding or lack of understanding. Talk about your grievances against your husband or wife, says the marital counselor; tell me about yourself, about the conditions of your marriage, your childhood, your relations with your parents. *A second operation* consists in the technician's relying on this account *to show the link between the problem at hand and a series of communication gaps* between the members of the group concerned. Can't you see, then, that if your child is not applying himself at school, this is because his father does not take an interest in his scholastic activity, does not communicate his feelings to the child except in the form of anger when faced with failures? Or if your daughter, though very intelligent, is uninterested in school, this is because you have been so concerned with her future that you have not taken what she wants into account; you have prevented her from positing her desire. And what is the inflation of mutual reproaches in marital conflicts, if not the refusal to take into consideration what each of the partners is trying to get the other to understand? What is sex education, if not precisely an activity for preventing the risks of failure by affirming that sexuality is useful, first and foremost, for communicating? *A third operation,* finally, is *the identifying of the causes of these gaps.* For what can disturb communications, split up messages, and distort perceptions in this way? *These are precisely false perceptions, screen images,* psychical concretions pieced together as much from archetypes as from the taking into account of the reality of others, projections as much as or more than recognitions: realize that these artifacts command the organization of our relations, that the measure of blindness that is present in our conflicts and our failures results from the vitality of an old desire that is capable of hiding a present reality, and you will have the means of readjusting your relations, of reassessing a situation.[31]

In this approach, the key concept is that of the image. By bringing it to the fore, one can turn the subject around, get him to accept responsibility for expertise, since it is he who reveals his own, get him at the same time to accept what he was refusing to hear, to see, to do, since it no longer has to do with morality, laws, or merits, with the possible or the impossible; it involves his own being, his relational equilibrium, his psychical and sexual fulfillment. Hence the whole effort of the technician bears upon the means of evoking these images.

Example: the *drawing of the family* in the C.M.P.P. Take a child eight to twelve years old suffering from scholastic maladjustment. Give him a piece of paper, a black pencil, and some colored pencils. Ask him to draw his family. No risk of refusal in this age group; they always agree. You are already aware that in the case of a normal family, the figures are generally distributed in two horizontals rows, the higher ones (the parents) and the lower ones (the children), and that they are drawn symmetrically with their colors serving to mark their distinctive attributes, their serious or light polarity. Thus, if the child positions all the members of the family on a single line, you can already suspect that the family is poorly structured. If he leaves out this or that member, you have the sign of a relational difficulty with the person in question, which the child wants to resolve by symbolically rubbing him out. The order in which the figures succeed one another also says a great deal about the place that the child sees himself given in the family. The dissymmetry he may assign to certain figures, himself included, the murky or clear coloring, and the

---

31. I base this description on an inquiry concerning the C.M.P.P. and groups of marital counselors, as well as on works such as *L'Enfant et les relations familiales,* by Maurice Porot (Paris: Presses Universitaires de France, 1954); *La Consultation conjugale,* by Guy Rucquoy (Brussels: Dessart, 1974); *Le Conseil conjugal et familial,* by Rolande Dupont (Paris: Casterman, 1972).

mutilation of members make it possible to refine further the child's representation of his family. A particular figure has no hands, for example: couldn't this be because the person in real life only uses them to hit the child? Another figure has no arms: isn't this because the person depicted transmits no affection, despite the desire which the child feels for it? The drawing of the family thus enables one to throw all the family anomalies, large and small, into relief. A child lies, steals, is aggressive and quick-tempered, or on the contrary is inhibited and passive. There are so many signs of a protest against what is out of kilter in the family structure, something the drawing will reveal. Besides expressing his malaise, his situation, through the drawing, the child at the same time furnishes a means of evaluating the family environment.

The medico-psycho-pedagogical centers are undoubtedly the best places for appreciating the pervasive capacity of psychoanalysis in the family sphere. By designating a poor regulation of images as the root cause of scholastic failure, the "psy" technique does not point the finger at any particular person or wrong behavior; it places the blame, rather, on the relations that obtain within the family and on the unconscious mental representations of its members. A child is suffering from a neurotic inhibition in relation to schoolwork: psychotherapy reveals a link between this inappetence and the discourse of the father. The latter is a driver for the R.A.T.P.* and regards his job as pointless, as leading nowhere. This way the father has of depicting his work is not denounced as bad in itself. The reality of the father's work will not be discussed with him, but rather its psychical repercussions on the child. The father will be induced to reassess his appreciation of reality as it bears on familial affects. As for the little girl who, in spite of being quite intelligent, is inattentive in class, spending her time in needless mischief, her drawing of the family shows that her relationship with her father is that of a little sister to an older brother who keeps

---

* Régie autonome des transports parisiens, the public transportation company that operates the buses in Paris. [Translator's note]

her in a state of empty-headed immaturity. But why does the father need to (re)play a role that is not his? What is this dissatisfaction that nags at his mind to the point of detracting from his official aims? What does this mean at the level of the couple? Another child is unstable at school and stays away from home. The mother brings him to the C.M.P.P. She talks at length about the child, about herself and her worries, but says nothing about her husband, apart from a few casual references. The fact that the father does not exist in the mother's discourse, that she does not refer to him as a holder of authority, isn't this lack of a paternal image in the mind of the mother the cause of the child's instability? And what does that say about the quality of the conjugal relationship, the share of dissatisfaction that is perpetuated in it? The C.M.P.P. is led to exercise a marital counseling function. The child is the element that proves the existence of a dysfunctioning of the family, the ideal element for bringing about alterations within it, since he is situated at the point where social desire and familial desire intersect. Some 10 to 20 percent of parents with children being treated in a C.M.P.P. are themselves undergoing psychotherapy at the center. And it is not unusual to see a child who shows no signs of serious disturbances being kept in psychotherapy solely in order to provide an administrative cover for the care and treatment of the parents.

Marital consultation employs a method that is equivalent in every respect. Here the symptoms are, in order of frequency: impotence, frigidity, psychosomatic illnesses, and the disturbances of children. The reference grid for normal behaviors can be represented by listing the matching needs of the couple, a complementarity in the economic and sexual spheres, as well as in the sphere of ego reinforcement and reorientation. I will take the example of the table constructed by Pollak describing the nature of the functions that each member of the couple must fill with respect to the other in all these areas, in every phase of his or her existence, before the arrival of the children, with them, and after their departure. The explanatory link between the nonfulfillment of these roles and the appearance of the symptom, between the sphere of needs and the complaint, is furnished by an analysis of the projections the partners placed on one another at the time of the initial choice, or by the modifications of the coordinates based on this choice made at the start. The orientation of these projections or images is subject to variations that the interviews and questionnaires make it possible to weigh in terms of two criteria: their greater or lesser proximity to what parental figures ought to be, and their distance from the behavioral range of the partner. Depending on the extent to which this construction is obscured by the initial images, or is out of line with the partner's dispositions, the marital relation will be normal (complementarity), neurotic (impotence, frigidity, extramarital inclinations), or homosexual (the partner's anxiety over his or her sexual identity). Hence the work of the marital counselor consists entirely in translating a suffering into a dysfunction and in relating this dysfunction to a maladjustment of images and realities, saying in effect: If you do not want to change your reality, then change your images; if you do not want to change your desires (your images), then change your reality; the important thing is that it work.

What was dysfunctional in the old family regime? (1) The family's attention was directed exclusively toward the matrimonial ratification of its influence, its importance, that is, toward the *exterior, visible form of its power.* (2) Correlatively, the family held children in a tight grip; they were the instruments of its perenniality and of its ambitions; in short, there was a *primacy of filiation.* Now, all the activity around the Parents' School consisted in bringing about a *tactical displacement of the old powers* of family, of its external powers, which were mainly concerned with self-aggrandizement, with the contraction of marriages useful to itself, *onto its internal powers,* so as to safeguard a specifically familial effect in the distribution of cultural qualities and social positions. *A crucial shift away from the family's external appearance toward internal relational ways and means.* Grafting itself onto this displacement, the operationalism of psychoanalysis contributed a flexible formula for resolving the frictions between social urgencies and familial ambitions. *Familial behaviors and social norms were "floated" in relation to one another; the theory of the role of images provided them with a principle of conversion into one another.* Between the risk of a juridical stiffening of the family and that of a costly and leveling imperialism of social norms, the discourse on the socializing role of parental images introduced a principle of automatic readjustment of the two authorities. It did not quash either one, but lessened the risks of conflict and combined their functions. It brought the child's freedom and the woman's sexuality into play against the strangle hold of the family. The child's relationship to his family is no longer described in terms of heredity or transmission but of his structuration relative to the norm, his more or less successful liberation from the family unit. Filiation is not decided by fate, but by the parents' offer to the child of improvable identificatory images. Maturation is not the acceptance of a heritage, a destiny, but the fading significance of one's family, escape from its desires, liberation from the possessive desires of one's parents. Thus the proper structuration of the child presupposes the destruction of the dual morality that distorts his perception of adults and furnishes images of them that evidence a pathogenic duplicity. Liberation implies a slackening of the family circle and hence of the sacrificial role of the mother—where the child was the main possible object of investment—*in favor of her sexuality.*

D. The Advanced Liberal Family: Freud and Keynes

Why such a concern with history, one might ask—why dwell so much on the familialist mysteries of the introduction of psychoanalysis and sexual liberation, since the latter have triumphed in any case and we are now living in the midst of a crisis of the family?

No one still regards the family as the essential form of

social organization, an unalterable figure to be protected at all costs. A sudden reticence has come over the very people who used to sing its praises. The directors of the Parents' School state that "from our observation post, we cannot see at present any ideal family arrangement emerging. The most important problem is that of the emotional investment made at the level of that gathering under the same roof, which, by virtue of its very power, risks hindering the respective autonomy of its members. In short, all the components of the group should now seek to avoid being pinned with a label, be it that of 'child' or that of 'parents,' and simply be 'persons' who learn to accept one another mutually in their roles and their desires, that is, to love one another."[32] "Gathering under one roof"—such a taste for euphemism; a pair of tongs are needed in order to talk about the family! And there is not much "family" left in Family Planning either. Since 1973, it has been steering toward the "revalorization of the person, the development of his entire psychosomatic being, outside traditional roles," the "reintegration of sexuality into all levels of everyday life," the "sexualization of society."[33] All those groups who once desired to defend the family against the assaults of an authoritarian normalization now think only of finding the best means of coping with its harmful effects. They want to efface this marking by the family, the labels it assigns to its members at the expense of their social autonomy. But they also endeavor to make up for its deficiencies, to socialize at least a portion of its affective, sexual functions, which it assumes only imperfectly, upsetting the balance of individuals, hindering their "psychosexual" unfolding. Their findings and criticisms point out the same risk of failure in two opposite dangers: the chilly withdrawal of the family into itself, which may make it a locus of passive resistance, a shel-

32. Presentation of the Parents' School in the issue of the review *Autrement* entitled "Finie la Famille?" (1976)

33. Simone Iff (president of Family Planning), *Demain la société sexualisée* (Paris: Calmann-Lévy, 1975).

ter protecting its members from the risks of the outside but seriously inhibiting them in their social life; or else its dislocation, its atomization through the growth of bachelorhood, of casual relationships that offer individuals too little security to permit them to function in a socially autonomous way. In these discourses the family has changed from being a pillar of society to being the place where society constantly threatens to come unglued.

Facing this disarray, there is only the little army of counselors and psychologists, and they are always insufficient in number to meet the demand of defenseless parents, of lost children and unhappy couples, of the misunderstood, of those who have not learned how to live. This is the place, then, where one should get involved, find solutions, make a positive contribution, take notice of all this suffering, join one's voice to the chorus of redeemers, or hold one's peace. Do you have a scenario, a plan, an experimental project, a little formula for self-management, a vision of the family of tomorrow, some proposal you would like to make? Don't hold back; the state is buying, and right-thinking people are interested. You say you have nothing to offer? Communitarian formulas seem illusory to you, mere transpositions of familial egocentrism to a broader scale? You decry the solitude to which individuals find themselves, the poverty of their emotional life, the insipidity of their existence? In that case, you will admit that something has to be done, that the counselors and "psy" people are the very ones who have set themselves to the task, as best they can, with the greatest honesty and neutrality. With them, there is no longer any question of moralism, of dogmatism, unless it be in a residual form. They do not assign anyone, dictatorially, to family life, any more than it is their aim to destroy family life. They simply want to help people live their situation in a shifting set of circumstances where fixed signposts have vanished and where the individual feels the need to be backed up but not led.

Nothing can be said against this argumentation if one accepts the terms in which it is deployed, the crisis of the family as the result of an evolution of mores, the development of psychologism and psychoanalysm as the solution, the least objectionable response to the situation. But what becomes of this line of argument when we challenge its assumptions, when we identify the emergence of the modern family and the expansion of "psy" organizations as a single process, and one that is not politically innocent in the least? What remains of this persuasive discourse if one is able to consider the process anew in the light of this discovery? Such a long detour had become necessary in order to challenge the kind of circular inquiry in which all reflection concerning both the family and the professions that flourished in its vicinity was confined. We should be able to use what we have learned from this genealogy of "counselism" to shift the question around. Instead of being lured into the search for a solution to the obvious malaises that develop around and within family life, we shall ask ourselves: This crisis of the family, *together with* this proliferation of "psy" activities, are themselves the solution to what problem?

First and foremost, they are a means of evading the first political formulation of the problem of the normalization of sexuality, both in its "socialist," hygienist, and antifamilial form and in its Pétainist, moralist, and traditionalist form. When the question of the liberalization of sexuality and that of voluntary procreation returned to the political stage in the fifties, the terms of the debate were fundamentally changed through the effect of the tactical encounter between, on the one hand, the qualitative politics of comfortably-off families, their withdrawal into themselves, their search for an optimization of their internal ties, and on the other hand, teachings that were adapted from psychoanalysis and its derivatives. From being a locus of resistance to medical norms that threatened its integrity and the interplay of its privileges, the bourgeois family became the best surface of reception of these norms. There was no further need for a central decision since the appeal came from those micro-centers of initiative, from that periphery which the family had become. Birth control, psycho-pedagogy, and the preoccupation with relational life were added to a store that was already stocked with the bourgeois "quality of life." After a period of hesitation, when business was bad, the new items sold quite well in that micromilieu which had already been organized in the eighteenth and nineteenth centuries on the model of spontaneist liberalism, the model of the contractual option. The "protected liberation" that characterized the education of children came to full flower in the applications of the teachings of Decroly, Montessori, Spitz, and above all, Freud. Recommended reading for parents who wanted to avoid traumatizing their children, good referrals when there was a problem—all this was the prolongation of something that had already been seen and done: the tactical closing up of parents around children, defending them against the educative prejudices and blunders of servants, against the dangers and corruptions of the street. Birth control and the "liberation" of women rested on women's old social vocation, on their function as ambassadresses of culture. And of course, as in the past, it was upon working-class families that they were to perform their mission of propagating these new norms that had done so well by them. "Sexual freedom," birth control, the relational demand, and pedagogy were to be spread along the same lines, according to the same technocratic interventionism that was once used to sell savings banks and schooling: the promotional goading and attendant blaming of families who, through their resistance, were ruining the members' chances. The launching of Family Planning echoed a discourse that was more than two centuries old, that of those men and women who had undertaken to struggle against the obscurantism of mores, to free the masses from their mental fetters, from miseries that used to be material and moral but now were sexual and emotional, so that they would produce fewer children, and above all, fewer social misfits.

Hence this recombination of sex with good philanthropic form dissipated the political rigidification the latter had provoked. There were no longer all-encompassing, "sociatricidal" issues at stake; there were resistances, rather, those of the established bodies, of groupings and corporations interested in perpetuating the old order of things: the Communist Party, the Church, and the leadership of the Medical Council.

The attitude of the Communist Party is indicative of this displacement of the problem of sexuality. One will recall the violent hostility of the French Communist Party to the newly formed Family Planning organization, the vigorously "anti-Malthusian" declarations of Jeannette Vermeersch and Maurice Thorez, expressing the old fear of an individualist solution to the social question. The workers' organizations had this retractile position with regard to practically all the innovations that appeared in the area of social technology. The Guesdists (ancestors of the Communist Party in the years from 1880 to 1890) had begun by denouncing compulsory education as a means of dominating and dividing the working class. A hostility that was soon followed by a reverse attitude: it was no longer schooling that was bad but insufficient funding; the resources allocated to education were inadequate; there were not enough schools. The same thing was repeated at the beginning of the 1960s as regards voluntary childbirth and, generally speaking, as regards all the related techniques for improving familial and relational life. One can read in the books of Bernard Muldworf, a Communist Party psychoanalyst, the procedure whereby "demands" relating to family life and psychological services were given a "Marxist" canonization.

Every time the Communist Party contracts in this way against a reform, then undertakes to assimilate it by demanding that it be speeded up and broadened, transforming a theoretical refusal into a quantitative demand, one can be certain that philanthropy has just scored a point. The game is a strange one where, in order to protect its function as the representative of popular discontent, the agent of resistance to "bourgeois" manipulation becomes the best advertising agent for means of individual advancement; while demanding the extension of the latter, the party will scurry about defending the belief in their intrinsic merits.

With the resignation of the Communist Party, the last political hurdle had been crossed. There remained only the corporatist opposition of the Church and the conservative faction of the Medical Council. At first glance, their opposition too looks ideological. The Church defends the moral values on which the family was founded, and the Medical Council opposes abortion in the name of respect for life. But in practice, everyone knows of the professional, social, and political benefits to which these options correspond. By abnegating its function as an ally and tutor of the family, the Church loses the solid basis of its inscription in the social body. The figure of the family doctor is just as threatened by the modernization of the family, which relegates him to a more mundane and public exercise of his art. The Medical Council clings to its old posture as a body of notables, to a relationship with its clientele that is closely related to political clientelism and the source of a power that is in fact reflected in the latter. As for the branch of the medical profession which, since the days of neo-Malthusianism, had looked forward to becoming the age of a hygienic liberalization of the family, it has participated actively in the movement, despite the difficulties it has encountered in deriving the benefits it once expected from this activity. For what has become plain to see since the last war is that the lines of transformation of the family are bringing about a disqualification of its old medical and religious entourage in favor of a new professional setting, that of the "psy" specialists. Ménie Grégoire was interviewd by Paul Giannoli in *France-Soir,* November 9, 1976, concerning her relations with "people of the profession," and this was her response: "The psychoanalysts know me and they recognize that what I am doing belongs to 'their family.' My fiercest adversaries, in the beginning, were doctors, because their clients did not always say good things about them on the air. Some doctors even thought that I would drive away their patients. Some of the church people were not very happy either. Confession was on the decline, and they had the impression that I was competing with them by doing something a little different, but where my interlocutors were looking for the same thing. Other priests, however, wrote to me, saying, 'By listening to you, I am learning how to hear a confession.' "

A first line of transformation of the family can be traced back to the confluence of the two original dimensions of the familial *aggiornamento*. The family's tactical withdrawal into itself and the diffusion of new norms brought about an *intensification* of family life. Concentrated on itself, more attentive than before to the least details of the children's education, the family became an avid consumer of everything that might help it to "realize itself." Vitia Hessel, a psychoanalyst and a novelist to boot, devoted a book entitled *Le Temps des parents* to the description of this frenetic activation of family life. She could just as well have called the book *Le Temps des psy,* for it explains the process of psycho-pedagogical sophistication of the family that has been developing, mainly in the middle classes, since the end of the last war. It is a process in which children constitute a kind of gilt-edged investment. Of course, the old type of parents had ambitions for their children too, but their motivations were rather primal and their speculations quite straightforward. They offered their sons an education in order to see them rise in the social scale, in order to be able to depend on their material support when the time came. They maintained very careful control over the future of the patrimony. For the new parents, who have a right to retirement and to the pension that goes with it, things are not so simple, and it no longer makes a great deal of sense to regard children as a prop for one's old age or as the instruments of precise ambitions. "In them, parents begin to cherish promises of success, a compensation, or more accurately, the permissible part of the dream that society has consented to leave to them. So the parents speculate over these heads tousled from sleep, these cheeks smeared with jam, just as their fore-bears speculated over their good Russians, and, like all specu-lations, theirs are marked by the most docile sort of conformism. Society dictates its models; they try to reproduce them. . . . Parents no longer have the right, as they had in the Dark Ages, to turn their children into failures. The Parents' School is standing by, and there is guidance counseling, and mass-circulation magazines to consult. A new science was born in the psychological optimism and relational fever of the postwar years. The European of the thirties and forties partly succeeded in ignoring it; his counterpart in the fifties and sixties was now receiving the full force of its contradictory thrusts." Discourses on the faults of children were replaced by such works as *The Child, Mirror of the Parents* by Roland Jaccard. The "parent" was continually called upon to fight an enemy that was none other than himself. " 'It is forbidden to make the child anxious,' said the psychologists. 'Don't let him fall asleep,' the professors said. 'He is worried and that is why he is working poorly,' the pediatrician remarked. The parent would hang his head: if the child was anxious, the parent was to blame. He was not motivated, the sociologists discovered. The parent would panic: if the child was not motivated, the parent had failed. Was there still time to make up for it? 'Don't scare the child,' he was told. 'Make him understand that life is a battle,' it was added. 'Protect him,' it was or-dered. 'Expose him, or you'll turn him into a zombie.' Don't brood over him. Don't traumatize. Don't project your own outdated dreams on the child. Don't give up. Don't inter-fere."[34] Everyone is aware of how the mass-circulation maga-zines such as *Parents, Psychologie,* and *Marie-Claire* use this knowingly contradictory character of "psy" advice to come out in turn with startling revelations regarding the dangers of the disappearance of family initiative, and with equally star-tling revelations regarding the dangers of the inhibiting effect of its excesses.

34. Vitia Hessel, *Le Temps des parents* (Paris: Mercure de France, 1969).

A second line of transformation, in apparent contradiction to the first, went in the direction of a *destabilization* of the family. The same ingredients were at work in both instances, however: the focus on childhood, and the concern with the quality of sexual and emotional life. But in this case, the effects they produced worked against the narrow limitations of family life, against the juridical immobility of contractual ties. The process is easy to understand, for there had been a more or less camouflaged misunderstanding in the encounter between familialism and psychoanalysis. It was not for nothing that the family shifted its interest from the exterior toward the interior, that it recentered itself on the refinement of internal ways of adjusting the parent-child and man-woman relationships. It was a question of rediscovering, on this private terrain, a specific power of the family, a vital hold on its members, a capacity for qualifying its children that it was in the process of losing on the public terrain. This was a compensatory and tactical stance that was bound to generate an *overinvestment*. However, relational normalization, the operationalism of psychoanalysis, would seem rather to go in the direction of a functional "disempowerment" of the family. Psychoanalysis does not "reveal," does not give "theoretical expression" to an a priori relationship of complicity between the family and society, a pre-established harmony, an interlocking relationship of the microcosm-macrocosm type. The difference between the power regime of the family and that of society as a whole is sufficiently great that all attempts at a precise codification of familial behavior are doomed ultimately to fail. The strength of psychoanalysis is precisely in capitalizing on this in order to show how the family can be responsible for the inadequate socialization of one or another of its members. In its practice, it accuses the family only occasionally. In its theory, it acknowledges the family to be a fundamental agency, but in a form that implies the latter's devitalization, the invalidation of its will to be an autonomous social protagonist. Psychoanalysis ratifies and valorizes the conventional family arrangements, the role of the father, the role of the mother, but at the same time it reduces their former strategic disposition to a mere skeleton, serving only as a constellation of images, a surface of induction for relations, a *functional simulacrum.*

This explains why psychoanalysis was able both to buy into the theme of the "happy family" at the start of Family Planning, and to serve as a reference for the critique of the family that followed. Through its formal reduction of familial powers to mere role playing, it could throw in with and—if the need arose—serve as a justification for outside temptations, for the individual game, the search for more harmonious, more balancing combinations. In a context in which the effective power of the family was diminishing, in which its self-absorption threatened to immobilize its members, psychoanalysis could encourage the revolt of those who were becoming sensitive to the most minimal differences of degree in the sacrifices that were to be made on the altar of that uncertain god. The promotion of relational quality served as a supporting framework for women who wished to seek their identity in a professional and not just familial activity, and for adolescents who saw themselves leading the life of *lycée* students, of young people, as much as that of the descendants of their parents.

The pathology of the modern family appears on either side of these two lines of transformation. Its margin of autonomy being reduced at the same time as its internal life is in demand, the family makes use of a psychological redoubling of its bonds in order to maintain a hold on its members, a tactic that may go so far as to prevent them from functioning outside its boundaries. More and more, it brings about, in the hollow of its intimacy, a merging of its members, an affective coalescence designed to resist the destructive temptations of the outside. It seems that this produces psychotics. Moreover, with its saturation by hygienic, psychological, and pedagogical norms, it becomes harder to distinguish the family from the disciplinary continuum of the social apparatuses. It thus appears as the troubled site of social subjection, of the impossibility of social autonomy, arousing the repulsion of those who do not want to give in to that dismal injunction, leading them to live outside its ties. It seems that these people are neurotics. The family is pathogenic, then, whether it resists exterior norms or does not resist them enough. Always the same alternating quantity of reproaches. Thus the slender furrow of the socialization of familial mores heaps up an ever greater number of victims on each of its two banks: those who cannot get free of the process, and those who are neither willing nor able to enter into it. Hence, in the space of a few decades, a strange reversal has occurred in the danger that is said to be lurking in the family. Because of its evasion of medical norms in the choice of alliances, and because of the duplicity of its sexual ethic, it was accused of manufacturing, in the shelter of its sovereignty, a whole population of *abnormals,* of physical and mental defectives. Now it is accused of being the original site of *madness,* owing to the excessive intensity of its ties or, on the other hand, to their dangerous fragility. It was condemned for its social extraterritoriality, its "primitive" rules, and its egocentrism. The attempt, at the beginning of modern-day society, to charge it with the function of normalization by trading on its ambitions and manipulating its fears only succeeded in turning it into this society's first disappointment.

This is the advanced liberal family, then: a residue of feudalism whose internal and external contours are blurred through the effect of an intensification of its relations and a contractualization of its bonds; a sort of endless whirl in which the standard of living, educational behavior, and the concern with sexual and emotional balance lead one another around in an upward search that concentrates the family a little more on itself with every turn; an unstable compound that is threatened at any moment with defection by its members, owning to that relational feverishness which exposes them to the temptations of the outside, as well as to that overvaluing of the inside which makes escape all the more necessary; a half-open place, constantly obsessed with the desire for a withdrawal into itself that would restore its old power at the cost of the individual integrity of its members, or—inversely—obsessed with the temptation of a renunciation that would deprive them of that last vestige of identity which it secures for them outside the sphere of social discipline.

The historical good fortune of the "psy" forces consists, therefore, in this dual—centrifugal and centripetal—tendency of the family, which reveals an intermediary space between the "intrafamilial" and the "extrafamilial," a zone undergoing an expansion and one furrowed by the ceaseless coming and going of those tormented within the family and those lost without it. A strategic position, between opposite and circular temptations, which only the "psy" agencies would be able to occupy, for they alone were prepared to manage instability.

This is *a position that their providential neutrality has enabled them to monopolize.* They do not have the handicap of the priest, who is riveted to the defense of moral values. They do not suffer from the deontological hesitation of the doctor, whose code prohibits him from harming life (abortion), or if he decides to go ahead with it in the name of service to others, presents him with choices where the way his diagnoses are produced has no real bearing on the situation, so that it is necessary to bring in a specialist in indecision, a "psy" who, prior to the operation, will verify that this is indeed what the individual wants. Only the "psy" specialist furnishes a neutral terrain for the resolution of differences of regime between the management of bodies and the management of populations. The regulation of images hegemonizes and harmonizes the regulation of corporal flows and that of social flows. There no longer exist social spaces for the management of sexuality like the old public dance, where the sexes, ages, and classes came into contact with one another, where choices of partners were made under the gaze and control of family and social-adherence groups [*groupes d'appartenance*]. There remain precious few of those aleatory spaces such as the vacant lot and the street, where sexual and amorous initiations were carried out.

Now there are "clubs," that is, private spaces organized in such a way as to facilitate sexual *rapprochements* between individuals of the same age group and standard of living, and protected by bouncers and police against the invasion of an incompatible clientele. There are prefabricated "adventure grounds" and sex-education courses in the schools. Images float in the emptiness that separates these "realities": public images, those of the movies, the photo-novels, and the newspapers; and private images, images of parents. Between the illusions engendered by the all-too-visible nature of the former and the disillusions engendered by the invisible significance of the latter, the "psy" specialists always find a way to put everyone back in touch with their true desire, and their "clients" can always find a solution in the "realities" they are offered.

Their discourse allows them to *circumscribe this position, to mark out its circuits and block its exits.* This discourse is a fortunate one, since it credits the family with being both the only model for socialization and the source of all dissatisfactions. An excess or deficiency is always imputed to a family in order to explain the oppressions and frustrations of individuals within it. In the suffering or pride of those who flee, there is always something that points back to a singular, baleful experience of the family, which invalidates or excuses the action taken but refers the subject of it back to the family. There is a total mastery of the terrain which enables this discourse to turn back against the family the "double moral standard" wherein its strength, and its social harmfulness, used to lie. It protected its members, cloistered its daughters, and sent its sons out in quest of jobs, marriages, and amorous adventures. It coupled sexuality and protection like a weapon and armor, constituting a little war machine designed to preserve the patrimony and conquer exterior riches. Nowadays, sexuality and protection are both oriented toward the quest for a harmony within the family, a satisfying complementarity. In this arrangement, each individual, each sex, is meant to find its share of preservation; everyone discovers an equal measure of assistance and repression in the other. A difficult balance, one that is virtually impossible to achieve, since the very demand for it generates instability. But this is precisely where the positive effect of the "psy" movement, its social utility, resides. It makes possible a situation in which the family disappears as a social protagonist but continues to exist as a means of individual attainment, as a place where ambitions are inscribed, a real origin of failures and a virtual horizon of successes. The Don Juan figure, that of the libertine who defies the familial order with its rules combining the seduction of persons and the coveting of things, disappears in favor of a continuous liberatory drift, a game that is replayed in houses, groups, and countries over and over again. His was a resolutely tragic departure, for—as with Jean Genet and his prisons—he called out in the end for an adversary worthy of his audacity. In the limbo of the new order that is emerging, his place seems to be reserved for a personage who has not yet found his letters of nobility, although he has already been identified as the chief enemy. This would be the "latent" homosexual, that individual who can never bring himself to accept the norm of conjugal complementarity, that maker of twin couples, of "troubled children."

Freud like Keynes, we said. Perhaps there is something more than a simile in this juxtaposition. Keynes theorized about the characteristic ways in which Western societies combined the social and the economic. He indicated the means by which they could be functionally adjusted, showing how the distribution of social subsidies could be organized in such a way that renewed consumption would ensue, production would be stimulated, and economic crises as well as the social ills they engendered would be averted. He managed to broaden the economic sphere precisely where its laws seemed to be swept aside by chance, giving way to insouciance, suffering, and revolt. In short, he made it possible to integrate the social sphere into the general regulation of the market, providing Western societies with the means of avoiding the alternative of anarchic liberalism or authoritarian centralism.

Where before there had only been the search for an always shaky and difficult compromise between free enterprise and the problems of social welfare, repression, and management, Keynes contributed a positive solution through the formation of a circular functionality between the two registers of the production of goods and the production of the producers (and consumers). He constituted the provisional point of completion of a search that had started with industrialization and the beginnings of philanthropy.

Could we not say that Freudianism made a similar operation possible by offering a flexible mechanism of adjustment of the juridical sphere and the medical sphere? There too, it was a matter of escaping a dangerous alternative between, on the one hand, a statist consecration of privileges through the power of juridical assets, particularly those contained in the family, and on the other hand, the setting up of a central mechanism of coercion, shoring up acquired positions and obstructing initiatives undertaken in the name of health norms. This question of joining the social and the economic was an old debate, and an old search as well: the nineteenth century never gave up trying to find a principle of balance between the necessity of imposing social norms of health and education and that of maintaining the autonomy of individuals and the ambitions of families as a principle of free enterprise. Now what did Freudianism contribute, if not the means of injecting the need for norms into the family, leaving the latter always "justified" in theory and always suspect in practice, suspected of pressing too heavily on its members, of frustrating them with the very thing it tried to offer them? An injection that did not sterilize the familial register but rather intensified it, since the family remained the horizon of all individual paths.

Might we not also be justified in seeing a certain complementarity between the two operations that go under the names of Keynes and Freud? The first saved the principle of private initiative, of individual, self-centered motivation in social organization, by discovering a technique that not only dressed the wounds produced by this anarchy but also fitted the faltering social zones back into the economic circuit in a way that worked. The second saved the familial reference without which "possessive individualism" had no functional possibilities; it cast suspicion on the family of origin, with its defects, and replaced faulty appraisals of this family with the concept of the family as a horizon for individuals to conquer, a place where they might steady their trajectories and inscribe their results. The disposition thus produced with regard to the family was an admirable one, for it made it possible to avoid the real dangers of the family's autonomy while facilitating social regulation by referring the frustrations of individuals to the family, by attaching their dreams and ambitions to it. What other site could offer so many resources?

People are going to say, "So yet another one of those irresponsible, hence facile, denunciations, a contempt for techniques which conceals a contempt for those in need of them; and such a fear behind the contempt!" They will be completely mistaken. I have not expressed any hostility in principle toward psychoanalysis—not in the least. I have tried to show in what context of problems and incentives, by what process, psychoanalysis was made "operational." Its usefulness to institutions was discerned in its ability to justify and renovate the two major frames of reference of a social order that functioned on the basis of a maximum avoidance of political issues: *the social norm as a reality principle* and *the family,* its effacement and its privileges, *as a value principle.* Those who were the agents of this operation are free to claim that they are applying a subversive theory by joining an aseptic norm to a phantasmal family. This only reveals their blindness before the transformations which these frames of reference are now undergoing, and their political will to continue them in their old forms. It is a way to avoid looking at the current shift from the reality principle of the decreed social norm toward the thing it was meant to control, to rule,

namely, *the body*. Not the hygienic body of the matadors of
equilibrium, nor the ventriloqual body of the "psy" specialists, but the one that is extricating itself from the familial
archi-bodies through the revolt of women; the body that resists the disciplinary architectures by means of countless invisible or spectacular insurrections; the body that affirms the
reality of a life and denounces the unreality of that by which
it would be encircled and reduced to silence. It is also a way
not to see another notion of value emerging on the side of
history. Not the absence of history of happy people, nor history in the eternal "psy" past, but the capacity for history as
it is affirmed in the face of the *metahistory* of the political
apparatuses, against the glue of familial genealogies, history
as that which is worth being recounted and whose enigma
derives from the aleatory positivity of its train of events.
There is no question of imagining some kind of pre-established or desired harmony between these two registers. The
separation between them is wide, rich in the interworking
operations of relay and shift, in the very processes that come
into play in that space which separates living from what
makes one want to live.

At Easter time in 1976, an obscure inmate of a provincial
prison died as the result of a long hunger strike that he had
embarked upon because, in his judicial dossier, only his
faults, his deviations from the norm, his unhappy childhood,
his marital instability, had been noted down, but not his endeavors, his searchings, the aleatory train of his life. It seems
that this was the first time a prison hunger strike had ended in
a death, the first time too that one had been undertaken for so
bizarre a motive.

Index

About The Author

Jacques Donzelot has taught sociology at the universities of Vincennes and Nanterre. He founded, with Michel Foucault, the Prison Information Group (G.I.P.).